Women's Fashions
of the Early 1900s

AN UNABRIDGED REPUBLICATION OF
"NEW YORK FASHIONS, 1909"

NATIONAL CLOAK & SUIT CO.

DOVER PUBLICATIONS, INC., NEW YORK

Copyright © 1992 by Dover Publications, Inc.
All rights reserved under Pan American and International Copyright Conventions.

Published in Canada by General Publishing Company, Ltd., 30 Lesmill Road, Don Mills, Toronto, Ontario.
Published in the United Kingdom by Constable and Company, Ltd., 3 The Lanchesters, 162–164 Fulham Palace Road, London W6 9ER.

This Dover edition, first published in 1992, is an unabridged republication of *New York Fashions, Vol. 12, No. 2, March, 1909,* first published by the National Cloak & Suit Co., New York, in 1909. A new publisher's note has been written for this edition.

Manufactured in the United States of America
Dover Publications, Inc., 31 East 2nd Street, Mineola, N.Y. 11501

Library of Congress Cataloging-in-Publication Data

Women's fashions of the early 1900s : an unabridged republication of "New York fashions, 1909" / National Cloak & Suit Co.
      p.   cm.
   ISBN 0-486-27276-1 (pbk.)
   1. Costume—United States—History—20th century. 2. Fashion—United States—History—20th century. 3. Costume—New York (State)—New York—History—20th century. 4. Fashion—New York (State)—New York —History—20th century. I. National Cloak & Suit Co. II. Title: New York fashions.
GT617.N4W66 1992
391′.2′097309041—dc20
                                                                        92-21805
                                                                        CIP

Publisher's Note

IN ITS 1909 mail-order catalog, the 21-year-old National Cloak & Suit Co. of New York assured women that they could "Dress Fashionably at Moderate Cost" by ordering from the "largest ladies' outfitting establishment in the world." No expense was spared, the company said, in producing the catalog; over $200,000 was spent in gathering and designing the new styles—and in having a cover drawn by well-known illustrator Howard Chandler Christy.

The company went to considerable lengths to cater to its customers. According to the catalog, orders for ready-made items were filled the day they were received while orders for made-to-measure garments were filled within ten days. Items could be returned at the company's expense with no questions asked and the company paid full transportation charges for all prepaid orders. There were separate order blanks for made-to-measure garments and ready-made items and the company obviously expected—or at least hoped for—repeat orders, since two of each order blank were included in the catalog.

The catalog featured practical styles for the middle-class woman, including the growing number of women joining the work force in offices and shops. No evening or formal wear was offered, although a special illustrated pamphlet of bridal sets was available. Separate pamphlets were also available for riding skirts and nurses' uniforms.

The first section of the catalog is devoted to made-to-measure suits and skirts. These garments could be made up in six different qualities of cloth and samples were available on request. Combining the jacket from one style with the skirt from another posed no problem, nor did extra large or extra long sizes, although these did involve an extra charge.

The fashions shown are extremely typical of the period. Although not quite as exaggerated as at the very beginning of the century, the forward-tilted, "S-shaped" silhouette, with its emphasis on a full bosom and rounded hips, is quite evident. Skirts are slightly shorter than previously, reaching just to the instep, and they fit smoothly over the hips, flaring out below. Jackets, for the most part, are long and semifitted. Collars are uniformly high and sleeves are long (although a few styles feature three-quarter-length sleeves), moderately full at the shoulder and fitted at the wrist. Waists, as well as lightweight dresses, petticoats, corset covers, chemises and slips, were lavishly trimmed with tucks, lace and embroidery. White was the color of choice for these, although some waists were offered in black or other colors.

Rounding out the catalog are sections devoted to children's clothing and to women's hats, hose, neckwear and other accessories. Also featured are two pages of tourist coats—needed as protection from the elements when riding in one of the growing number of automobiles.

NEW YORK
FASHIONS
1909

Drawn by HOWARD CHANDLER CHRISTY expressly for

NATIONAL
CLOAK &
SUIT CO.
NEW YORK CITY

Howard Chandler Christy · 1909

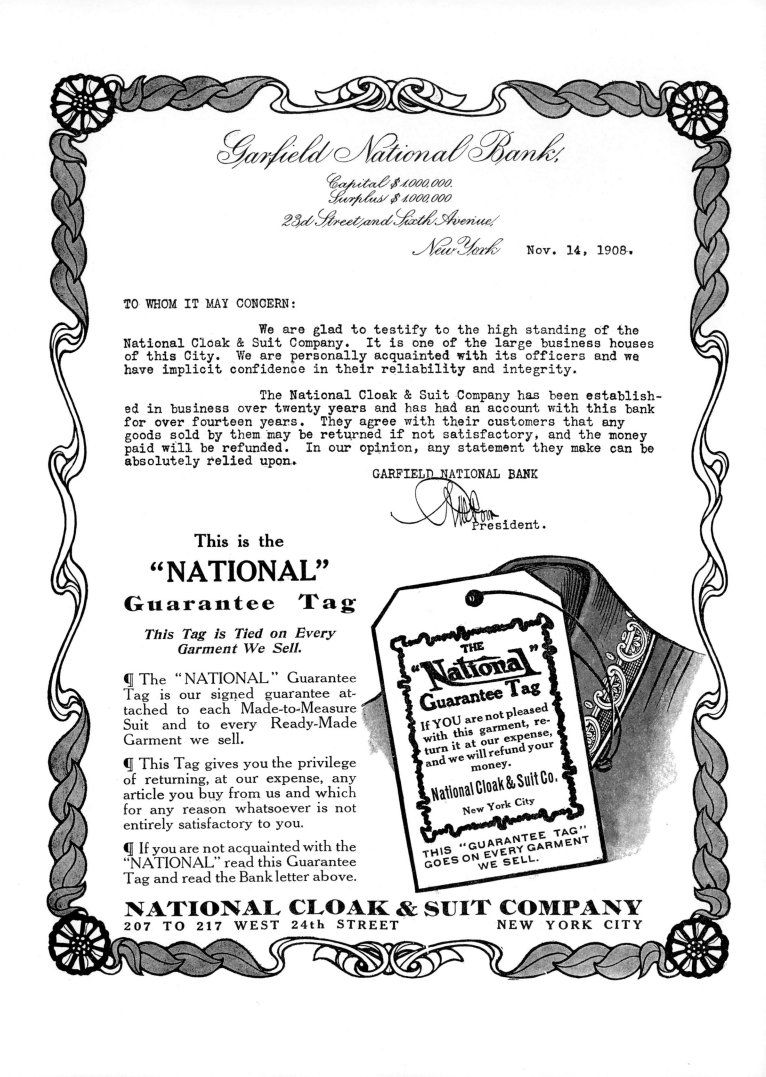

Garfield National Bank,

Capital $ 1.000.000.
Surplus $ 1.000.000

23d Street and Sixth Avenue,

New York Nov. 14, 1908.

TO WHOM IT MAY CONCERN:

    We are glad to testify to the high standing of the National Cloak & Suit Company. It is one of the large business houses of this City. We are personally acquainted with its officers and we have implicit confidence in their reliability and integrity.

    The National Cloak & Suit Company has been established in business over twenty years and has had an account with this bank for over fourteen years. They agree with their customers that any goods sold by them may be returned if not satisfactory, and the money paid will be refunded. In our opinion, any statement they make can be absolutely relied upon.

GARFIELD NATIONAL BANK

President.

This is the
"NATIONAL"
Guarantee Tag

This Tag is Tied on Every Garment We Sell.

¶ The "NATIONAL" Guarantee Tag is our signed guarantee attached to each Made-to-Measure Suit and to every Ready-Made Garment we sell.

¶ This Tag gives you the privilege of returning, at our expense, any article you buy from us and which for any reason whatsoever is not entirely satisfactory to you.

¶ If you are not acquainted with the "NATIONAL" read this Guarantee Tag and read the Bank letter above.

THE
"National"
Guarantee Tag
If YOU are not pleased with this garment, return it at our expense, and we will refund your money.
National Cloak & Suit Co.
New York City
THIS "GUARANTEE TAG" GOES ON EVERY GARMENT WE SELL.

NATIONAL CLOAK & SUIT COMPANY
207 TO 217 WEST 24th STREET   NEW YORK CITY

THE "NATIONAL" PERFECT FIT CHART

FILL IN PARTICULARS, CUT OUT THIS SHEET AND SEND IT TO US.

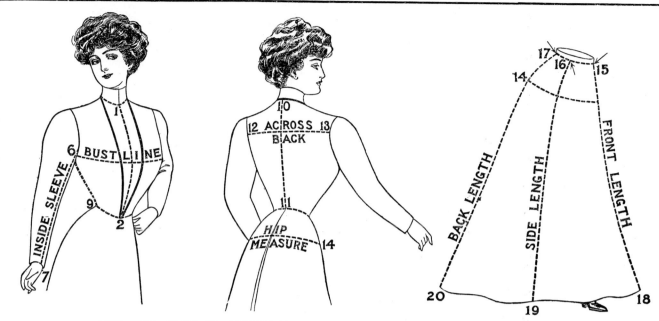

FOR USE ONLY IN ORDERING GARMENTS SHOWN ON PAGES 9 TO 29.

These measurements must be taken directly from your figure — not from an old garment.
Use an accurate tape measure. Make no allowance for seams.

NOTE. { Tie a cord around your waist to locate the NATURAL WAIST-LINE.
{ Do not remove it until your measurements are completed. THIS IS IMPORTANT.

MEASUREMENTS FOR MADE-TO-MEASURE JACKET.

Bust Measure:—All around body, well up under arms, over largest part of bust. (Do not allow tape measure to slip down in back. If your bust measure is **over 44 inches**, there will be an extra charge of 10 per cent. See paragraph 12, page 6.) ....

Waist Measure:—(Make no allowance for dip or for lapping.) ....

Hip Measure:—Around body six inches below waist-line. Do not allow tape measure to slip up or down. ....

Neck Measure:—Around neck over dress collar at bottom of collar. (See 1 in illustration above.) ....

Neck to Waist, Front:—From collar seam (1) to cord at waist-line (2). Read "NOTE" above. Do not give this measurement too long. ....

Special Measurement:—Begin at center of waist-line (point 2) and measure up and around back of neck and return to point 2, as shown by the heavy line. ....

Length of Sleeve, Inside Seam:—(Not Outside Seam.) Take this measurement from armhole to **length desired** with arm hanging in position as shown. ....

Do you wish Long or Three-Quarter Length Sleeves? ....

Length Under Arm:—From armhole seam (6) to cord at waist-line (9). Read "NOTE" above. Do not raise your arm when this measurement is being taken. ....

Neck to Waist, Back:—From collar seam (10) to waist-line (11). Read "NOTE" above. Be careful that you do not give this measurement too long. ....

Across Back:—Between armhole seams from (12) to (13). (Four inches below collar seam in back.) ....

Length Jacket:—From collar seam in back (10) to length desired. If jacket is wanted longer than described, read paragraph 14, page 6. ....

Mark X in front of Jacket Lining desired:

	Good Satin (no extra charge).
	Silk (extra charge). $............
	Skinner's Guaranteed Satin (extra charge).$............

There is an extra charge for lining with Silk or Skinner's Guaranteed Satin as stated below each description of Tailor-Made Suits on pages 9 to 27.

Color of Lining Desired in Jacket:—

With 1st choice of material ....

With 2d choice of material ....

We will furnish any color of Lining desired, but we recommend only Black, White and Gray, as they do not crock.

MEASUREMENTS FOR MADE-TO-MEASURE SKIRT.

Do Not Use this Blank to Order READY-MADE Skirts Shown on Pages 68 to 79.

Waist Measure:—Remove outside belt when taking this measurement. Do not allow for dip or for lapping. ....

Hip Measure:—Around body six inches below waist-line. Do not allow tape measure to slip up or down. If your hip measure is **more than 50 inches**, there will be an extra charge of 10 per cent. See paragraph 12, page 6. ....

Front Length:—From bottom of waist band in front (15) to desired length (18). ....

Side Length:—From bottom of waist band on side (16) to desired length (19). ....

Back Length:—From bottom of waist band in back (17) to desired length (20). ....

BE SURE TO READ CAREFULLY PAGES 6, 7 AND 8 BEFORE SENDING US YOUR ORDER.

² Use this Order Blank only for Made-to-Measure Garments

SHOWN ON PAGES 9 TO 29 INCLUSIVE

* (Order Blank for our **Ready-Made Goods** shown on pages 30 to 116 will be found in BACK of this Style Book)

NATIONAL CLOAK AND SUIT CO.

207 TO 217 WEST TWENTY-FOURTH STREET
NEW YORK CITY

I send you this order with the understanding that if the garment you make for me does not fit, or is not entirely satisfactory, I may return it in good condition within three days of its receipt, at your expense, and you will refund my money, alter it free of charge, or you will make me another garment, whichever I prefer.

Mrs. or Miss.. No.. Street or Avenue

(If married, use husband's initials)

Town.. County.. State..........................

(State here your post office address.)

In what town is your Express Office?.. What is the name of Express Company?..

STYLE No.	PAGE	QUALITY		QUALITY		Do not write anything in this space.
		1st Choice	Price	2nd Choice	Price	
Suit......................	....					
Jacket....................	....					
Skirt......................	....					

In ordering a suit to be made to measure, if you wish the jacket of one style and the skirt of another, please state your selections clearly. See page 8 for particulars as to prices.

What is your height?.. Weight?............................

Do you stand unusually erect? ....

If there is any peculiarity or irregularity in your figure, please describe fully in a letter to accompany this order.

Have you had any previous correspondence relative to this order? ....

Have you read paragraphs 1, 2, 3 and 4 below?..

May we substitute if our stock of the materials you have selected is sold out?.................................... Should it be necessary to substitute, we will use similar material of greater value, without extra charge. Please answer this question.

1.—**Please attach samples of the materials you select** in the spaces provided for them on this sheet. We always use the first selection if we have the material when the order reaches us. Do not make a second selection unless you are willing that we should use it, if necessary.

If your second choice of cloth is of a higher quality than your first choice, and we are compelled to use your second, we will put the garment in work and promptly advise you and you may remit the balance, if any.

2.—**We urge you to carefully examine your order** before mailing it, to make sure that the correct style numbers are mentioned and that the order is complete in every detail. We require the measurements taken from your figure—not from an old garment. Do not attempt to take your own measurements; any one in your own home can do it for you. Please read carefully the description of the garment you order.

3.—**In our endeavor to fill orders promptly,** we usually start to make the garment the same day the order is received; therefore we cannot comply with requests sent later to have changes made.

4.—**MOURNING GARMENTS.**—When ordering a garment for mourning or second mourning wear, kindly state this fact distinctly, so that we may use the proper linings and trimmings.

Enclosed find $..................

(Read paragraphs 6 and 7 page 6, regarding Our Terms and How to Remit)

FIRST CHOICE OF CLOTH.

Pin sample like this, using two (2) pins

SECOND CHOICE OF CLOTH.

Pin sample like this, using two (2) pins.

Please send your Style Book to my friends named below:

NAME	ADDRESS
....	....
....	....
....	....
....	....

FILL IN PARTICULARS, CUT OUT THIS SHEET AND SEND IT TO US.

FILL IN PARTICULARS, CUT OUT THIS SHEET AND SEND IT TO US.

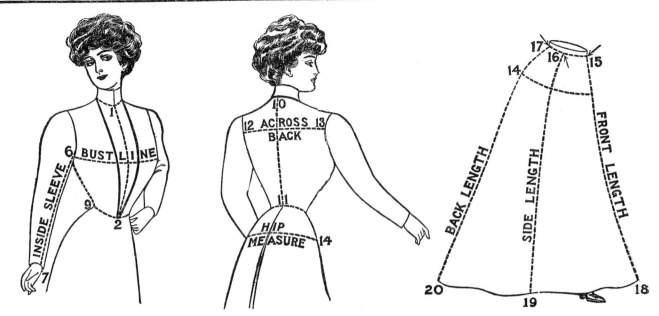

FOR USE ONLY IN ORDERING GARMENTS SHOWN ON PAGES 9 TO 29.

These measurements must be taken directly from your figure—not from an old garment. Use an accurate tape measure.   Make no allowance for seams.

NOTE. { Tie a cord around your waist to locate the NATURAL WAIST-LINE. Do not remove it until your measurements are completed. **THIS IS IMPORTANT.**

MEASUREMENTS FOR MADE-TO-MEASURE JACKET.

Bust Measure:—All around body, well up under arms, over largest part of bust. (Do not allow tape measure to slip down in back. If your bust measure is **over 44 inches**, there will be an extra charge of 10 per cent. See paragraph 12, page 6.)

Waist Measure:—(Make no allowance for dip or for lapping.)

Hip Measure:—Around body six inches below waist-line. Do not allow tape measure to slip up or down.

Neck Measure:—Around neck over dress collar at bottom of collar. (See 1 in illustration above.)

Neck to Waist, Front:—From collar seam (1) to cord at waist-line (2). Read "NOTE" above. Do not give this measurement too long.

Special Measurement:—Begin at center of waist-line (point 2) and measure up and around back of neck and return to point 2, as shown by the heavy line.

Length of Sleeve, Inside Seam:—(Not Outside Seam.) Take this measurement from armhole to **length desired** with arm hanging in position as shown.

Do you wish Long or Three-Quarter Length Sleeves?

Length Under Arm:—From armhole seam (6) to cord at waist-line (9). Read "NOTE" above. Do not raise your arm when this measurement is being taken.

Neck to Waist, Back:—From collar seam (10) to waist-line (11). Read "NOTE" above. Be careful that you do not give this measurement too long.

Across Back:—Between armhole seams from (12) to (13). (Four inches below collar seam in back.)

Length Jacket:—From collar seam in back (10) to length desired. If jacket is wanted longer than described, read paragraph 14, page 6.

Mark X in front of Jacket Lining desired:

| | **Good Satin** (no extra charge). |
| **Silk** (extra charge). $............ |
| **Skinner's Guaranteed Satin** (extra charge).$............ |

There is an extra charge for lining with Silk or Skinner's Guaranteed Satin as stated below each description of Tailor-Made Suits on pages 9 to 27.

Color of Lining Desired in Jacket:—

With 1st choice of material............

With 2d choice of material............

We will furnish any color of Lining desired, but we recommend only Black, White and Gray, as they do not crock.

MEASUREMENTS FOR MADE-TO-MEASURE SKIRT.

Do Not Use this Blank to Order READY-MADE Skirts Shown on Pages 68 to 79.

Waist Measure:—Remove outside belt when taking this measurement. Do not allow for dip or for lapping.

Hip Measure:—Around body six inches below waist-line. Do not allow tape measure to slip up or down. If your hip measure is **more than 50 inches**, there will be an extra charge of 10 per cent. See paragraph 12, page 6.

Front Length:—From bottom of waist band in front (15) to desired length (18).

Side Length:—From bottom of waist band on side (16) to desired length (19).

Back Length:—From bottom of waist band in back (17) to desired length (20).

BE SURE TO READ CAREFULLY PAGES 6, 7 AND 8 BEFORE SENDING US YOUR ORDER.

⁴ Use this Order Blank only for Made-to-Measure Garments
SHOWN ON PAGES 9 TO 29 INCLUSIVE
(Order Blank for our **Ready-Made Goods** shown on pages 30 to 116 will be found in BACK of this Style Book)

NATIONAL CLOAK AND SUIT CO.
207 TO 217 WEST TWENTY-FOURTH STREET
NEW YORK CITY

I send you this order with the understanding that if the garment you make for me does not fit, or is not entirely satisfactory, I may return it in good condition within three days of its receipt, at your expense, and you will refund my money, alter it free of charge, or you will make me another garment, whichever I prefer.

Mrs. or Miss.. (If married, use husband's initials.)   No. .... Street or Avenue

Town .... (State here your post-office address.)   County.................................... State.............................

In what town is your Express Office? ....   What is the name of Express Company? ....

STYLE No.	PAGE	QUALITY 1st Choice	Price	QUALITY 2nd Choice	Price
Suit............	....	....	....	....	....
Jacket.........	....	....	....	....	....
Skirt.........	....	....	....	....	....

› In ordering a suit to be made to measure, if you wish the jacket of one style and the skirt of another, please state your selections clearly. See page 8 for particulars as to prices.

What is your height: .... Weight? ....

Do you stand unusually erect? ....

If there is any peculiarity or irregularity in your figure, please describe fully in a letter to accompany this order.

Have you had any previous correspondence relative to this order? ....

Have you read paragraphs 1, 2, 3 and 4 below? ....

May we substitute if our stock of the materials you have selected is sold out? .... Should it be necessary to substitute, we will use similar material of greater value, without extra charge. Please answer this question.

1.—Please attach samples of the materials you select in the spaces provided for them on this sheet. We always use the first selection if we have the material when the order reaches us. Do not make a second selection unless you are willing that we should use it, if necessary.

If your second choice of cloth is of a higher quality than your first choice, and we are compelled to use your second, we will put the garment in work and promptly advise you and you may remit the balance, if any.

2.—We urge you to carefully examine your order before mailing it, to make sure that the measurements are accurate, that the correct style numbers are mentioned and that the order is complete in every detail. We require the measurements taken from your figure—not from an old garment. Do not attempt to take your own measurements; any one in your own home can do it for you. Please read carefully the description of the garment you order.

3.—In our endeavor to fill orders promptly, we usually start to make the garment the same day the order is received; therefore we cannot comply with requests sent later to have changes made.

4.—MOURNING GARMENTS.—When ordering a garment for mourning or second mourning wear, kindly state this fact distinctly, so that we may use the proper linings and trimmings.

Do not write anything in this space.

Enclosed find $..................

(Read paragraphs **6** and **7**, page **6**, regarding Our Terms and How to Remit.)

FIRST CHOICE OF CLOTH.

Pin sample like this, using two (2) pins.

SECOND CHOICE OF CLOTH.

Pin sample like this, using two (2) pins.

Please send your Style Book to my friends named below:

NAME	ADDRESS
....	....
....	....
....	....
....	....

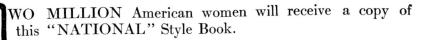

This is THE "NATIONAL" STYLE BOOK

What Will It Mean to You?

TWO MILLION American women will receive a copy of this "NATIONAL" Style Book.

Hundreds of thousands of women who get this Style Book will USE it to secure becoming new styles and to save money on their wearing apparel. There are others who will marvel at the "NATIONAL'S" Low Prices. And this, without stopping to think that this benefit may just as well be THEIRS.

We have spent for this edition of the "NATIONAL" Style Book $214,782—almost a quarter of a million dollars. Yet all this expense, all this labor in gathering the new styles, in designing new garments—all this wealth of beauty and becomingness, all this OPPORTUNITY will have no meaning to you, unless you take advantage of it.

The most fashionable gown will not become you unless you WEAR it. This Style Book is USELESS to you unless YOU USE IT.

Before you lay this book aside, with all the pleasure and profit it really holds for you, let us tell you what this "NATIONAL" Style Book can do for you—what it will mean to you if You USE IT.

FIRST: It will help you to even greater becomingness in dress, by giving you all of the desirable New York Styles for your selection.

SECOND: The "NATIONAL" Style Book gives you the benefit of "NATIONAL" Low Prices.

THIRD: Every garment you order from this Style Book will be sent you with all postage or express charges prepaid by us, no matter in what part of the United States you live.

FOURTH: Every "NATIONAL" garment illustrated in this Style Book will come to you with our Signed Guarantee attached. This Guarantee says: "We will give you your money back if you ask for it, and when you ask for it, and we will pay express charges both ways."

Buying by mail at the "NATIONAL" is no longer new. In Twenty-One Years the "NATIONAL'S" customers have increased, until To-day, we have friends in every town in the United States.

And so YOU too, will come to realize the benefits the "NATIONAL" offers. EVENTUALLY, you are going to buy at the "NATIONAL"—Why Not NOW ?

New York Fashions
Vol. 12, No. 2, March, 1909

All Rights Reserved

Copyright, 1909, by
National Cloak & Suit Company

READ BEFORE ORDERING

1. How to Learn the Cost of a Made-to-Measure Garment.

Under the descriptions of our Made-to-Measure Suits and Skirts, shown on pages 9 to 29, are given prices for making them to measure from our various grades of materials. To distinguish the value of our materials, we have graded them according to quality. Our samples are labelled Quality C, D, E, F, G and H, the lowest grade being marked Quality C.

For example: Should you wish a suit made like Style No. 4013 from any of our fabrics labelled Quality C, the price would be $17.50. If made from Quality D material, the price would be $20.00, and so on up to $32.00 for the garment if made from Quality H material.

2. Our Materials.

We have the largest stock in New York of the most desirable imported and domestic materials. These we use in making to measure the Suits, Skirts and Jackets shown on pages 9 to 29 of this Style Book. Our materials are graded according to quality, samples being labelled from Quality C to Quality H.

In selecting our stock of Spring and Summer materials, we found that the goods of the A and B grades contained cotton and shoddy. We therefore decided to discontinue those grades from our line, as we do not handle any materials we cannot recommend

However, the great increase in the volume of our business during the past year enables us to offer the C and D grades at practically as low prices as were formerly charged for A and B qualities. At the same time, our customers will be receiving a very much better article.

All our fabrics are thoroughly sponged and shrunk by us, and every one is guaranteed. We do not handle anything we cannot recommend.

We cannot undertake to make garments from materials furnished by customers.

3. Special Samples.

SAMPLES OF MADE-TO-MEASURE MATERIALS. Our stock of materials used in the making of the Suits, Skirts and Jackets shown on pages 9 to 29 of this Style Book includes over 400 different kinds. If you desire samples of any of these materials and will specify the colors you prefer, we will gladly send a generous assortment free, upon receipt of your request. Do not overlook the importance of telling us just the kind and colors of materials you desire.

SAMPLES OF READY-MADE GOODS. In cases where we can furnish samples of the Ready-Made goods, this fact is stated clearly at the bottom of the page illustrating the garments. The materials in all our Ready-Made goods will be found exactly as described, and it is therefore advisable that you should order at once from this Style Book, rather than request samples. Remember you take no risk, as our Guarantee protects you.

4. Our Workmanship.

"I have never seen better workmanship" is the expression used by thousands of our customers in writing about "NATIONAL" suits. The reason is plain. We have the largest, most skilful and best trained organization of men tailors, cutters and designers in America. Some of these men have been with the "NATIONAL" twenty years, each year becoming more capable of affording you nearer perfect work. It has become second nature to them to give attention to the little things that together result in a well-made and properly finished garment. No detail in a "NATIONAL" suit is neglected.

5. We Pay Postage and Express Charges.

Remember that the "NATIONAL" pays postage and express charges. This is one of the distinct features of our policy. It means that, in addition to the saving you make by means of the "NATIONAL" low prices, you will also save all postage and express charges when you deal with us.

Always bear this fact in mind and also please inform your friends that no matter where they live, and that whatever they order from the "NATIONAL"—whether a handkerchief or a Made-to-Measure suit—all express charges or postage is prepaid by us to any part of the United States on every order accompanied by the full list price of the goods ordered. We do not pay express charges on goods sent C.O.D.

6. How to Send Money.

Remit either by Post Office Money Order, Express Money Order, New York Bank Draft or Check, payable to "**National Cloak and Suit Company, New York City.**" We recommend either Post Office Money Orders or Express Money Orders, as they are absolutely safe, and a convenient way to send money; moreover, in case of loss in the mails you are protected.

It is not safe to send cash; but if you cannot remit in any other way, enclose the money in a strong envelope, seal it securely, **and be sure to have it registered.**

Always send an amount sufficient to cover the cost of your order; better send too much than too little. All sums in excess of your purchase will be promptly refunded after your order is filled.

7. Our Terms.

We do a strictly cash business and carry no charge accounts. If an amount sufficient to cover the full list price of the goods desired accompanies the order, we will pay transportation charges to any part of the United States. **If you wish goods sent C.O.D. we require a deposit of at least one-third the amount of your order,** in which case they will be sent by express C.O.D. for the balance; but on such shipments the customer must pay the express charges and also the express company's charge for sending the money to us. We do not ship C.O.D. without the required deposit. Goods sent C.O.D. must go by express as they cannot be mailed. All orders for points outside the United States must be fully paid for in advance.

We can accept orders only on the above terms.

8. Acknowledgment of Orders.

Every order for a Made-to-Measure garment will be acknowledged the day it reaches us. If you do not receive our acknowledgment within a reasonable time after mailing your order, please notify us. Be sure to state the exact date you sent the order, the amount enclosed, and whether the remittance was in the form of a Bank Draft, Post Office Money Order or Express Money Order. State number of Post Office or Express Money Order.

Orders for Ready-Made goods are usually filled the day they are received; therefore, no acknowledgment of the receipt of such orders is necessary.

9. Time Required to Fill Orders.

Orders for Ready-Made goods are usually filled the same day as received.

Orders for Made-to-Measure garments, shown on pages 9 to 29, are usually filled within 10 days from the time we receive your order, notwithstanding that we cut and make them to your measure.

In our endeavor to fill all Made-to-Measure orders promptly, we start to make the garments the same day your order is received; therefore we cannot comply with requests sent later to have changes made.

10. Correspondence.

Letters are answered by women of experience in matters of dress, and you can write us fully with the assurance that your communications will be handled by these experts who can appreciate your requirements. Do not hesitate to ask for any information in reference to our garments or methods, which is not given in this Style Book. Always date your letters and write the names of your Post Office, County and State distinctly.

Read the Questions and Answers on page 7. This may save you the trouble of writing us.

11. Always Sign Your Name the Same Way.

Please be very careful how you sign your name. It is often a cause of serious mistakes and delay to receive letters from the same person signed Mrs. Wm. T. Smith, the next time Ella M. Smith, and again Mrs. E. M. Smith. Always sign your name the same way, and if you are married, always use your husband's initials, thus: Mrs. William T. Smith.

Note: If you change your address, please advise us, giving your old as well as your new address.

If you receive our Style Books or letters addressed in more than one way or receive two of our Style Books of the same edition, you will be doing us a favor to advise us promptly.

12. Extra Large Made-to-Measure Garments.

Extra size garments require extra material. Therefore on our Made-to-Measure Suits and Jackets shown on pages 9 to 27 where the bust measure is over 44 inches, there will be an extra charge of ten per cent. on the price of the suit or separate jacket. On Made-to-Measure Skirts, shown on pages 9 to 29, when ordered with a hip measure of over 50 inches, there will be an additional charge of ten per cent. of the price of the skirt.

For instance, should you order a suit Style No. 4014, and your bust measure is over 44 inches, the price should be figured as follows:

Suit Style No. 4014, Quality C, Price.........$18.00
10 per cent. extra charge for bust measure over
44 inches 1.80

Price of Suit, $19.80

These extra charges apply to all Made-to-Measure Suits or Jackets shown on pages 9 to 27 which are ordered with a bust measure of over 44 inches, or on Made-to-Measure Skirts on pages 9 to 29 with a hip measure of over 50 inches.

13. Mourning Garments.

When ordering a garment for mourning or second mourning wear, kindly state this fact distinctly, so that we may use the proper linings and trimmings.

14. Extra Long Jackets.

For the prices quoted, the **Made-to-Measure** Jackets shown on pages 9 to 27 will be made any length up to that mentioned in the description. If a jacket is wanted longer than stated in its description, there will be a reasonable charge for the extra length desired, as per schedule below:

If Jacket is to be made of
Quality C cloth add 20 cents for each additional inch desired.
"   D   "   "   25   "   "   "   "   "   "   "
"   E   "   "   30   "   "   "   "   "   "   "
"   F   "   "   35   "   "   "   "   "   "   "
"   G   "   "   40   "   "   "   "   "   "   "
"   H   "   "   45   "   "   "   "   "   "   "

(No change can be made in the lengths of our **Ready-Made** Jackets.)

15. Riding Skirts, Nurses' Uniforms, Bridal Sets.

Special Illustrated Leaflets describing these articles will be sent free on request.

ANSWERS TO QUESTIONS YOU MAY WISH TO ASK

Read Carefully : It may save you the trouble of writing us

Question:—Will you guarantee to fit me ?

Answer:—We positively will For over twenty years the energy, ability and experience of this establishment have been devoted to perfecting and improving our system of making garments to order from measurements sent by mail. If the directions on our measurement charts in the front of this Style Book are carefully followed, any garment we make to measure for you will fit you perfectly.

Question:—In case you do not satisfy me, will you refund my money ?

Answer:—Yes, we will refund your money immediately and without argument and pay express charges or postage both ways. Every garment bears our signed guarantee to this effect. We ask no questions as to why you return a garment. If you are not satisfied, and ask for your money back, it will be returned to you at once. There will be no unpleasantness or no correspondence about it. If you are dissatisfied with our goods, we want you to return them and get your money back. Remember, we pay express charges both ways.

Question:—In ordering a Made-to-Measure suit, may I select the jacket or waist of one style and the skirt of another ?

Answer:—Yes: if you order any of the styles shown on pages 9 to 29 of this Style Book. The models shown on these pages are made to measure, and you may make any combinations you desire. Full particulars regarding combinations will be found on page 8. Please remember, however, that we will not make a suit combining one of our Ready-Made styles with one of our Made-to-Measure models.

Question:—Do you make special designs not illustrated by you ?

Answer:—We do not.

Question:—Do you employ agents ?

Answer:—*No agents whatever are employed by us.* Anyone claiming to represent us is a swindler, and is endeavoring to obtain money under false pretenses. All orders should be mailed direct to us at 207 to 217 West 24th Street, New York City.

Question:—Do you allow commissions or discounts ?

Answer:—We do not. Our prices are so very reasonable that we can allow no reductions, regardless of the amount of goods ordered.

Question:—Do you pay postage or express charges ?

Answer:—We prepay postage and express charges to any part of the United States provided an amount sufficient to cover the full list price of the goods desired accompanies the order ; therefore, you need send us only the price of each article ordered, as we will prepay transportation charges, no matter how large or how small your order. We do not pay express charges or return money charges on goods shipped C. O. D.

Question:—Do you sell your materials by the yard ?

Answer:—Yes: but only the materials used in our Made-to-Measure garments. A price list will be furnished on request.

Question:—Do you sell patterns ?

Answer:—We do not sell patterns of any of our garments, nor those of any other make.

Question:—Do you make riding habits ?

Answer:—We have a special leaflet illustrating and describing Ready-Made riding skirts, which we will be pleased to send you free on request. We will send you at the same time samples of the materials from which these skirts are made and quote prices for any of our jackets shown on pages 9 to 27, which are suitable for a riding coat.

Question:—Have you skirts for maternity wear ?

Answer:—You will find illustrations and descriptions of skirts for maternity wear by referring to styles 4752 and 4754 on page 76.

Question:—Will you buy for me any goods which you do not carry ?

Answer:—We will, as a matter of accommodation to our customers, but the full amount necessary to pay for the desired merchandise must accompany the order. *In such cases the goods cannot be returned, and we do not pay express charges or postage on them.*

$100 REWARD: We will pay this sum for information leading to the arrest and conviction of any person claiming to be our agent. We have no agents or branches.

Index

DON'T BE AFRAID OF MAKING A MISTAKE.

Every day we receive hundreds of orders from women who have never ordered by mail before. So don't hesitate for fear of making a mistake. Just write us in your own way what you want, and in any language. We will understand and ship your order promptly. Remember, you take no risk whatever.

Have you requested Samples of the Materials used for our Made-to-Measure Suits and Skirts? If not, sit down and write us for them at once. We will gladly send them to you free. Just say: "Please send me Samples of your new Spring and Summer materials for your Made-to-Measure Garments." Specify colors if you have any preference. We will send you a large assortment of Samples entirely free by return mail.

Don't spoil your Style Book. Don't cut out the illustrations. Simply write us the style numbers of the garments you wish. Keep your Style Book. If you mislay it, there will be many occasions when you will be sure to regret it.

Keep this Style Book where you can find it readily. Keep it so that you can use it frequently—so that you can shop from it. It will help you to save money in the buying of your wearing apparel. Experience in ordering from it will prove that this Style Book brings the convenience of a New York Department Store into your own home. It gives you New York's greatest advantage in variety, in style and in price. We pay postage and express charges.

Instructions for Ordering the MADE-TO-MEASURE Garments

Illustrated on Pages 9 to 29.

1. How to Order a Made-to-Measure Garment. **First**: Make your selections from the models shown on pages 9 to 29 of this Style Book. **Second**: Choose a material from any of our samples labelled Quality C, D, E, F, G and H. **Third**: Have your measurements taken at home according to our simple instructions on the Order Blank in **front** of this Style Book. **Fourth**: Carefully fill out the Order Blank, enclose your remittance and mail to us. **As we conduct a mail-order business, we receive orders by mail only.**

2. How to Select a Style. Select from pages 9 to 29 the style of garment you prefer. In ordering a suit to be made to your measure, you have the privilege of selecting the jacket of one style and the skirt of another, but only those shown on pages 9 to 29. To learn the price of a suit consisting of two Made-to-Measure styles, read the instructions given in paragraph 5 on this page

3. How to Select a Material for a Made-to-Measure Garment. Choose from our samples labelled Quality C, D, E, F, G and H, the material you like best, and note the quality printed on the pin-ticket attached. You can ascertain the price of your garment when made in that quality by referring to the figures under its description in this Style Book. If when you write us for samples, you do not find just exactly what you want among those we send you, write us stating the colors and qualities you prefer, and we will very gladly send you another assortment.

In selecting our stock of Spring and Summer materials, we found that the goods of the A and B grades contained cotton and shoddy. Therefore, we decided to discontinue those grades from our line, as we do not handle any materials we cannot recommend.

However, the great increase in the volume of our business during the past year enables us to offer the C and D grades at practically as low prices as were formerly charged for A and B qualities. At the same time, our customers will be receiving a very much better article.

4. How to Take Your Measurements for a Made-to-Measure Garment. Turn to the Order Blank in the front of this Style Book. The instructions printed thereon tell you exactly how your measurements can be taken by any one in your own home. It is not necessary to go to a dressmaker for this purpose. These instructions should be carefully read by you, as well as by the person who is to take your measurements. Remember, the measurements should be taken from your figure, and not from an old garment. Use an accurate tape measure, and do not make any allowance for seams. If you have any special instructions to give us as to how you wish your garment made or trimmed, or if there is any peculiarity about your figure, write us fully on a separate sheet and enclose it with the order. Do not fail to securely pin or sew samples of the materials you select in the spaces provided for them on our Order Blank.

5. How to Learn the Cost of a Made-to-Measure Suit Consisting of the Jacket and Skirt of Different Styles Shown on Pages 9 to 29. In ordering a suit to be made to your measure, you may combine the features of any of the styles shown on pages 9 to 29 of this Style Book. That is, if you are pleased with the jacket of one style, but prefer the skirt of another, we will make the suit exactly as you wish, combining the styles selected. **Please remember, however, that we will not make a suit combining one of our Ready-Made styles with one of our Made-to-Measure garments.**

The price of each jacket and skirt illustrated on pages 9 to 29 of this Style Book, is given separately under its description, and you can easily ascertain the cost of a suit consisting of the jacket of one style and the skirt of another, by adding the price of the jacket desired to that of the skirt you wish, in the same quality of material.

For example, if you wish a suit made of Quality C material, to consist of a jacket like style No. 4037 with a skirt like style No. 4039, you can ascertain the price of the suit by adding the cost of the jacket and skirt, as follows:

Jacket Style No. 4037, Quality C..$11.00
Skirt Style No. 4039, Quality C.. 5.50

Price of suit complete.......$16.50

Should you wish a suit made of Quality H material, with a jacket like style No. 4037, and the skirt like style No. 4039, the price would be figured as follows:

Jacket Style No. 4037, Quality H..$18.25
Skirt Style No. 4039, Quality H.. 12.75

Price of suit complete.......$31.00

The prices of all **Made-to-Measure** suits consisting of the jacket of one style and the skirt of another style must be figured according to these instructions.

6. Sleeves. If when ordering a Made-to-Measure garment, you do not fancy the sleeve shown with the style selected, we will substitute that of any other garment illustrated on pages 9 to 27 without extra charge, provided the sleeve you prefer does not require additional trimming.

4001   4002   4003

WE MAKE THESE GARMENTS TO MEASURE ONLY.
WRITE FOR FREE SAMPLES OF MATERIALS.

No. 4001 . . . $18.00 up

The symmetrical lines and tasteful adornment of this elegant London model make it in every way a splendid selection.

The **Coat** is semi-fitted with a lap-over cutaway front. For prices quoted below it can be made any length up to 32 inches in back. The chic silk tie is drawn through the collar in plaited effect and ends in tassels. Cuffs inlaid with silk and trimmed with buttons.

The **Skirt** has ten gores, and is trimmed, as pictured, with buttons. Wide bias fold around the bottom.

* For prices quoted Coat will be lined throughout with Good Satin. Skirt unlined.

Made of Quality	Price of Suit	Price of Coat	Price of Skirt
C cloth.......	$18.00	$10.75	$7.75
D "	20.50	12.00	9.00
E "	23.00	13.25	10.25
F "	26.00	14.75	11.75
G "	29.00	16.25	13.25
H "	32.50	18.00	15.00

No. 4002 . . . $16.50 up

A suit of distinct individuality, which bears unmistakably the indefinable stamp of perfect taste.

The **Coat** is a modified Robespierre model with chic revers and Directoire pockets. Collar is of silk edged with fancy braid. For prices quoted below it can be made any length up to 30 inches in back. It is semi-fitted both front and back.

The **Skirt** is side-plaited and comprises seven gores. A strap of the material extends down the front and two similar straps are applied around the bottom.

* For prices quoted Coat will be lined throughout with Good Satin. Skirt unlined.

Made of Quality	Price of Suit	Price of Coat	Price of Skirt
C cloth.......	$16.50	$9.50	$7.50
D "	19.00	10.75	8.75
E "	21.50	12.00	10.00
F "	24.50	13.50	11.50
G "	27.75	15.25	13.00
H "	31.50	17.25	14.75

No. 4003 . . . $20.00 up

The exquisite Directoire Costume illustrated here is a reigning favorite and cannot fail to elicit admiration.

The **Coat** is in pronounced cutaway outline with a lap-over front. It is semi-fitted and can be made any length up to 36 inches in back for prices quoted below. The collar and cuffs are of silk edged with fancy braid, and the chic silk tie reappearing above waist line is finished with tassels.

The **Skirt** is a flaring model, made with nine gores. Two folds of the material forming plaits, extend down the front.

* For prices quoted Coat will be lined throughout with Good Satin. Skirt unlined.

Made of Quality	Price of Suit	Price of Coat	Price of Skirt
C cloth.......	$20.00	$13.50	$7.00
D "	22.50	14.75	8.25
E "	25.50	16.50	9.50
F "	28.50	18.00	11.00
G "	32.00	20.00	12.50
H "	36.00	22.25	14.25

*Add 2.25 to the above prices if extra quality Silk or Skinner's Guaranteed Satin lining is desired in Coat 4001; add $2.00 if desired in Coat 4002; add $2.50 if desired in Coat 4003. You may select the Coat of one style and the Skirt of another; see page 8 for particulars as to prices.

4004

4006

4004

4005

4006

WE MAKE THESE GARMENTS TO MEASURE ONLY—WRITE FOR FREE SAMPLES OF MATERIALS.

No. 4004 . . . $18.00 up

This natty Coat Suit conforms in every way to the latest whims of Fashion.

The **Coat** has a single-breasted cutaway front and is semi-fitted. For prices quoted below it can be made any length up to 32 inches in back. Collar is inlaid with silk.

The **Skirt** is four-gored with folds and tailored straps of the material as pictured, and is trimmed down the front with buttons to accord with those used on Coat.

* For prices quoted Coat will be lined throughout with Good Satin. Skirt unlined.

Made of Quality	Price of Suit	Price of Coat	Price of Skirt
C cloth	$18.00	$10.50	$8.00
D "	20.50	11.75	9.25
E "	23.00	13.00	10.50
F "	26.00	14.50	12.00
G "	29.50	16.25	13.75
H "	33.00	18.00	15.75

No. 4005 . . . $13.00 up

Good taste and refinement are delightfully exemplified in this jaunty Suit.

The **Jacket** is single-breasted with a fly front closing. It is semi-fitted and displays straps of the material and buttons. For prices quoted it can be made any length up to 27 inches in back.

The **Skirt** is finished with tailored seams and is trimmed with buttons. It is an up to date four-gored model.

* For prices quoted Jacket will be lined throughout with Good Satin. Skirt unlined.

Made of Quality	Price of Suit	Price of Jacket	Price of Skirt
C cloth	$13.00	$8.50	$5.00
D "	15.50	9.75	6.25
E "	18.00	11.00	7.50
F "	21.00	12.50	9.00
G "	24.00	14.00	10.50
H "	27.50	15.75	12.25

No. 4006 . . . $19.00 up

Silk Hercules braid applied on all edges lends a picturesque charm to this handsome model.

The **Coat** can be made any length up to 32 inches in back for prices quoted below. It is semi-fitted, slashed at the sides and trimmed with soutache braid and buttons. The collar and cuffs are of silk edged with braid.

The **Skirt** is eight-gored, in flaring outline, with a slot seam down the front. A wide fold embellishes the lower edge.

* For prices quoted Coat will be lined throughout with Good Satin. Skirt unlined.

Made of Quality	Price of Suit	Price of Coat	Price of Skirt
C cloth	$19.00	$12.50	$7.00
D "	21.50	13.75	8.25
E "	24.00	15.00	9.50
F "	27.00	16.50	11.00
G "	30.00	18.00	12.50
H "	33.50	19.75	14.25

*Add $2.25 to the above prices if extra quality Silk or Skinner's Guaranteed Satin lining is desired in Coat 4004 or 4006; add $1.75 if desired in Jacket 4005. We will make any of these Coats or Skirts separately; see prices given under each description.

4007 4008 4009

WE MAKE THESE GARMENTS TO MEASURE ONLY—WRITE FOR FREE SAMPLES OF MATERIALS.

No. 4007 . . . $16.50 up

Graceful cutaway Coat Suits of this character are in high favor this season.

The **Coat** is single-breasted, semi-fitted, and can be made any length up to 36 inches in back for prices quoted below. It is neatly completed with lapped seams. The collar and cuffs are of taffeta silk, tailor stitched.

The **Skirt** is a stylish four-gored model, trimmed with buttons down the front and with a fold around the bottom.

* For prices quoted Coat will be lined throughout with Good Satin. Skirt unlined.

Made of Quality	Price of Suit	Price of Coat	Price of Skirt
C cloth	$16.50	$10.50	$6.50
D "	19.00	11.75	7.75
E "	21.50	13.00	9.00
F "	24.50	14.50	10.50
G "	27.50	16.00	12.00
H "	31.00	17.75	13.75

No. 4008 . . . $7.50 up

This chic model is remarkably effective considering the simplicity of the design.

The **Eton Jacket** is single-breasted, tight-fitting both front and back. Lapped seams supply an appropriate tailored completion.

The **Skirt** has seven gores in flaring outline, with lapped seams to match jacket.

* For prices quoted Jacket will be lined throughout with Good Satin. Skirt unlined.

Made of Quality	Price of Suit	Price of Jacket	Price of Skirt
C cloth	$7.50	$5.50	$5.00
D "	10.00	6.75	6.25
E "	12.50	8.00	7.50
F "	15.50	9.50	9.00
G "	18.50	11.00	10.50
H "	22.00	12.75	12.25

No. 4009 . . . $17.50 up

A handsome model is depicted here combining grace, beauty and practical adaptability.

The **Coat** is in lap-over effect in front and can be made any length up to 32 inches in back for prices quoted below. It is in semi-fitted outline. The jaunty roll collar is of the material handsomely edged with taffeta silk.

The **Skirt** is a flare design with nine gores. A wide fold is applied around the bottom. Skirt is finished with buttons and braid loops to match those on Coat.

* For prices quoted Coat will be lined throughout with Good Satin. Skirt unlined.

Made of Quality	Price of Suit	Price of Coat	Price of Skirt
C cloth	$17.50	$10.50	$7.50
D "	20.00	11.50	9.00
E "	22.50	12.75	10.50
F "	25.50	14.25	12.00
G "	28.50	15.75	13.50
H "	32.00	17.50	15.25

* Add $2.50 to the above prices if extra quality Silk or Skinner's Guranteed Satin lining is desired in Coat 4007; add $1.25 if desired in Jacket 4008; add $2.25 if desired in Coat 4009. You may select the Coat of one style and the Skirt of another; see page 8 for particulars as to prices.

WE MAKE THESE GARMENTS TO MEASURE ONLY—WRITE FOR FREE SAMPLES OF MATERIALS.

No. 4010 . . . $16.50 up

Suits with long graceful lines like the one pictured will be worn extensively this season.

The **Coat** is single-breasted, and can be made any length up to 30 inches in back for prices quoted below. It is semi-fitted and attractively trimmed with soutache loops and buttons on the lapels and pockets. The collar is inlaid with taffeta silk.

The **Skirt** is one of the new four-gored models, trimmed with two straps of the material, loops and buttons.

* For prices quoted Coat will be lined throughout with Good Satin. Skirt unlined.

Made of Quality	Price of Suit	Price of Coat	Price of Skirt
C cloth	$16.50	$10.00	$7.00
D "	19.00	11.25	8.25
E "	21.50	12.50	9.50
F "	24.50	14.00	11.00
G "	27.50	15.50	12.50
H "	31.00	17.25	14.25

No. 4011 . . . $16.50 up

Excellent taste is displayed in this smart London model, which is the acme of good style.

The **Coat** is semi-fitted, single-breasted, and finished with lapped seams. For prices quoted below, it can be made any length up to 32 inches in back.

The **Skirt** is nine-gored in flaring outline with a fold of the material around the lower edge.

* For prices quoted Coat will be lined throughout with Good Satin. Skirt unlined.

Made of Quality	Price of Suit	Price of Coat	Price of Skirt
C cloth	$16.50	$10.00	$7.00
D "	19.00	11.25	8.25
E "	21.50	12.50	9.75
F "	24.50	14.00	11.50
G "	27.50	15.50	13.00
H "	31.00	17.25	14.75

No. 4012 . . . $17.00 up

A decidedly chic suit which will appeal to women who appreciate clothes of character.

The **Coat** is in cutaway outline, semi-fitted and single-breasted. It is adorned with buttons and soutache loops. For prices quoted below it can be made any length up to 32 inches in back.

The **Skirt** is finished with lapped seams and has a flounce of the material trimmed with buttons and loops. Skirt is a nine-gored flaring model.

* For prices quoted Coat will be lined throughout with Good Satin.

Made of Quality	Price of Suit	Price of Coat	Price of Skirt
C cloth	$17.00	$9.50	$8.00
D "	19.50	10.75	9.25
E "	22.00	12.00	10.50
F "	25.00	13.50	12.00
G "	28.00	15.00	13.75
H "	31.50	16.75	15.50

*Add $2.00 to the above prices if extra quality Silk or Skinner's Guaranteed Satin lining is desired in Coat 4010; add $2.25 if desired in Coat 4011 or 4012. We will make any of these Coats and Skirts separately; see prices given under each description.

4013

4014

4015

WE MAKE THESE GARMENTS TO MEASURE ONLY—WRITE FOR FREE SAMPLES OF MATERIALS.

No. 4013 . . . $17.50 up

The **Coat** of this charming Suit can be made any length up to 32 inches in back. It is semi-fitted with a single-breasted front in cutaway effect. The collar and cuffs are of taffeta silk edged with Hercules and soutache braid. The tie is of silk ending in tassels.

The **Skirt** is six-gored, trimmed with straps of the material and buttons.

* For prices quoted Coat will be lined throughout with Good Satin. Skirt unlined.

Made of Quality	Price of Suit	Price of Coat	Price of Skirt
C cloth.......	$17.50	$11.00	$7.00
D "	20.00	12.25	8.25
E "	22.50	13.50	9.50
F "	25.50	15.00	11.00
G "	28.50	16.50	12.50
H "	32.00	18.25	14.25

No. 4014 . . . $18.00 up

The **Coat** of this modish Suit is single-breasted and semi-fitted. For prices quoted below it can be made any length up to 32 inches in back. Pockets and all edges are bound with tailor braid, and collar and cuffs are inlaid with taffeta silk. If braid is omitted, deduct $1.50 from prices quoted.

The **Skirt** comprises seven gores, and has three straps of the material around the bottom. Trimmed down front with buttons.

* For prices quoted Coat will be lined throughout with Good Satin. Skirt unlined.

Made of Quality	Price of Suit	Price of Coat	Price of Skirt
C cloth.......	$18.00	$11.50	$7.00
D "	20.50	12.75	8.25
E "	23.00	14.00	9.50
F "	26.00	15.50	11.00
G "	29.00	17.00	12.50
H "	32.50	18.75	14.25

No. 4015 . . . $18.50 up

A stunning Suit cut in the modified Directoire style now so much in vogue.

The **Coat** is single-breasted, in pronounced cutaway outline. Cuffs, collar and arm-holes of taffeta trimmed with soutache braid. Soutache loops and buttons applied front and back. Can be made any length up to 30 inches in back for prices quoted below.

The **Skirt** is four-gored, trimmed with buttons and straps of the material.

* For prices quoted Coat will be lined throughout with Good Satin. Skirt unlined.

Made of Quality	Price of Suit	Price of Coat	Price of Skirt
C cloth.......	$18.50	$12.00	$7.00
D "	21.00	13.25	8.25
E "	23.50	14.50	9.50
F "	26.50	16.00	11.00
G "	29.50	17.50	12.50
H "	33.00	19.25	14.25

*Add $2.25 to the above prices if extra quality Silk or Skinner's Guaranteed Satin lining is desired in Coats 4013 or 4014; add $2.00 if desired in Coat 4015. You may select the Coat of one style or the Skirt of another; see page 8 for particulars as to prices.

4016

4017

4017   4018

WE MAKE THESE GARMENTS TO MEASURE ONLY—WRITE FOR FREE SAMPLES OF MATERIALS.

No. 4016 · · · $17.50 up

This design will impress women of discrimination with its practical features.

The **Coat** is a popular cutaway model, semifitted, and can be made any length up to 32 inches in back for prices quoted below. The pocket flaps, sleeves and the back are trimmed with buttons.

The **Skirt** consists of thirteen gores, falling in side-plaits, and has a fold of the material around the bottom.

* For prices quoted Coat will be lined throughout with Good Satin. Skirt unlined.

Made of Quality	Price of Suit	Price of Coat	Price of Skirt
C cloth.......	$17.50	$9.50	$8.50
D "	20.50	11.00	10.00
E "	23.50	12.50	11.50
F "	26.50	14.00	13.00
G "	30.00	15.50	15.00
H "	34.00	17.50	17.00

No. 4017 · · · $16.00 up

A jaunty Suit appropriate for visiting, shopping or general utility, is shown above.

The **Jacket** is single-breasted and semifitted, and for prices quoted below can be made any length up to 27 inches in back. Collar is inlaid with taffeta silk edged with braid.

The **Skirt** has nine gores arranged in side-plaits. There is a wide fold around the bottom.

* For prices quoted Jacket will be lined throughout with Good Satin. Skirt unlined.

Made of Quality	Price of Suit	Price of Jacket	Price of Skirt
C cloth.......	$16.00	$9.00	$7.50
D "	18.50	10.25	8.75
E "	21.00	11.50	10.00
F "	24.00	13.00	11.50
G "	27.00	14.50	13.00
H "	30.50	16.25	14.75

No. 4018 · · · $16.00 up

This type of Coat Suit is extremely popular and will insure its wearer being smartly dressed.

The **Coat** is in decided cutaway outline with a single-breasted front. It is semi-fitted and can be made any length up to 30 inches in back for prices quoted below. The chic Tuxedo collar is inlaid with taffeta silk and finished with braid.

The **Skirt** is a graceful side-plaited model with the fulness stitched to below the hips. It consists of nine gores.

* For prices quoted Coat will be lined throughout with Good Satin. Skirt unlined.

Made of Quality	Price of Suit	Price of Coat	Price of Skirt
C cloth.......	$16.00	$10.00	$6.50
D "	18.50	11.25	7.75
E "	21.00	12.50	9.00
F "	24.00	14.00	10.50
G "	27.00	15.50	12.00
H "	30.50	17.25	13.75

*Add $2.25 to the above prices if extra quality Silk or Skinner's Guaranteed Satin lining is desired in Coat 4016; add $1.75 if desired in Jacket 4017; add $2.00 if desired in Coat 4018. We will make any of these Coats or Skirts separately; see prices given under each description.

4019

4021

4019　　　4020　　　4021

WE MAKE THESE GARMENTS TO MEASURE ONLY—WRITE FOR FREE SAMPLES OF MATERIALS.

No. 4019 . . . $17.00 up

A jaunty Suit, practical and smart, which will appeal to every up to date woman.

The **Coat** is cut in semi-fitted outline, with a single-breasted cutaway front, and can be made any length up to 32 inches in back for prices quoted below. The sleeves are trimmed with buttons.

The **Skirt** has nine gores arranged in graceful side-plaits, and displays a fold of the material around the bottom.

* For prices quoted Coat will be lined throughout with Good Satin. Skirt unlined.

Made of Quality	Price of Suit	Price of Coat	Price of Skirt
C cloth........	$17.00	$10.00	$7.50
D "	19.50	11.25	8.75
E "	22.00	12.50	10.00
F "	25.00	14.00	11.50
G "	28.00	15.50	13.00
H "	31.50	17.25	14.75

No. 4020 . . . $15.50 up

An attractive Tuxedo collar inlaid with silk and edged with fancy braid provides a chic decorative finish on the Jacket of this model.

The **Jacket** is double-breasted and can be made any length up to 24 inches in back for prices quoted below. It is semi-fitted and finished with straps of the material on the edges.

The **Skirt** is modeled in nine-gored outline, flaring at the lower edge, where it is trimmed with buttons.

* For prices quoted Jacket will be lined throughout with Good Satin. Skirt unlined.

Made of Quality	Price of Suit	Price of Jacket	Price of Skirt
C cloth........	$15.50	$10.00	$6.00
D "	18.00	11.25	7.25
E "	20.50	12.50	8.50
F "	23.50	14.00	10.00
G "	26.50	15.50	11.50
H "	30.00	17.25	13.25

No. 4021 . . . $18.00 up

The delightful style features of this fetching Costume will be immediately apparent to discerning women.

The **Coat** is made in lap-over effect with a cutaway front. It is semi-fitted and can be made any length up to 36 inches in back for prices quoted below. The collar is attractively inlaid with silk and edged with braid. The silk tie is finished with tassels.

The **Skirt** is nine-gored; flaring. The fold around the bottom is finished with buttons and loops in front.

* For prices quoted Coat will be lined throughout with Good Satin. Skirt unlined.

Made of Quality	Price of Suit	Price of Coat	Price of Skirt
C cloth........	$18.00	$11.50	$7.00
D "	20.50	12.75	8.25
E "	23.50	14.25	9.75
F "	26.50	16.00	11.00
G "	30.00	18.00	12.50
H "	34.00	20.00	14.50

*Add $2.25 to the above prices if extra quality Silk or Skinner's Guaranteed Satin lining is desired in Coat 4019; add $1.50 if desired in Jacket 4020; add $2.50 if desired in Coat 4021. You may select the Coat of one style and the Skirt of another; see page 8 for particulars as to prices.

4022

4024

4023

4024

WE MAKE THESE GARMENTS TO MEASURE ONLY.
WRITE FOR FREE SAMPLES OF MATERIALS.

No. 4022 . . . $19.00 up

An up-to-date Suit in cutaway outline is shown here, which is in its way a masterpiece.

The **Coat** can be made any length up to 30 inches in back for prices quoted below. Semi-fitted model with cutaway front, trimmed with tailored straps and loops of braid trimmed with buttons. Collar is inlaid with taffeta silk edged with fancy braid. Cuffs and collar finished with loops and buttons.

The **Skirt** consists of nine flaring gores and has three straps of the material around the bottom.

* For prices quoted Coat will be lined throughout with Good Satin. Skirt unlined.

Made of Quality	Price of Suit	Price of Coat	Price of Skirt
C cloth........	$19.00	$11.75	$7.75
D "	21.50	13.00	9.00
E "	24.00	14.25	10.25
F "	27.00	15.75	11.75
G "	30.50	17.50	13.50
H "	34.00	19.00	15.50

No. 4023 . . . $16.00 up

Smart simplicity characterizes this beautiful Suit which is correct and up-to-date in every detail.

The **Jacket** is single-breasted and semi-fitted. Collar, cuffs and pockets are inlaid with taffeta silk. Model is slashed at the sides. For prices quoted below it can be made any length up to 24 inches in back.

The **Skirt** is trimmed in front with buttons and simulated button holes of soutache braid. It consists of eight gores in flaring outline, and has a wide fold around the bottom.

* For prices quoted Jacket will be lined throughout with Good Satin. Skirt unlined.

Made of Quality	Price of Suit	Price of Jacket	Price of Skirt
C cloth........	$16.00	$9.25	$7.25
D "	18.50	10.50	8.50
E "	21.00	11.75	9.75
F "	24.00	13.25	11.25
G "	27.00	14.75	12.75
H "	30.50	16.50	14.50

No. 4024 . . . $17.50 up

As a smart visiting costume, this design is perfect. It exhibits excellent taste in every line.

The **Coat** is semi-fitted and displays the fashionable lap-over front. For prices quoted below it can be made any length up to 30 inches in back. Collar and cuffs of taffeta edged with fancy braid. The chic tie ends in tassels.

The **Skirt** has six gores in flaring effect, uniquely trimmed with straps of the material, buttons and soutache loops.

* For prices quoted Coat will be lined throughout with Good Satin. Skirt unlined.

Made of Quality	Price of Suit	Price of Coat	Price of Skirt
C cloth........	$17.50	$12.50	$5.50
D "	20.00	13.75	6.75
E "	22.50	15.00	8.00
F "	25.50	16.50	9.50
G "	28.50	18.00	11.00
H "	32.00	19.75	12.75

*Add $2.00 to the above prices if extra quality Silk or Skinner's Guaranteed Satin lining is desired in Coats 4022 or 4024; add $1.50 if desired in Jacket 4023. We will make any of these Coats or Skirts separately; see prices given under each description.

4025

4026

4027

WE MAKE THESE GARMENTS TO MEASURE ONLY.
WRITE FOR FREE SAMPLES OF MATERIALS.

No. 4025 . . . $18.00 up

A chic silk tie ending in tassels, gives distinction to this stunning Directoire costume.

The **Coat** is single-breasted, and can be made any length up to 32 inches in back for prices quoted below. It is a semi-fitted model, extremely stylish in cut. Collar and cuffs are of taffeta silk edged with braid.

The **Skirt** has seven gores in flaring effect, and is trimmed with soutache loops and buttons to match those used on the coat. A wide fold appears around the bottom.

* For prices quoted Coat will be lined throughout with Good Satin. Skirt unlined.

Made of Quality	Price of Suit	Price of Coat	Price of Skirt
C cloth........	$18.00	$11.00	$7.50
D "	20.50	12.25	8.75
E "	23.00	13.50	10.00
F "	26.00	15.00	11.50
G "	29.00	16.50	13.00
H "	32.50	18.25	14.75

No. 4026 . . . $16.00 up

Soutache loops and buttons are employed with striking effect on both the skirt and coat of this charming cutaway model.

The **Coat** can be made any length up to 30 inches in back for prices quoted below. It is semi-fitted. Pockets, sleeves and all edges are trimmed with tailor braid.

The **Skirt** is one of the modish four-gored designs.

* For prices quoted Coat will be lined throughout with Good Satin. Skirt unlined.

Made of Quality	Price of Suit	Price of Coat	Price of Skirt
C cloth........	$16.00	$10.50	$6.00
D "	18.50	11.75	7.25
E "	21.00	13.00	8.50
F "	24.00	14.50	10.00
G "	27.00	16.00	11.50
H "	30.50	17.75	13.25

No. 4027 . . . $14.50 up

This double-breasted model, in cutaway outline, is an adaptation of one of the newest London styles.

The **Coat** is semi-fitted, finished with tailor stitching. For prices quoted below it can be made any length up to 30 inches in back.

The **Skirt** is in four-gored effect, distinctly new in cut, and is trimmed with buttons.

* For prices quoted Coat will be lined throughout with Good Satin. Skirt unlined.

Made of Quality	Price of Suit	Price of Coat	Price of Skirt
C cloth........	$14.50	$10.00	$5.00
D "	17.00	11.25	6.25
E "	19.50	12.50	7.50
F "	22.50	14.00	9.00
G "	25.50	15.50	10.50
H "	28.50	17.00	12.00

* Add $2.25 to the above prices if extra quality Silk or Skinner's Guaranteed Satin lining is desired in Coat 4025; add $2.00 if desired in Coat 4026 or 4027. You may select the Coat of one style and the Skirt of another; see page 8 for particulars as to prices.

4028

4029

4030

WE MAKE THESE GARMENTS TO MEASURE ONLY—WRITE FOR FREE SAMPLES OF MATERIALS.

No. 4028 . . . $15.00 up

An air of smartness distinguishes this mannish tailored Suit.

The **Jacket** is in double-breasted effect, and can be made any length up to 27 inches in back for prices quoted below. It is semi-fitted and finished with lapped seams.

The **Skirt** comprises nine gores, arranged in deep side-plaits. It is trimmed with a wide fold of the material.

* For prices quoted Jacket will be lined throughout with Good Satin. Skirt unlined.

Made of Quality	Price of Suit	Price of Jacket	Price of Skirt
C cloth..	$15.00	$8.00	$7.75
D "	17.50	9.25	9.00
E "	20.00	10.50	10.50
F "	23.00	12.00	12.00
G "	26.00	13.50	13.75
H "	29.50	15.00	15.50

No. 4029 . . . $16.50 up

The charming sleeveless Jumper Dress and Prince Chap Jacket shown here is ideal for Summer wear.

The **Jacket** is semi-fitted, and can be made any length up to 24 inches in back.

The One-Piece **Jumper Dress** is plaited, finished with fancy braid and buttons. Closes in back. The flare Skirt has four gores, and is attached to jumper. Lace guimpe [not included.

* For prices quoted Jacket will be lined throughout with Good Satin. Skirt unlined.

Made of Quality	Price of Suit	Price of Jacket	Price of Jumper Dress
C cloth........	$16.50	$7.00	$10.00
D "	19.00	8.25	11.25
E "	21.50	9.50	12.50
F "	24.50	11.00	14.00
G "	27.50	12.50	15.50
H "	31.00	14.25	17.25

No. 4030 . . . $17.50 up

The modish cutaway model pictured above is eminently suitable for smart outdoor wear.

The **Coat** is semi-fitted, and can be made any length up to 32 inches in back for prices quoted below. It is single-breasted. Stitched straps of the material and buttons provide an appropriate tailored finish.

The **Skirt** has nine gores, stitched to below the hips and from there falling in side-plaits. The wide fold around the bottom is trimmed with buttons.

* For prices quoted Coat will be lined throughout with Good Satin. Skirt unlined.

Made of Quality	Price of Suit	Price of Coat	Price of Skirt
C cloth........	$17.50	$10.25	$7.75
D "	20.50	11.75	9.25
E "	23.50	13.25	10.75
F "	26.50	14.75	12.25
G "	30.00	16.50	14.00
H "	33.50	18.25	15.75

* Add $1.75 to the above prices if extra quality Silk or Skinner's Guaranteed Satin lining is desired in Jacket 4028; add $1.50 if desired in Jacket 4029; add $2.25 if desired in Coat 4030. We will make any of these Coats or skirts separately; see prices given under each description.

4031

4032

4033

WE MAKE THESE GARMENTS TO MEASURE ONLY—WRITE FOR FREE SAMPLES OF MATERIALS.

No. 4031 . . . $16.50 up

The lines of this smart street Suit make it generally becoming, and it is in every way an ideal selection.

The **Coat** is double-breasted, and can be made any length up to 30 inches in back for prices quoted below. It is semi-fitted and finished with tailored straps of the material. Collar and cuffs are inlaid with silk, and a detachable vestee of white piqué at the neck affords a smart completion.

The **Skirt** consists of seven gores, flaring at the lower edge where a wide fold is applied.

* For prices quoted Coat will be lined throughout with Good Satin. Skirt unlined.

Made of Quality	Price of Suit	Price of Coat	Price of Skirt
C cloth	$16.50	$9.50	$7.50
D "	19.00	10.75	8.75
E "	22.00	12.25	10.25
F "	25.00	13.75	11.75
G "	28.50	15.50	13.50
H "	32.00	17.25	15.25

No. 4032 . . . $19.75 up

A handsomely tailored Jumper Dress in semi-princess effect and a chic Prince Chap Jacket are included in this attractive style.

The **Jacket** is semi-fitted, single-breasted, and can be made any length up to 27 inches in back. Patch pockets give a smart finish.

The sleeveless **Jumper Dress** is plaited and finished with loops and buttons. Collar trimmed with narrow fancy braid. Silk tie ends in tassels. Closes in back. Lace guimpe not included. Skirt portion has nine gores with wide fold and is attached to Jumper.

* For prices quoted Jacket will be lined throughout with Good Satin. Jumper unlined.

Made of Quality	Price of Suit	Price of Jacket	Price of Jumper Dress
C cloth	$19.75	$8.00	$12.25
D "	22.50	9.25	13.75
E "	25.50	10.50	15.50
F "	28.75	12.00	17.25
G "	32.25	13.50	19.25
H "	36.00	15.00	21.25

No. 4033 . . . $17.50 up

This effective Costume exhibits in its shaping the essentials of the latest vogues.

The **Coat** is single-breasted and decidedly cutaway in outline. For prices quoted it can be made any length up to 32 inches in back. It is fancifully trimmed with loops and buttons on fronts, back and on the novel pocket flaps. The collar is inlaid with silk and trimmed with buttons.

The **Skirt** is a side-plaited model, made with nine gores and displays a fold of the material around the bottom.

* For prices quoted Coat will be lined throughout with Good Satin. Skirt unlined.

Made of Quality	Price of Suit	Price of Coat	Price of Skirt
C cloth	$17.50	$10.50	$7.50
D "	20.00	11.75	8.75
E "	22.50	13.00	10.00
F "	25.50	14.50	11.50
G "	29.00	16.25	13.25
H "	33.00	18.25	15.25

*Add $2.00 to the above prices if extra quality Silk or Skinner's Guaranteed Satin lining is desired in Coat 4031; add $1.75 if desired in Jacket 4032; add $2.25 if desired in Coat 4033. You may select the Coat of one style and the Skirt or Jumper Dress of another; see page 8 for particulars.

4034   4035   4036

WE MAKE THESE GARMENTS TO MEASURE ONLY—WRITE FOR FREE SAMPLES OF MATERIALS.

No. 4034 . . . $16.50 up

This smart Suit, conservative in line and development, is in exquisite taste and the style is perfect.

The **Coat** is single-breasted and for prices quoted below can be made any length up to 32 inches in back. It is semi-fitted both front and back and made with lapped seams. Collar and cuffs are inlaid with taffeta silk.

The **Skirt** is a graceful model, made in the new four-gored style with a lapped seam down the front, which is trimmed with soutache loops and buttons. A wide fold is applied around the bottom.

* For prices quoted below Coat will be lined throughout with Good Satin. Skirt unlined.

Made of Quality	Price of Suit	Price of Coat	Price of Skirt
C cloth	$16.50	$10.00	$7.00
D "	19.00	11.25	8.25
E "	21.50	12.50	9.50
F "	24.50	14.00	11.00
G "	27.50	15.50	12.50
H "	31.00	17.25	14.25

No. 4035 . . . $12.50 up

A charming Prince Chap model is shown here, the youthful lines of which explain its popularity.

The **Jacket** is single-breasted and is made half loose-fitting both front and back. For prices quoted below it can be made any length up to 24 inches in back. The stylish notched collar and the button-trimmed cuffs are of the material.

The **Skirt** is made in flaring effect with nine gores, and is finished with lapped seams and trimmed with buttons.

* For prices quoted below Jacket will be lined with Good Satin. Skirt unlined.

Made of Quality	Price of Suit	Price of Jacket	Price of Skirt
C cloth	$12.50	$7.00	$6.00
D "	15.00	8.25	7.25
E "	17.50	9.50	8.50
F "	20.50	11.00	10.00
G "	23.50	12.50	11.50
H "	27.00	14.25	13.25

No. 4036 . . . $18.00 up

A modish Suit which is not too elaborate for ordinary uses, but is nevertheless appropriate for afternoon or church wear.

The **Coat** is single-breasted and can be made any length up to 32 inches in back for prices quoted below. It is a semi-fitted model finished with tailor-stitched seams and modishly trimmed with loops and buttons. The chic collar is inlaid with striped silk.

The **Skirt** is seven-gored in flaring effect and has a strap of the material around the bottom. Soutache loops and buttons down the front provide a smart completion.

* For prices quoted below Coat will be lined with Good Satin. Skirt unlined.

Made of Quality	Price of Suit	Price of Coat	Price of Skirt
C cloth	$18.00	$11.50	$7.00
D "	20.50	12.75	8.25
E "	23.00	14.00	9.50
F "	26.00	15.50	11.00
G "	29.00	17.00	12.50
H "	32.50	18.75	14.25

*Add $2.25 to the above prices if extra quality Silk or Skinner's Guaranteed Satin lining is desired in Coats 4034 or 4036; add $1.50 if desired in Jacket 4035. We will make any of these Coats or Skirts separately; see prices given under each description.

WE MAKE THESE GARMENTS TO MEASURE ONLY—WRITE FOR FREE SAMPLES OF MATERIALS.

No. 4037 . . . $16.50 up

A graceful Suit which has received enthusiastic approbation from the élite of Fashion.

The **Coat** can be made any length up to 30 inches in back for prices quoted below. It is semi-fitted both front and back and attractively trimmed with tailored straps of the material. Taffeta silk and soutache braid form the collar effect, and are used on the sleeves to simulate cuffs.

The **Skirt** has six flaring gores, is ornamented with straps of the material, and trimmed with buttons and loops.

* For prices quoted below Coat will be lined with Good Satin. Skirt unlined.

Made of Quality	Price of Suit	Price of Coat	Price of Skirt
C cloth	$16.50	$11.00	$6.00
D "	19.00	12.25	7.25
E "	21.50	13.50	8.50
F "	24.50	15.00	10.00
G "	27.50	16.50	11.50
H "	31.00	18.25	13.25

No. 4038 . . . $17.00 up

This modish semi-fitted cutaway coat will appeal to women who seek smart effects.

The **Coat** is semi-fitted both front and back, and can be made any length up to 32 inches in back for prices quoted below. It is distinctly up-to-date in cut, and is finished with the new Directoire pockets.

The **Skirt** is finished with lapped seams to match coat and has a flounce of the same material, trimmed with loops and buttons. It is made in flaring effect with nine gores.

* For prices quoted below Coat will be lined with Good Satin. Skirt unlined.

Made of Quality	Price of Suit	Price of Coat	Price of Skirt
C cloth	$17.00	$10.00	$7.50
D "	19.50	11.25	8.75
E "	22.00	12.50	10.00
F "	25.00	14.00	11.50
G "	28.00	15.50	13.00
H "	31.50	17.25	14.75

No. 4039 . . . $12.00 up

This mannish model will meet with the approval of the most discriminating wearer.

The **Jacket** is single-breasted and made with a fly front. It is semi-fitted both front and back. For prices quoted below it can be made any length up to 24 inches in back.

The **Skirt** is one of the modish flaring models comprising seven gores, and is smartly finished with lapped seams to match Jacket.

* For prices quoted Jacket will be lined throughout with Good Satin. Skirt unlined.

Made of Quality	Price of Suit	Price of Jacket	Price of Skirt
C cloth	$12.00	$7.00	$5.50
D "	14.50	8.25	6.75
E "	17.00	9.50	8.00
F "	20.00	11.00	9.50
G "	23.00	12.50	11.00
H "	26.50	14.25	12.75

*Add $2.00 to the above prices if extra quality Silk or Skinner's Guaranteed Satin lining is desired in Coat 4037; add $2.25 if desired in Coat 4038; add $1.50 if desired in Jacket 4039. You may select the Coat of one style and the Skirt of another; see page 8 for particulars as to prices.

WE MAKE THESE GARMENTS TO MEASURE ONLY—WRITE FOR FREE SAMPLE OF MATERIALS.

No. 4040 . . . $12.00 up	No. 4041 . . . $18.00 up	No. 4042 . . . $19.50 up
A jaunty Suit of this kind always holds its own in the esteem of practical women.	A stunning model with the elaborate style characteristic of the present season.	This becoming Suit displays all of the Season's salient style features.
The **Jacket** is double-breasted, and can be made any length up to 24 inches in back for prices quoted below. It is a semi-fitted model, smartly finished with tailor-stitched seams.	The **Coat** displays the new lap-over front and is bound on all edges with Hercules braid paralleled by one row of soutache braid. Collar is embellished with silk and is also braid-trimmed. The coat is semi-fitted, and for prices quoted below can be made any length up to 30 inches in back.	The **Coat** can be made any length up to 32 inches in back. It is semi-fitted, and the collar, cuffs and revers are of taffeta relieved with braid.
The **Skirt** is a graceful seven-gored, flaring design with the seams stitched to match Jacket.	The **Skirt** comprises seven gores, flaring at the lower edge, and is ornamented with tailored straps finished with buttons.	The **Skirt** has two folds of the material and is trimmed down the left side with buttons and soutache loops. It consists of seven gores.
* For prices quoted Jacket will be lined throughout with Good Satin. Skirt unlined.	* For prices quoted Coat will be lined throughout with Good Satin. Skirt unlined.	* For prices quoted Coat will be lined throughout with Good Satin. Skirt unlined.

Made of Quality	Price of Suit	Price of Jacket	Price of Skirt	Made of Quality	Price of Suit	Price of Coat	Price of Skirt	Made of Quality	Price of Suit	Price of Coat	Price of Skirt
C cloth	$12.00	$7.00	$5.50	C cloth	$18.00	$12.00	$6.50	C cloth	$19.50	$12.50	$7.50
D "	14.50	8.25	6.75	D "	20.50	13.25	7.75	D "	22.00	13.75	8.75
E "	17.00	9.50	8.00	E "	23.00	14.50	9.00	E "	25.00	15.50	10.00
F "	20.00	11.00	9.50	F "	26.00	16.00	10.50	F "	28.00	17.25	11.50
G "	23.00	12.50	11.00	G "	29.00	17.50	12.00	G "	31.50	19.00	13.25
H "	26.50	14.25	12.75	H "	32.50	19.25	13.75	H "	35.00	20.75	15.00

*Add $1.50 to the above prices if extra quality Silk or Skinner's Guaranteed Satin lining is desired in Jacket 4040; add $2.00 if desired in Coat 4041; add $2.25 if desired in Coat 4042. We will make any of these Coats or Skirts separately; see prices given under each description.

4044

4045

4044

4043

4044

4045

WE MAKE THESE GARMENTS TO MEASURE ONLY—WRITE FOR FREE SAMPLES OF MATERIALS.

No. 4043 . . . $17.50 up

A faultless design which responds to every requirement of style and utility.

The **Coat** is single-breasted and can be made any length up to 32 inches in back for prices quoted below. It is semi-fitted and smartly trimmed with buttons and tailored straps of the material.

The **Skirt** is nine-gored with the fulness disposed in graceful side-plaits. Buttons finish the front and a wide fold extends around the bottom.

* For prices quoted Coat will be lined throughout with Good Satin. Skirt unlined.

Made of Quality	Price of Suit	Price of Coat	Price of Skirt
C cloth........	$17.50	$10.00	$8.00
D "	20.00	11.25	9.25
E "	22.50	12.50	10.50
F "	25.50	14.00	12.00
G "	28.50	15.50	13.75
H "	32.00	17.25	15.50

No. 4044 . . . $17.50 up

One of the stunning new slashed coats is shown here, attractively trimmed with soutache loops and buttons.

The **Coat** can be made any length up to 32 inches in back for prices quoted below. It is semi-fitted and has a single-breasted front.

The **Skirt** has nine gores in flaring effect with straps of the material applied around the bottom.

* For prices quoted Coat will be lined throughout with Good Satin. Skirt unlined.

Made of Quality	Price of Suit	Price of Coat	Price of Skirt
C cloth......	$17.50	10.50	7.50
D "	20.00	11.75	8.75
E "	22.50	13.00	10.00
F "	25.50	14.50	11.50
G "	28.50	16.00	13.00
H "	32.00	17.75	14.75

No. 4045 . . . $18.50 up

A high Consulat collar and a chic silk tie ending in tassels distinguish this handsome Coat Suit.

The **Coat** is semi-fitted and has a single-breasted cutaway front. For prices quoted it can be made any length up to 32 inches in back. Silk braid outlined by soutache provides a smart touch both front and back.

The **Skirt** has nine gores with a wide fold around the bottom.

* For prices quoted Coat will be lined throughout with Good Satin. Skirt unlined.

Made of Quality	Price of Suit	Price of Coat	Price of Skirt
C cloth........	$18.50	$11.50	$7.50
D "	21.00	12.75	8.75
E "	23.50	14.00	10.00
F "	26.50	15.50	11.50
G "	29.50	17.00	13.00
H "	33.00	18.75	14.75

* Add $2.25 to the above prices if extra quality Silk or Skinner's Guaranteed Satin lining is desired in any of these Coats. You may select the Coat of one style and the Skirt of another; see page 8 for particulars as to prices.

4047

4048

4047

4048

4046

WE MAKE THESE GARMENTS TO MEASURE ONLY.
WRITE FOR FREE SAMPLES OF MATERIALS.

No. 4046 . . . $19.50 up

This is one of this Season's charming combination Jumper Dress and Coat Costumes.

The **Coat** is single-breasted, and can be made any length up to 30 inches in back for prices quoted below. It is semi-fitted and modishly trimmed with straps of the material.

The **Jumper Dress** is sleeveless and is made in Princess effect. The neck is outlined with a strap of the material trimmed with buttons. The Skirt is attached to Jumper, and is made with seven gores. It has a strap of the material around the bottom. Lace guimpe is not included. Dress closes in back.

* For prices quoted Coat will be lined throughout with Good Satin. Skirt unlined.

Made of Quality	Price of Suit	Price of Coat	Price of Jumper Dress
C cloth........	$19.50	$10.50	$9.50
D "	22.25	11.75	11.00
E "	25.25	13.00	12.75
F "	28.50	14.50	14.50
G "	32.00	16.00	16.50
H "	35.50	17.50	18.50

No. 4047 . . . $16.50 up

Soutache loops and buttons provide the chic embellishment on this delightful Coat Suit.

The single-breasted **Coat** is in cutaway effect with long graceful lines. For prices quoted below it can be made any length up to 36 inches in back.

The **Skirt** is a flare design with six gores. It has a slot seam down the center of the front. It is trimmed with loops and buttons.

* For prices quoted Coat will be lined throughout with Good Satin. Skirt unlined.

Made of Quality	Price of Suit	Price of Coat	Price of Skirt
C cloth........	$16.50	$11.50	$5.50
D "	19.00	12.75	6.75
E "	21.50	14.00	8.00
F "	24.50	15.50	9.50
G "	27.50	17.00	11.00
H "	31.00	18.75	12.75

No. 4048 . . . $20.00 up

Tailor braid has been used on the edges of this design with striking effect, and its becoming lines place it at once above the ordinary.

The **Coat** is in double-breasted effect and is semi-fitted. It can be made any length up to 30 inches in back for prices quoted below. It has two plaits on each side of both front and back. Collar and cuffs are of taffeta silk edged with braid.

The **Skirt** consists of nine gores with the fulness arranged in side-plaits. A fold of the material is applied around the bottom.

* For prices quoted Coat will be lined throughout with Good Satin. Skirt unlined.

Made of Quality	Price of Suit	Price of Coat	Price of Skirt
C cloth...	$20.00	$12.50	$8.00
D "	22.50	13.75	9.25
E "	25.50	15.50	10.50
F "	28.50	17.25	11.75
G "	32.00	19.00	13.50
H "	36.00	21.00	15.50

*Add $2.00 to the above prices if extra quality Silk or Skinner's Guaranteed Satin lining is desired in Coat 4046 or 4048; add $2.50 if desired in Coat 4047. We will make any of these Coats, Skirts or the Jumper Dress separately; see prices given under each description.

4049   **4050**   **4051**

WE MAKE THESE GARMENTS TO MEASURE ONLY.
WRITE FOR FREE SAMPLES OF MATERIALS.

No. 4049 . . . $20.00 up

A serviceable Jumper Dress with a natty separate Coat is one of the most convenient styles of the present season.

The **Coat** is single-breasted, semi-fitted, and can be made any length up to 32 inches in back for prices quoted below.

The **Jumper Dress** is sleeveless and is tucked and trimmed with buttons and straps of the material; closes in back. The nine-gored, side-plaited Skirt portion has a strap of the material around the bottom. Lace guimpe is not included.

* For prices quoted Coat will be lined throughout with Good Satin. Jumper unlined.

Made of Quality	Price of Suit	Price of Coat	Price of Jumper Dress
C cloth........	$20.00	$10.00	$10.50
D "	23.00	11.50	12.00
E "	26.00	12.75	13.75
F "	29.50	14.25	15.75
G "	33.00	15.75	17.75
H "	37.00	17.25	20.25

No. 4050 . . . $17.00 up

Straps of silk on all edges and down the fronts give a dressy air to the exquisite model pictured above.

The **Jacket** is single-breasted, semi-fitted, and can be made any length up to 27 inches in back for prices quoted below.

The **Skirt** has seven gores, in flaring outline. The fold of the material is edged with silk and finished with soutache loops and buttons to match those on the Jacket.

* For prices quoted Jacket will be lined throughout with Good Satin. Skirt unlined.

Made of Quality	Price of Suit	Price of Jacket	Price of Skirt
C cloth........	$17.00	$10.50	$7.00
D "	19.50	11.75	8.25
E "	22.00	13.00	9.50
F "	25.00	14.50	11.00
G "	28.00	16.00	12.50
H "	31.50	17.75	14.25

No. 4051 . . . $19.00 up

The **Coat** of this smart Suit is a cutaway design in double-breasted effect. It is semi-fitted, and finished with straps of the material and buttons. The neck displays a collar effect of silk combined with rich fancy garniture and tailor braid. For prices quoted below it can be made any length up to 30 inches in back.

The **Skirt** comprises seven gores with three plaits at each seam. It has one fold of the material.

* For prices quoted Coat will be lined throughout with Good Satin. Skirt unlined.

Made of Quality	Price of Suit	Price of Coat	Price of Skirt
C cloth........	$19.00	$11.00	$8.50
D "	21.50	12.25	9.75
E "	24.00	13.50	11.00
F "	27.00	15.00	12.50
G "	30.50	16.75	14.25
H "	34.00	18.50	16.00

*Add $2.25 to the above prices if extra quality Silk or Skinner's Guaranteed Satin lining is desired in Coat 4049; add $1.75 if desired in Jacket 4050; add $2.00 if desired in Coat 4051. You may select the Coat of one style and Skirt or the Jumper Dress of another; see page 8 for particulars.

4052

4053

4054

WE MAKE THESE GARMENTS TO MEASURE ONLY—WRITE FOR FREE SAMPLES OF MATERIALS.

No. 4052 . . . $15.00 up

This trim Suit is unobtrusive in design, extremely smart and will appeal to conservative dressers.

The **Jacket** is single-breasted and semi-fitted; made any length up to 27 inches in back for prices quoted below. It is finished in the approved manner with lapped seams.

The **Skirt** is side-plaited and is made with nine gores. A fold of the material is applied around the bottom, also extending upward on the sides; trimmed with buttons.

* For prices quoted Jacket will be lined throughout with Good Satin. Skirt unlined.

Made of Quality	Price of Suit	Price of Jacket	Price of Skirt
C cloth	$15.00	$7.50	$8.00
D "	17.50	8.75	9.25
E "	20.00	10.00	10.50
F "	23.00	11.50	12.00
G "	26.00	13.00	13.50
H "	29.50	14.75	15.25

No. 4053 . . . $14.50 up

The modest simplicity of this modish Suit serves to accentuate the beauty of its faultless lines.

The **Jacket** is single-breasted with a fly front. It is semi-fitted both front and back, and for prices quoted below it can be made any length up to 24 inches in back.

The **Skirt**, which comprises nine gores, is in flaring outline and has a fold of the material paralleled by a narrow strap around the bottom.

* For prices quoted Jacket will be lined throughout with Good Satin. Skirt unlined.

Made of Quality	Price of Suit	Price of Jacket	Price of Skirt
C cloth	$14.50	$8.00	$7.00
D "	17.00	9.25	8.25
E "	19.50	10.50	9.50
F "	22.50	12.00	11.00
G "	25.50	13.50	12.50
H "	29.00	15.25	14.25

No. 4054 . . . $13.50 up

A chic vestee of white piqué which outlines the silk Tuxedo collar of this Suit provides an attractive touch of individuality.

The **Jacket** is single-breasted and can be made any length up to 24 inches in back for prices quoted below. It is semi-fitted and closes with a fly front.

The **Skirt** consists of seven gores, flaring smartly at the bottom, and is finished with lapped seams.

* For prices quoted Jacket will be lined throughout with Good Satin. Skirt unlined.

Made of Quality	Price of Suit	Price of Jacket	Price of Skirt
C cloth	$13.50	$9.00	$5.00
D "	16.00	10.25	6.25
E "	18.50	11.50	7.50
F "	21.50	13.00	9.00
G "	24.50	14.50	10.50
H "	28.00	16.25	12.25

*Add **$1.75** to the above prices if extra quality Silk or Skinner's Guaranteed Satin lining is desired in Jacket 4052; add $1.50 if desired in Jackets 4053 or 4054. We will make any of these Jackets or Skirts separately; see prices given under each description.

4055   4056   4057

WE MAKE THESE GARMENTS TO MEASURE ONLY—WRITE FOR FREE SAMPLES OF MATERIALS.

No. 4055 . . . $13.00 up

The natty mannish model pictured here is a splendid selection for serviceable wear.

The **Jacket,** which is single-breasted, can be made any length up to 27 inches in back for prices quoted below. It is semi-fitted. The collar is trimmed with tiny buttons.

The **Skirt** consists of seven gores, stitched to a little below the hips, and from there falling in side-plaits.

* For prices quoted Jacket will be lined throughout with Good Satin. Skirt unlined.

Made of Quality	Price of Suit	Price of Jacket	Price of Skirt
C cloth	$13.00	$7.50	$6.00
D "	15.50	8.75	7.25
E "	18.00	10.00	8.50
F "	21.00	11.50	10.00
G "	24.00	13.00	11.50
H "	27.50	14.75	12.25

No. 4056 . . . $20.00 up

This handsome creation will respond to the most exacting demands of style in dress.

The **Coat** displays a vest effect of fancy garniture, and is trimmed with tailor braid. Collar and cuffs are of silk edged with braid. Silk tie finished with tassels. For prices quoted below it can be made any length up to 32 inches in back.

The **Skirt** has seven gores stitched to a little below the hips, with three plaits on each seam.

* For prices quoted Coat will be lined throughout with Good Satin. Skirt unlined.

Made of Quality	Price of Suit	Price of Coat	Price of Skirt
C cloth	$20.00	$12.75	$7.75
D "	23.00	14.50	9.00
E "	26.25	16.50	10.25
F "	29.75	18.50	11.75
G "	33.25	20.50	13.25
H "	37.00	22.50	15.00

No. 4057 . . . $15.50 up

The original design of this handsome street Suit has gained for it instant popularity.

The **Jacket** is single-breasted and can be made any length up to 27 inches in back for prices quoted below. It is a semi-fitted model trimmed around the neck and down the front with straps of the material. Neck is further ornamented with soutache braid.

The **Skirt** is side-plaited and consists of nine gores. A bias fold contributes an appropriate tailored completion.

* For prices quoted Jacket will be lined throughout with Good Satin. Skirt unlined.

Made of Quality	Price of Suit	Price of Jacket	Price of Skirt
C cloth	$15.50	$8.25	$7.75
D "	18.00	9.50	9.00
E "	20.75	11.00	10.25
F "	23.75	12.50	11.75
G "	27.00	14.25	13.25
H "	30.50	16.00	15.00

*Add $1.75 to the above prices if extra quality Silk or Skinner's Guaranteed Satin lining is desired in Jackets 4055 or 4057; add $2.25 if desired in Coat 4056. You may select the Coat of one style and the Skirt of another; see page 8 for particulars as to prices.

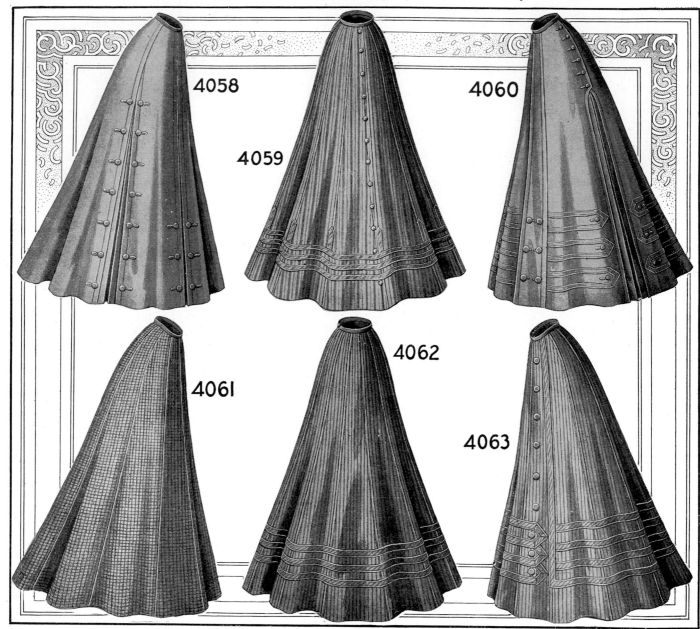

WE MAKE THESE SKIRTS TO MEASURE ONLY—WRITE FOR FREE SAMPLES OF MATERIALS.

No. 4058 . . . $8.00 up

This stunning Skirt is one of the new four-gored models now so popular among devotees of Fashion. It has a slot seam down the front and double inverted plaits at the sides. Soutache loops and buttons furnish an appropriate tailored finish.

Made of Quality		Made of Quality	
C cloth....	$8.00	F cloth....	$12.00
D "	9.25	G "	13.50
E "	10.50	H "	15.25

No. 4061 . . . $5.50 up

This attractive English walking Skirt is severely plain, but the lines are perfect and it is admirable for all around wear. It comprises seven gores in flaring outline and is finished with lapped seams.

Made of Quality		Made of Quality	
C cloth....	$5.50	F cloth....	$9.50
D "	6.75	G "	11.00
E "	8.00	H "	12.75

No. 4059 . . . $7.75 up

Flare Skirts are exceedingly fashionable this season. This pleasing example is made with nine gores and finished with lapped seams. Buttons trim the front, and parallel straps of the material are applied around the bottom with points extending upward on each gore.

Made of Quality		Made of Quality	
C cloth....	$7.75	F cloth....	$11.75
D "	9.00	G "	13.25
E "	10.25	H "	15.00

No. 4062 . . . $7.50 up

This charming flare model is strictly tailored throughout and will be found to answer all requirements of style and dress. It consists of nine gores strictly tailor stitched and has three straps of the material applied in parallel rows around the bottom.

Made of Quality		Made of Quality	
C cloth....	$7.50	F cloth....	$11.50
D "	8.75	G "	13.00
E "	10.00	H "	14.75

No. 4060 . . . $8.50 up

Anyone desiring a smart Skirt will immediately be attracted to the up to date model shown here. It comprises five gores with inverted plaits admitted at the sides. Straps of the material appear around the bottom, and soutache loops and buttons provide an agreeable decorative device.

Made of Quality		Made of Quality	
C cloth....	$8.50	F cloth....	$12.50
D "	9.75	G "	14.00
E "	11.00	H "	15.75

No. 4063 . . . $8.25 up

One of the popular nine-gored flaring Skirts is shown here. A serviceable tailored Skirt of this kind is a necessity, and the chic embellishment of straps and buttons applied as pictured provides a desirable touch of individuality.

Made of Quality		Made of Quality	
C cloth....	$8.25	F cloth....	$12.25
D "	9.50	G "	13.75
E "	10.75	H "	15.50

Any Skirt shown with the Suits on pages 9 to 27 will be made to your order separately at prices quoted.
All our Skirts are unlined, and made with a ribbon band.

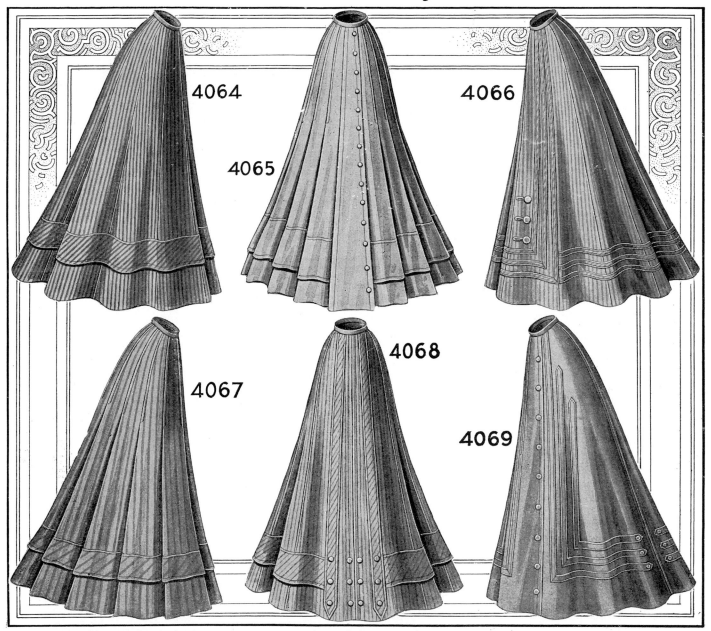

WE MAKE THESE SKIRTS TO MEASURE ONLY—WRITE FOR FREE SAMPLES OF MATERIALS.

No. 4064 . . . $6.25 up

The smart construction pictured here is designed to answer the requirements of dress and service. It is made with seven gores, flaring stylishly, and has a bias fold of the material around the bottom.

Made of Quality		Made of Quality	
C cloth....	$6.25	F cloth....	$10.25
D "	7.50	G "	11.75
E "	8.75	H "	13.50

No. 4067 . . . $7.75 up

This beautiful Skirt is remarkably effective considering the simplicity of the design. It is made with nine gores with the fulness stitched to below the hips and disposed in deep side-plaits all around. There is a wide fold of the material around the bottom.

Made of Quality		Made of Quality	
C cloth....	$7.75	F cloth....	$11.75
D "	9.00	G "	13.25
E "	10.25	H "	15.00

No. 4065 . . . $8.00 up

This stylish plaited Skirt consists of nine gores with the fulness stitched down to a little below the hips and from there falling in deep side-plaits. The panel effect in front is trimmed with buttons and a wide fold is applied around the lower edge.

Made of Quality		Made of Quality	
C cloth....	$8.00	F cloth....	$12.00
D "	9.25	G "	13.50
E "	10.50	H "	15.25

No. 4068 . . . $9.00 up

An extremely dressy Skirt constructed on straight mannish lines in accordance with the tendencies of the present season. It is an eight-gored flaring design, finished with lapped seams, and trimmed down the front with straps and buttons. One fold of the material is applied as pictured.

Made of Quality		Made of Quality	
C cloth....	$9.00	F cloth....	$13.00
D "	10.25	G "	14.50
E "	11.50	H "	16.25

No. 4066 . . . $8.00 up

A nine-gored flaring Skirt faultlessly finished is shown here. Straps of the material combined with soutache loops and buttons add to the neat tailored appearance.

Made of Quality		Made of Quality	
C cloth....	$8.00	F cloth....	$12.00
D "	9.25	G "	13.50
E "	10.50	H "	15.25

No. 4069 . . . $7.50 up

The woman who desires something new will immediately be attracted by this smart four-gored model, which is tastefully ornamented with tailored straps of the material combined with buttons. A trimming of buttons extends down left side as pictured.

Made of Quality		Made of Quality	
C cloth....	$7.50	F cloth....	$11.50
D "	8.75	G "	13.00
E "	10.00	H "	14.75

In selecting a Suit, you may order any of these Skirts with any Coat on pages 9 to 27. See page 8 for particulars as to prices. An extra, separate belt of the same material will be furnished for 25 cents.

4101—Child's Hat of fine quality Mexican Braid, closely woven and very pliable so that it may be shaped to suit the fancy. It is extremely durable and attractively trimmed with a plaid silk scarf, finished with fancy gilt buttons. In natural straw color only, with scarf of red, blue or green plaid. $1.98

4102—Child's Hat of fine quality Tuscan Straw. This extremely dressy little hat is daintily trimmed with a wreath of flowers and green leaves combined with bows of satin ribbon. This hat is particularly appropriate for dress wear. In natural straw color only, with trimming of white, pink, red or light blue. $2.49

4103—Girl's Hat of fine quality Java Braid, closely woven, extremely pliant and particularly durable. It is made with a very wide brim, and the crown is trimmed with a scarf of taffeta, draped in soft folds with fringed ends, as pictured. Gilt buttons provide an effective finish. In natural straw color only, with scarf of navy blue, Copenhagen blue, rose or red. . . . $2.98

4104—Child's Hat of fine quality Panama Braid, closely woven. Just the thing for wear during the warm weather; light weight; very pretty in appearance and wears splendidly. The roll brim may be worn as pictured, or shaped as the fancy suggests. The hat is trimmed with a scarf of taffeta which has a soft knot at the sides and two fringed ends. In natural straw color only, with pink or light blue scarf. $2.98

4105—Girl's Hat of fine quality Milan Straw, with the wide brim beautifully woven in lacy effect. The scarf of taffeta silk, which trims the crown, is edged with silk fringe and draped at the side with a large fancy of silk in rosette effect. A very chic and stylish hat. In natural straw color only, with pink or light blue trimming. $3.98

4106—Misses' or Ladies' Hat of fine quality rough Satin Straw, in sailor shape. This jaunty adaptation of the ever popular sailor style is tastefully trimmed with satin, which appears in folds around the crown with the satin draped in a soft twist at the side, where it is further adorned with two handsome curled quills. Colors: black, red, navy blue, Copenhagen blue or brown; with trimming to match. $3.98

4107—Misses' or Ladies' Hat of very fine quality rough Satin Straw. A natty sailor shape tastefully trimmed with a broad Alsatian bow of handsome wide velvet ribbon which also extends around the crown. A stylish gilt buckle in front gives a handsome finish to what is a thoroughly charming and attractive hat. Colors: black, red, burnt straw or natural straw; trimmed with black; also in navy blue or brown, with trimming to match. $3.98

Special Note: Hats 4106 and 4107 are suitable for Misses or Ladies. They are admirable selections for Summer wear.

4108—An extremely dressy Hat, in a becoming shade with the brim slightly drooping in accordance with so many of the smart hats seen this season. The hat is hand-made of fancy braid, and the crown is draped with chiffon taffeta; this material also edges the brim. Silk wild roses in delicate shades of pink, combined with foliage, loops and ends of taffeta, trim the front and side. Fancy gilt buckle in front. Hat can be furnished in black, navy blue, pale blue, white or champagne; trimmed in each case with pink flowers. $2.98

4109—For a jaunty tailored Hat nothing surpasses the useful Turban, as it is both comfortable and becoming. This chic little model is made of fine quality hair braid, on a wire frame. The brim displays pipings of chiffon. The wing effect at the side is of fancy net bound with braid, and the braid buckle is intertwined with chiffon, as pictured. Hat can be furnished in black, brown, navy blue or gray. The black is suitable for mourning wear. $2.98

4110—A natty Hat in Charlotte Corday contour, is pictured here, the stylish outlines of which make it ideal for fashionable wear. It is a hand-made hat of fluted hair braid with soft draping of mull around the crown and a shirred mull rosette at the side, which is combined with two jaunty quills. The hat can be furnished in black, brown, navy blue or Copenhagen blue. The black can be used for mourning wear. $2.98

4111—A Hat of attractive style, hand-made and nicely finished, which will appeal to conservative dressers. The hair braid which forms the entire hat is applied in folds. The crown is embellished in rosette effect, formed of braid with chiffon drawn through the center, as pictured. Folds of chiffon are also used around the crown. The model is tastefully trimmed with a pair of natural wings of iridescent coloring. It can be had in black, navy blue, brown or gray. $3.98

4112—This Hat is made of fancy braid combined with folds of Chiffon. A pleasing shape effectively trimmed with two large roses of a beautiful shade of pink intermingled with deep green foliage. The trimming around crown is caught at the left side with an attractive buckle of brilliant steel. The model is altogether extremely attractive, and we offer it at an unusually low price. It can be had in black, white, navy blue, champagne or brown; with pink roses. $3.98

4113—This fashionable Hat is a general favorite, because of its splendid style and finish. It is made of fancy braid with the brim drooping and dented as pictured. The soft crown is trimmed with chiffon and taffeta folds, deftly draped and ending in a soft knotted effect at the side of front where the two stylish braid wings are garnished with taffeta. It can be had in black, champagne, gray, navy blue, Copenhagen blue or brown. The black may be used for mourning wear. . . $3.98

4114—This is a picturesque yet inexpensive Hat of delicate coloring, which will answer all requirements of dress. It is made of braid with a drooping brim, which is finished with a fluted edge. Satin draping in soft folds around the crown and caught at the side with a steel buckle is very effectively employed. Two very pretty roses and foliage adorn the model as pictured. It may be had in black, white, navy blue or champagne, trimmed in each case with pink roses. $3.98

4115—A Hat of the latest fashion, made of fine quality rough straw, picturesque in its shaping. Soft full draping of striped taffeta silk around the crown with a decidedly attractive aigrette effect appearing on one side. The hat can be had in black, burnt straw color, navy blue or brown; trimming of striped taffeta in harmonizing colors. . . **$3.98**

4116—A Hat of graceful contour, an immensely popular style in New York this season is pictured here. The silk poppies which are placed in a wreath effect around the front of the model are of a beautiful shade of blue and are combined with foliage. Soft folds of mull are artistically used around the crown, finished with a large bow, which is fastened in the center with a handsome buckle. Hat can be had in black, white, navy blue, champagne or brown, with folds of mull to match; excepting the black, which is trimmed with Copenhagen blue. The flowers in each case are blue. **$4.98**

4117—This hand-made Hat is of beautiful soft Tuscan straw, delightfully stylish in its shaping, and admirably trimmed with two handsome roses. The crown all around is banked with foliage. The hat can be had in natural straw color only, with red, pink or tea roses, as preferred. **$4.98**

4118—A chic little Hat, particularly stylish in effect, which may be worn appropriately on all occasions. The model is made of fancy braid in an extremely rich effect. The brim is turned upward on one side as pictured, and caught with soft folds of Messaline. Three braid wing effects are used to trim the other side, and in front the large rosette is of fluted braid, and has a gilt braid cabachon in the center. Can be had in black, brown, navy blue or gray. **$4.98**

4119—A particularly fascinating hand-made Hat, which is fashioned of fancy braid. Messaline of excellent quality is used as a trimming around the crown and in front. At the sides the braid is uniquely applied, forming an exceptionally chic effect. A large wing caught with a jet button further ornaments the model on the side. Can be had in black, navy blue, brown, white or smoke gray. **$4.98**

4120—The design of this becoming Hat is especially pleasing. It is strictly hand-made of very handsome braid. The crown is artistically formed of braid and combined with Messaline arranged in soft folds all around as pictured. Braid rosette in front has a satin button in the center and the two pair of natural wings at the side are intermingled with Messaline. Can be had in black, navy blue, brown or smoke gray. **$4.98**

4121—Fine Milan Straw is the material used to form this stunning hat. The shape is one of the reigning styles in New York this season. It is trimmed around the crown with a drapery of satin which is loosely knotted at the side as pictured. Two handsome curled quills provide a splendid finish to what is, in all respects, a very stylish hat. Can be had in black or natural color straw with trimming of black satin and dark green quills. **$4.98**

4122—A truly stylish Hat in turban shape, which is a wise selection on account of its general becomingness. It is made of fine quality imported satin straw braid, gracefully arranged over a wire frame, combined with shirrings of taffeta silk in an excellent quality to match. A dashing rosette of braid and taffeta appears on one side of the front, and two beautiful imported, shaded wings are artistically placed as pictured. Colors: black, navy blue, Alice blue, brown or gray. Remarkable value. **$4.98**

4123—This pleasing Hand-made Hat has a characteristic touch of style about it. It is made of fancy hair braid, and the slightly drooping brim is edged with taffeta silk. Chiffon deftly shirred adorns the crown which also displays a handsome jet ball pin. Nine small ostrich tips in color to match the foundation of the hat are placed to the side front with delightful effect. Colors: black, brown, navy blue or white. **$5.98**

4124—An extremely attractive Hat, strictly handmade, of fine quality fancy braid with a graceful brim drooping slightly in the back. The model is suitable for general wear. It is effectively trimmed with wide loops of very fine quality taffeta ribbon caught with an attractive buckle, and intermingled with silk flowers in a color to match the body of hat. Braid is fancifully applied around the crown. Colors: black, brown, navy blue or white. The black hat displays a buckle of jet and is appropriate for mourning wear. **$5.98**

4125—It is astonishing what delightful effects are produced by the use of fancy hair braid. This chic example is made of genuine imported fancy braid with the brim coquettishly turned up on the side. The trimming device consists of braid effects tastefully draped about the crown, combined with folds of chiffon. Chiffon, fancifully arranged, forms the top of crown and a very large chrysanthemum furnishes a pleasing finish. Colors: brown, navy blue, Copenhagen blue, white, or all black. . . **$5.98**

4126—It is impossible to convey in an illustration the splendid shape and the exquisite taste used in trimming this fashionable hat. It is made of fine quality chip straw, the brim drooping gracefully on one side and tilted upward on the other. The rosette effects which appear around the tall crown are of fine quality French Val lace knife-plaited. Three beautiful American Beauty roses are arranged on the left side combined with imported foliage of a rich green. The hat can be had in black, navy blue, Copenhagen blue, or white straw. . . . **$5.98**

4127—Of all the pleasing variety of beautiful Hats which we show this season this is perhaps the daintiest. It is made of a fine lacy braid, effectively applied. The model has a gracefully drooping brim trimmed with folds of satin ribbon caught with handsome steel buckles and ending in an exquisite rosette of fine satin ribbon. Sprays of lilacs and beautifully shaded foliage blend most agreeably with the delicate coloring of the hat. Can be furnished in solid white; in pink with white flowers; light blue with white flowers; or champagne with pink flowers. . **$5.98**

4128—This dainty Hat is of fine quality closely-woven Tuscan straw braid with the brim edged with Milan straw. The crown is enwreathed with beautiful silk poppies intermingled with foliage. On one side, a dashing rosette is formed of loops of fine quality satin ribbon. The hat can be furnished in natural straw color only, with poppies and ribbon trimming in either red or blue. **$5.98**

4133

4132

4130

4135

4134

4131

4129

4129—**This smart Turban is hand-made,** on a wire frame. The brim is formed of satin braid interwoven with chiffon and velvet to match, ending in knots on the left side, where a large shaded wing is applied with delightful effect. The entire crown consists of chiffon arranged in milliner's folds. Facing of chiffon. Colors: black, navy blue, brown or gray. **$7.98**

4130—**A stylish design in mushroom shape,** with a brim of fine Milan straw and a crown of closely woven Tuscan straw. The hat may be had in natural straw color only. The trimming consists of a wreath of roses in American beauty colorings from deepest dye to delicate glow, combined with foliage. A large bow to the side and back made of Panne velvet in two-tone effect to match roses, or with black velvet bow, if preferred. **$7.98**

4131—**There is a dash and freedom of style** about this attractive tailored hat which is altogether charming. It is strictly hand-made of fancy hair braid, the brim flaring slightly to one side. Fine satin Messaline is artistically draped over the crown, ending in front with a shirred rosette effect of Messaline. The model is further ornamented with a pair of fine, imported wings. Colors: black, brown, navy blue or gray; wings to match. **$7.98**

4132—**Nothing could be more fascinating than this beautiful Hat,** which has the chic of the true Parisian style. It is made of good quality Milan straw in natural color only. The trimming is of velvet, which is wound around the crown and is used in cord effect on the edge of the brim. Two large shaded silk and velvet roses with rosebuds and deep green imported foliage contribute

to the picturesque finish. The brim is slightly tilted to one side. This hat can be furnished with either Copenhagen blue, rose pink, or black velvet trimming. **$7.98**

4133—**A Hat indisputably effective in style,** and of splendid quality is shown here. The shape is of finest quality pressed Neapolitan straw with the brim attractively dented. It is a hat of a style which makes it appropriate for smart street wear and is sufficiently dressy for more formal occasions. The crown is draped with black satin with a handsome rosette in front exquisitely shirred. Two chic Mephisto quills add appreciably to the smartness. Can be had in black only, with black trimming and quills. **$7.98**

4134—**Fancy Hair Braid combined with folds of Chiffon,** in exquisite contour composes this entire hat. It is a hand-made design tastefully trimmed with nine ostrich tips; chiffon daintily shirred forms a soft rosette effect with a handsome jet ball pin thrust through the center. Colors: black, brown, navy blue or white. **$7.98**

4135—**A becoming Hat,** picturesquely laden with a wreath of imported flowers and foliage in exquisite colorings. The shape is generally becoming and the hat is a model of perfect taste. Silk velvet ribbon arranged in loops is very effectively placed around the crown. Can be furnished in two colors: burnt straw or black. In black, the hat will be trimmed with black velvet ribbon. The burnt straw hat will be trimmed with brown. **$8.98**

4136

4140

4139

4137

4141

4142

4138

4136—A charming Hat designed for dress wear, the light weight of which makes it especially adapted for the Summer months. It is strictly hand-made and formed of an exquisite lacy braid of silky texture interwoven with Tuscan. The graceful drooping brim is smartly dented, as pictured. It is trimmed with four handsome ostrich plumes and soft aigrette effect of cut ostrich. The soft crown is adorned with a taffeta ribbon. The hat is both stylish and dressy, and we offer it at a remarkably low price. It can be furnished in black or natural straw color only, with the trimming, in each case, of white. **$9.98**

4137—An exquisitely dainty Hat, made of a fine chip straw with a mushroom brim. The crown is adorned with Marabout, a form of trimming which has met with marked approval in the realm of Fashion. At the left side a Marabout fancy, combined with a pretty rosette of satin ribbon, contributes greatly to the dressy appearance. Satin ribbon is used in a fold around crown. Furnished in black with black trimming; natural straw color with tan Marabout trimming; or in white with white trimming. **$9.98**

4138—A bewitching model which bears the indefinable stamp of Paris. It is made of very fine quality Milan straw in a most becoming shape. Velvet ribbon trims the crown, and terminates at side-back in loops and ends. The floral adornment is ideal in its color harmony and wonderful in its naturalness. It consists of two large chrysanthemums combined with silk and velvet pansies, intermingled with foliage. The model can be had in either black or natural straw, with trimming as described. **$11.98**

4139—A small modish Hat, admirably adapted for wear on dress occasions is pictured here. It is a hand-made model, formed entirely of shirred chiffon with a twist of satin ribbon around the crown, caught in front with a handsome jet buckle. Two grace-

ful ostrich plumes provide a handsome completion. The hat can be had in black with one black and one white plume, or, if preferred, in all black; also in gray with gray plumes. . **$11.98**

4140—A truly artistic Hat, beautiful in its shaping, which is an admirable example of the prevailing style. It is a chip straw with a wide brim, gracefully tilted up on one side and finished on the under edge of brim with a velvet fold. The crown is covered with soft shirred satin Messaline of a splendid quality, with an attractive jet buckle in front. Two handsome ostrich plumes of generous length trim the model. The hat may be had in black straw only, with one white and one black plume. If preferred, it may be had in all black. **$11.98**

4141—This fascinating dress Hat is of finest quality Milan straw with the brim stylishly shaped, as pictured, and trimmed beneath with a fold of black velvet. Fine velvet ribbon in black extends around the crown with a large Alsatian bow in back. The flowers used to adorn the model are two very large silk and velvet roses in beautiful contrasting shades, with clusters of forget-me-nots and foliage in a very natural effect. The model can be had in natural straw color or black straw with trimming as described. **$11.98**

4142—This handsome Hat is distinctly up to date in its graceful contour. The entire hat is made of a fine quality imported braid, fancifully applied on the crown, intermingled with Maline. producing a truly charming effect. A soft twist of Maline and braid fastening with a jet ornament provides a Frenchy touch in front. Model is finished with two full, long ostrich plumes, which add greatly to its charming appearance. Can be had in black with two white plumes, or in black with black plumes, as preferred. **$12.98**

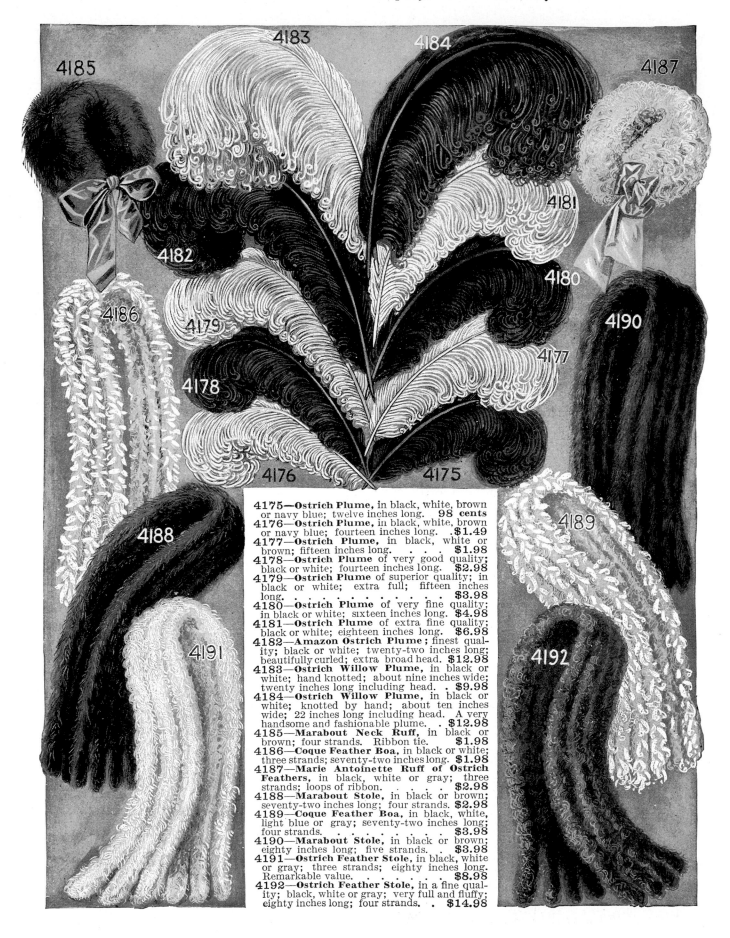

4175—Ostrich Plume, in black, white, brown or navy blue; twelve inches long. **98 cents**

4176—Ostrich Plume, in black, white, brown or navy blue; fourteen inches long. **.$1.49**

4177—Ostrich Plume, in black, white or brown; fifteen inches long. . . . **$1.98**

4178—Ostrich Plume of very good quality; black or white; fourteen inches long. **$2.98**

4179—Ostrich Plume of superior quality; in black or white; extra full; fifteen inches long. **$3.98**

4180—Ostrich Plume of very fine quality; in black or white; sixteen inches long. **$4.98**

4181—Ostrich Plume of extra fine quality; black or white; eighteen inches long. **$6.98**

4182—**Amazon Ostrich Plume**; finest quality; black or white; twenty-two inches long; beautifully curled; extra broad head. **$12.98**

4183—**Ostrich Willow Plume**, in black or white; hand knotted; about nine inches wide; twenty inches long including head. . **$9.98**

4184—**Ostrich Willow Plume**, in black or white; knotted by hand; about ten inches wide; 22 inches long including head. A very handsome and fashionable plume. . **$12.98**

4185—**Marabout Neck Ruff**, in black or brown; four strands. Ribbon tie. **$1.98**

4186—**Coque Feather Boa**, in black or white; three strands; seventy-two inches long. **$1.98**

4187—**Marie Antoinette Ruff of Ostrich Feathers**, in black, white or gray; three strands; loops of ribbon. . . . **$2.98**

4188—**Marabout Stole**, in black or brown; seventy-two inches long; four strands. **$2.98**

4189—**Coque Feather Boa**, in black, white, light blue or gray; seventy-two inches long; four strands. **$3.98**

4190—**Marabout Stole**, in black or brown; eighty inches long; five strands. . **$3.98**

4191—**Ostrich Feather Stole**, in black, white or gray; three strands; eighty inches long. Remarkable value. **$8.98**

4192—**Ostrich Feather Stole**, in a fine quality; black, white or gray; very full and fluffy; eighty inches long; four strands. . **$14.98**

LADIES' BELTS—SIZES 22 TO 30 INCHES WAIST MEASURE.

4201—Wash Belt of all-over embroidery; ocean pearl buckle. White only. . . . . **25 cents**

4202—Wash Belt of heavy mercerized gros-grain belting. White only. . . . . **25 cents**

4203—Elastic Belt; gilt buckle back and front. Black only. **25 cents**

4204—Tailored Belt of French kid, studded with steel nail heads. Harness buckle. Black, brown, navy blue, white or gray. **49 cents**

4205—Silk Elastic Belt, trimmed with Renaissance buckle of Roman gilt. Black, navy blue, brown, white, light blue or red. . **49 cents**

4206—Silk Elastic Belt, with buckle of Roman gilt in Florentine design. Black, navy blue, brown, light blue or white. **49 cents**

4207—Plaited Girdle of taffeta silk; front trimmed with satin-covered buttons. Black, navy blue, brown or white. . **49 cents**

4208—Wash Belt of linen; beautifully embroidered; hemstitched edge; pearl buckle. White only. . . . . **49 cents**

4209—Wash Belt of very fine imported linen, exquisitely embroidered; pearl buckle; scalloped edge. White only. . . **49 cents**

4210—Belt in Persian pattern. Art Nouveau buckle. Black, navy blue, brown, light blue or white. . . . . **49 cents**

4211—Tailored Belt of fine French kid; neat metal buckles front and back. Black, navy blue, brown, white or gray. . **59 cents**

4212—Silk Elastic Belt, studded with steel nail heads. Steel buckle. Black, brown, navy blue, light blue, white or gray. **59 cents**

4213—Elastic Belt, with shaped front of fine French kid; closes with patent clasps. Black or white. . . . . . . **59 cents**

4214—Plaited Belt of fine quality French kid; shaped in front; gilt buckle. Black, brown or white. . . . . **59 cents**

4215—Silk Elastic Belt, with handsome gilt buckle in front and back. Black, navy blue, light blue, brown or white. . . **59 cents**

4216—Jet Elastic Beaded Belt, with back and front buckle effect of jet. Black only. . . . . **59 cents**

4217—Belt of attractively embossed elastic; buckle of Roman gilt. Black, navy blue, light blue, brown, white or myrtle green. **79 cents**

4218—Silk Elastic Belt, decorated with cut-steel nail heads; steel buckle. Black, navy blue, light blue, brown or white. **79 cents**

4219—Silk Elastic Belt, with shaped front of French kid; studded with cut-steel nail heads; closes with patent clasps. Exceptional value. Black, white, navy blue, brown or light blue. . **79 cents**

4220—Belt of excellent quality plaited taffeta silk; trimmed with hemstitching, rosettes of taffeta and buttons. Black only. **98 cents**

4221—Silk Elastic Belt; Parisian novelty buckles of heavy gilt both front and back. Black, white, navy blue or light blue. . **98 cents**

4222—French Kid Belt; crushed in back and held in place by a gilt buckle to accord with front buckle. Black, white or brown. **98 cents**

4223—Elastic Beaded Belt of cut jet; girdle buckle on back and front of heavy cut jet in star design. Black only. . . **98 cents**

4224—Silk Elastic Belt; trimmed with steel nail heads; steel buckle. Black, white, navy blue, light blue or gray. . . . . **98 cents**

4225—Silk Elastic Belt; studded with steel nail heads; steel buckle front and back. Black, white, navy blue, light blue or brown. **$1.49**

4226—Silk Elastic Belt; cut-steel nail heads; buckle on back and front of cut steel. Black, white, navy blue, light blue or gray. . **$1.98**

The READY-MADE Dresses shown on this page can be furnished only as illustrated and described. SIZES—32 TO 44 BUST MEASURE. The skirts are made about 40 inches long in front and hang evenly all around. They have a three-inch basted hem so that they can be easily lengthened or shortened by the customer. WE CANNOT FURNISH SAMPLES OF THE MATERIALS.

4301—One-Piece Dress of finest quality Figured Satin Foulard, in black, navy blue, Copenhagen blue, or dark rose color, with white figure. A very dressy gown displaying all of the little style touches which stamp it unmistakably as being up-to-date. The chemisette is of white Oriental lace with tiny bows of Messaline in a contrasting color, and is bordered by handsome Persian garniture and folds of Messaline. The Gibson plaits which extend over the shoulders to the waist-line are also of Messaline, as also are the crushed girdle and the cuff effect. Sleeves are finely tucked and trimmed with Messaline-covered buttons. Tucked panels are introduced on the front, outlined by soutache braid. Cuffs are of lace and attached to the lawn sleeve lining. Plain gored skirt with two wide folds of Messaline to match color of material. Dress closes invisibly in back. Waist lined with lawn. . . . **$24.75**

4302—Two-Piece Dress of good quality Taffeta Silk, in black, navy blue or brown. The Gibson plaits over the shoulders are paralleled by tucks. Chemisette of cream-colored Oriental lace trimmed with braid ornaments. The collar effect is piped with Messaline to match and displays loops and buttons of Messaline, similar buttons being used down the front, and as a completion on the tucked sleeves. Attached plaited girdle of the material. The skirt has seven gores with the fulness disposed in side-plaits all around. Dress closes in back, and is unlined. . . **$12.98**

4303—Two-Piece Jumper Dress of Taffeta Silk, in black, navy blue or brown. The jumper is sleeveless, and the low neck both front and back is edged with a fold of satin with tiny revers in front, ending in a chic tie trimmed with buttons. Tucks extend to the waist-line in back, and over the shoulders to yoke depth in front. The Gibson effect over the shoulders is outlined by a satin fold. Plaited girdle of taffeta attached. The lace waist pictured is not included. Nine-gored flare skirt with a box-plait in front and an inverted plait in back. A wide fold of taffeta adorns the bottom. Dress closes in back. Unlined. . **$9.98**

4304—Two-Piece Dress of good quality Taffeta Silk, in black, navy blue or brown. Waist is tucked to yoke depth in front with full-length tucks in back. Deep V-shaped chemisette front and back of cream-colored dotted net, prettily tucked. The chic sleeves are tucked, trimmed with taffeta buttons, and edged with a frill of net to correspond with the Gibson collar. Plain nine-gored flare skirt with a plait down the front, which is finished with taffeta buttons. Dress closes invisibly in back. Unlined. **$11.98**

4305—Two-Piece Coat Suit of finest quality Shantung Silk, in natural Pongee color, brown, navy blue or reseda green. The jacket is single-breasted and is about 31 inches long in back. Notched collar of the material. Two flap pockets. Sleeves fancifully trimmed with the material, combined with self-covered buttons, a similar decoration appearing in back. Jacket richly lined throughout with white taffeta silk. The flare skirt comprises eight gores with an inverted plait both front and back, and a wide fold of the material around the bottom. This beautiful material is used this season for the smartest suits, its wearing qualities and extreme light weight, making it especially desirable. **$23.50**

4308

4306   4307

4309

4310

The READY-MADE Dresses shown on this page can be furnished only as illustrated and described.   SIZES—32 TO 44 BUST MEASURE.   The skirts are made about 40 inches long in front and hang evenly all around. They have a three-inch basted hem so that they can be easily lengthened or shortened by the customer.   WE CANNOT FURNISH SAMPLES OF THE MATERIALS.

4306—Coat Suit of very fine quality Taffeta Silk, in black or navy blue; also in fine Pongee silk in natural color only. The jacket is semi-fitting and about 35 inches long in back. Notched collar. The turn-back cuffs are trimmed with buttons which also ornament the pocket flaps and the back, where the seams are slit. Jacket lined throughout with white Peau de Cygne. Plain gored skirt with a plait down the front trimmed with self-covered buttons. Two wide folds of the material. **$24.75**

4307—Two-Piece Dress of Figured Satin Foulard, in black, navy blue, Copenhagen blue, brown or smoke gray. Chemisette of tucked net and Val lace. Piped around neck and down front with black satin combined with a frill of the material. Plaits over the shoulders. Tucked sleeves finished with a frill and piped with black satin. Closes in back. Plaited nine-gored skirt with satin piping around lower edge. Waist and skirt unlined. . **$12.98**

4308—Two-Piece Dress of good quality Taffeta, in black, navy blue or brown. The chemisette is of tucked dotted net in cream-white, outlined by an attractively braided collar effect. Blouse closes in front invisibly, and is tucked to yoke depth in front and down the full length of back. The chic tucked sleeves are trimmed with self-covered buttons, the latter being used in combination with loops of taffeta on the waist, also extending down the front of the plain gored skirt, where they are applied over a plait. Crushed girdle of taffeta. **$11.98**

4309—Two-Piece Dress of excellent Taffeta Silk, in black with all black yoke; also in navy blue, garnet, brown, or smoke gray with cream-white yoke. V-shaped chemisette of net over silk, trimmed with soutache braid and buttons and outlined by braided revers. Plaited over the shoulders in front and also in back, where the waist closes. The tucked sleeves are finished with taffeta-covered buttons and turn-back cuffs. Braided Gibson collar. Tie of taffeta. The flaring skirt is trimmed down the front with buttons applied on a plait. Belt of taffeta. Waist and skirt unlined. **$14.98**

4310—One-Piece Dress of finest quality Shantung Silk, in natural Pongee color, navy blue or brown. This is a beautiful Oriental silk, extremely fashionable and admirably adapted for Summer wear. Chemisette and Gibson collar of ecru tucked net, the latter being finished with a French novelty edging. Waist is handsomely braided around the neck, down front, and also on the tucked sleeves, where taffeta piping in a contrasting shade is employed. The same piping outlines the chemisette. Sleeves are of tucked net below the elbow, finished with edging. The gored-flaring skirt displays an inserted fan-plait in sheath effect below the knee, above which it is embellished with handsomely braided buttons to match those on the waist. Dress closes in back and is unlined, ... **$21.50**

4311 4312 4313 4314 4315

The READY-MADE Dresses shown on this page can be furnished only as illustrated and described. SIZES—32 TO 44 BUST MEASURE. The skirts are made about 40 inches long in front and hang evenly all around. They have a three-inch basted hem so that they can be easily lengthened or shortened by the customer. WE CANNOT FURNISH SAMPLES OF THE MATERIALS.

4311—One-Piece Dress and extra Coat of finest quality Taffeta Silk, in black with black silk lace yoke; also in navy blue, brown or smoke gray with cream lace yoke. The waist is prettily braided both front and back and trimmed with taffeta buttons. Plaited over shoulders. Yoke outlined by satin piping, which is also used on sleeves combined with buttons. Flare skirt with a simulated panel in front and a plait at each side. Wide fold of taffeta. Dress closes invisibly in back. Unlined. The coat closes with braided taffeta loops. Tuxedo collar of satin and Persian garniture. All seams finished with tailored straps of taffeta. Length in back about 39 inches. Seams are slashed and display buttons in back. Yoke lining of the material. . . . **$29.75**

4312—Two-Piece Dress of fine quality Satin Messaline, in black, navy blue, brown or smoke gray. The waist, front and back, also the sleeves, are tucked in all-over effect with the closing concealed beneath a box-plait in front. It has a Dutch collar of Messaline, also an extremely attractive additional collar of handsome imitation Irish lace. Sleeves edged with Val. Plain gored skirt with a deep plait down the front, which is trimmed with Messaline-covered buttons. **$15.98**

4313—Two-Piece Dress of very fine quality Figured Satin Foulard, in combinations of black and white, navy blue and white, brown and white, or rose and white. The waist is in blouse effect, plaited over the shoulders and trimmed with Messaline-covered buttons. V-shaped yoke of cream-colored net prettily tucked,

the same tucked net being employed for the lower part of sleeves. Yoke is outlined by folds of plain Messaline and soutache braid to match. Plain gored skirt finished with buttons to match those on waist, and piped around the bottom as pictured. Unlined. Closes in back. **$14.98**

4314—Two-Piece Dress of very fine quality Striped Taffeta Silk, in gray and white stripe; also in brown and white stripe. A particularly dressy costume heavily silk-embroidered by hand in front. Both waist and skirt are trimmed with tailored straps of black or brown taffeta, according to color of material selected. Yoke of cream-colored tucked net. Sleeves, collar and the rounded neck piped with taffeta in a contrasting color. Plain flare skirt with a panel down the front ornamented with buttons. Separate crushed girdle of taffeta. Dress closes invisibly in back. Unlined. **$19.75**

4315—Two-Piece Dress of very fine quality Figured Satin Foulard, in combinations of navy blue and white, green and white, catawba and white, or brown and white. This is a dress of extremely attractive style. Yoke and under-sleeves are of tucked dotted net in cream-color. The collar effect, which outlines the yoke, the front and the chic slashed sleeves, is edged with narrow folds of taffeta in a contrasting shade and tailor stitching. Loops and buttons of taffeta furnish a smart decorative touch. Similar loops and buttons ornament the skirt which is a plain gored flaring model. Waist closes in front. Plain tucked back. **$18.98**

4316   4317   4318   4319   4320 4321

The READY-MADE Dresses shown on this page can be furnished only as illustrated and described. SIZES 32 TO 44 BUST MEASURE. The skirts are made about 40 inches long in front and hang evenly all around. They have a three-inch basted hem so that they can be easily lengthened or shortened by the customer. WE CANNOT FURNISH SAMPLES OF THE MATERIALS.

4316—One-Piece Dress of very fine quality Figured Satin Foulard, in combinations of black and white, blue and white, green and white, or brown and white. A chic dress impressive in its faultless style. The yoke both back and front is of white Cluny lace. Gibson collar and yoke outlined with piping of Persian material affording an artistic color contrast. Plaits over the shoulders extending to the waist-line both front and back. Front displays Directoire pendants with tasseled ends. Waist and skirt joined by a crushed girdle of the material. Attractive tucked sleeves ending in cuffs of Cluny lace edged with Foulard. Plain gored skirt, with a plait down the front and a deep inverted plait in back. Waist lined with Japanese silk. Dress closes invisibly in back. $21.50

4317—Two-Piece Dress of fine quality Taffeta, in black, navy blue or brown. The yoke and the sleeves below the elbow are of cream-colored lace and embroidered Filet net. The yoke is outlined in a contrasting shade as also are the collar and the sleeves. Waist is richly embroidered around neck and on the front with silk soutache and fancy braid. Tucks appear to yoke depth on the front and extend down the full length of the back. Upper part of sleeves tucked as pictured. The plain gored skirt is trimmed with a Tunic fold. Separate boned crushed girdle. Waist closes in front. Dress is unlined. $15.98

4318—One-Piece Princess Dress of superior quality Taffeta Silk, in black, with black silk lace yoke; also in navy blue or champagne, with cream lace yoke. The Princess panel extending down the front is ornamented with parallel rows of soutache braid and taffeta-covered buttons. Braid is also used with attractive effect on the upper part of waist and on the Princess girdle; it also edges the tucked sleeves. Waist is finely tucked to yoke depth both front and back. Skirt is in flare effect, trimmed around the lower edge with a wide taffeta fold. Dress is unlined. Closes invisibly in back. $14.98

4319—One-Piece Dress of fine quality Messaline Silk, in navy blue or brown with ecru yoke; in taupe (smoke gray) with white yoke; also in black with all black yoke. The yoke both front and back and Gibson collar are of tucked net, trimmed in front with tiny bows, gilt buttons and Persian embroidery. Plaited girdle of Messaline. Shaped sleeves are tucked as pictured. Flaring skirt is finished with buttons down front, applied over a wide tuck. A fold of Messaline ornaments the lower edge. Waist lined with Japanese silk. Skirt unlined. Dress closes in back. . . $19.75

4320—Two-Piece Dress of good quality Satin Foulard, in combinations of black and white, navy blue and white, brown and white, or catawba and white. The chemisette which graces the front of this stylish model is of finely tucked net, bordered by pipings of Messaline in a contrasting color and relieved by handsome Persian trimming. The Gibson collar and the tucked, shirred sleeves are piped to correspond. Ornamental buttons trim the front. Short tucks both front and back provide desirable fulness. Skirt has an attached girdle of the material and is completed with fancy buttons to match those used on the waist. Dress is unlined. Waist closes invisibly in front. (See also 4321.) . . . $16.98

4321—Two-Piece Dress of fine quality Messaline Silk, in black, navy blue or brown. Exactly the same style as 4320, but in plain colors. $16.98

4401—**One-Piece Dress of fine Batiste,** in white only. This chic dress is elaborated with insertions of Italian Filet lace combined with embroidered dots and Cluny and French Val. Both back and front of waist are daintily-trimmed with lace and attractively tucked. Waist and skirt joined by a girdle in Empire effect of Filet insertion with a medallion of imitation Baby Irish lace. Filet insertion is also introduced down the front. Skirt is lavishly tucked. Tucked sleeves trimmed with Val lace and embroidered dots. Dress closes invisibly in back. Long sleeves only. **$9.98**

4402—**One-Piece Princess Jumper Dress of fine, durable Linene,** in white, natural linen color or cadet blue. This simple and effective little dress is made with a V-neck, tucked to yoke depth in front, with full-length tucks in back. It is tastefully ornamented around the neck, down the front and on the Empire girdle and sleeves with white soutache braid applied in scrolls and Greek border design. Short tucked sleeves. Plain gored skirt. Closes invisibly in back. Guimpe shown in the illustration is not included. Short sleeves as pictured only. **$5.98**

4403—**One-Piece Jumper Dress of good quality Linene,** in white, natural linen color or light blue. The low-cut neck is made with a rolling collar piped with linene in a contrasting color, and the same piping appears in combination with fancy buttons down the entire front, where the dress closes invisibly with hooks and eyes. The short sleeves are also piped and trimmed with buttons. Plaited over the shoulders. Piped around waist-line. Plain gored

skirt. We do not furnish the guimpe shown in the illustration. Short sleeves as pictured only. **$3.98**

4404—**One-Piece Princess Dress of fine quality fancy striped Chambray,** in white and black with light blue trimming; white and lavender with lavender trimming; white and light blue with light blue trimming; or white and natural linen color with tan trimming. The chemisette and collar are of white Swiss trimmed with crochet lace and insertion. Chemisette is outlined by folds of linene in a contrasting color. Colored linene also finishes the sleeves and forms the chic tie on the front. Waist is plaited over the shoulders as pictured, and attached to skirt by a girdle of the material. Tucked sleeves. Dress neatly trimmed with linene-covered buttons. A fold of the material around the bottom of skirt. Dress closes invisibly in back. Long sleeves only. . . . **$6.98**

4405—**One-Piece Princess Dress of very fine, soft Batiste,** in white only. Elaborate yoke, both front and back, of Val lace insertion ornamented in front with medallions of Swiss embroidery. Princess tucks are introduced below the yoke, and a wide panel of exquisite embroidery insertion outlined by Val extends down the front as pictured. Sleeves are tucked, trimmed with embroidery and Val lace, and are also frilled with lace at the wrist to correspond with collar. Princess girdle of Val insertion. Skirt has a deep flounce attractively tucked as pictured and ornamented with Val insertion. Dress buttons invisibly in back. Long sleeves only.
$12.98

These READY-MADE Dresses can be furnished only as illustrated and described. Sizes 32 to 44 Bust Measure. The Skirts are made about 40 inches long in front and hang evenly all around. They have a three-inch basted hem so that they can be easily lengthened or shortened by the customer. We cannot send samples of these materials. For Princess Slips to be worn beneath these dresses, see Page 91.

4406—**One-Piece Princess Dress of very fine quality Imported Batiste,** in white, light blue or pale pink. The Princess panel of fine tucks which extends down the entire front is a feature of this handsome dress. It is outlined by imitation Baby Irish insertion. The girdle is of insertion and tucks to correspond. Tucked batiste edged with Irish insertion and a frill of Val form á Bertha effect over the shoulders, as pictured, also being continued down the back to the waist-line. Back of waist is finely tucked and lace-trimmed exactly like the front. Back and front yoke and Gibson collar of Cluny and Val lace insertion. The elaborate sleeves are tucked and attractively trimmed with Cluny and frills of Val, Irish insertion also being applied with charming results. Skirt has a deep tucked flounce ornamented with Val lace headed by Cluny insertion. Dress closes invisibly in back. Long sleeves only.   **$16.98**

4407—**One-Piece Dress of fine Batiste,** in white, light blue or champagne. The entire waist is adorned with rich Point de Venise insertion combined with inserts of Princess tucks. Plaits over the shoulders are daintily frilled with Val paralleled by Val and Cluny insertion. They extend to the waist-line both front and back. The girdle is of Point de Venise insertion. The chic tucked sleeves display inserts and frills of French Val lace. Gibson collar and V-shaped yoke of Cluny and Val. Skirt finished with a deep tucked flounce with insertions of Val and Cluny lace. Closes invisibly in back. Long sleeves only. **$9.98**

4408—**Two-Piece Dress of Dotted Swiss,** in white only. The waist of this cool, summery model is tucked to yoke depth in front and down the entire back. Waist buttons invisibly in front beneath a plastron of eyelet embroidery. The epaulettes and the collar are of the same attractive embroidery frilled with Val lace. Sleeves tucked in all-over effect and edged with Val insertion and lace. Skirt is finished with a tucked flounce headed by Val insertion and displays a wide panel of eyelet embroidery down the front as pictured. Detachable belt. Long sleeves only.   . . **$4.98**

4409—**Two-Piece Dress of Batiste,** in white only. Waist is attractively tucked both front and back between inserts of Val lace. V-shaped yoke in front and Gibson collar of Val lace insertion. Sleeves below the elbow are trimmed with tucks and buttons and display insertions of Val lace. Skirt has three inserts of Val and a full, tucked bouffante flounce. Waist closes invisibly in back. Detachable belt. Long sleeves only. **$3.98**

4410—**Two-Piece Dress of fine Batiste,** in white only. Deep front yoke of imitation Baby Irish and Cluny insertion combined with French Val, the epaulettes and the panel effect down front being also of Irish insertion surrounded by Val lace. Waist is tucked to yoke depth in front and also in back where it buttons invisibly. The tucked flounce on the skirt is trimmed with Val insertion and headed by tucks and Val. Detachable girdle of Irish and Val lace. Long sleeves only.   . . . , . . . **$9.98**

These **READY-MADE** Dresses can be furnished only as illustrated and described.   Sizes 32 to 44 Bust Measure. The Skirts are made about 40 inches long in front and hang evenly all around. They have a three-inch basted hem so that they can be easily lengthened or shortened by the customer. We cannot send samples of these materials. For Princess Slips to be worn beneath these dresses, see page 91.

4411—One-Piece Princess Dress of fine Lawn Embroidery, in white only. This beautiful dress is composed almost entirely of panels of Swiss eyelet embroidery with insertions of French Val lace. The design is of unusual elegance and is carried out the same in back with the exception of the Princess panel. Waist displays a round yoke both front and back of Val lace outlined by Cluny insertion, the latter also being applied around embroidery on shoulders. Princess tucks and insertions of Val both front and back. Sleeves are of embroidery and lace insertion frilled with Val to match the Gibson collar. Bottom of skirt is elaborately trimmed with Val insertion and tucks. Dress closes in back. Long sleeves only. **$14.98**

4412—Two-Piece Dress of Lawn, in white only. The waist of this neat and serviceable dress is of eyelet embroidery, paralleled by rows of Val insertion, with crochet insertion down the center of the front, where the waist buttons invisibly. Tucked back. Sleeves are of tucks and Val insertion arranged alternately, finished at the wrist with Val lace to correspond with the Swiss embroidered Gibson collar. The skirt displays a deep flounce ornamented with clusters of Princess tucks, and is trimmed with insertions of Swiss embroidery and Val lace. Detachable belt. Long sleeves only. . . **$4.98**

4413—One-Piece Princess Dress of good quality Linene, in cadet blue or natural linen color. An extremely attractive and practical dress made with the folds of the material in Gibson effect over the shoulders, which are neatly piped in a contrasting color, as also is the Princess panel extending down the entire length of both front and back and the Tunic fold on the skirt. The dress buttons visibly down the left side of front with handsome pearl buttons, these buttons being also utilized as a trimming in back. Attached chemisette of Swiss embroidery and Val lace. Turn-back cuffs of embroidery and lace to match. Long sleeves only. **$4.98**

4414—Two-Piece Dress of fine Lawn, in white only. The waist of this chic little dress has a front of Swiss eyelet embroidery combined with Val and crochet insertion with baby tucks extending to the waist line. A lace panel of crochet and Val insertion is applied on the shoulders continued down the full length of the sleeves paralleled by clusters of tucks. The knife-plaited Louis XVI frills which finish the sleeves and the Gibson collar lend a unique, decorative touch. Tucked back trimmed with Val insertion. Waist buttons invisibly in back. Skirt is prettily trimmed with Val and crochet insertion as pictured, and has a deep, full, tucked flounce. Detachable belt. Long sleeves only. . . . **$7.98**

4415—One-Piece Dress of fine quality Batiste, in white only. This handsome dress is lavishly adorned with wide inserts of Point de Paris lace. The trimming both front and back is identical. Waist is tucked to yoke depth. Empire girdle of Point de Paris lace. The collar is finished with a knife-plaited frill and the sleeves display a cuff effect to correspond. The tucked flounce is lace-trimmed and headed by a wide band of insertion. Dress buttons invisibly in back. Long sleeves only. **$11.98**

These READY-MADE Dresses can be furnished only as illustrated and described. Sizes 32 to 44 Bust Measure. The Skirts are made about 40 inches long in front and hang evenly all around. They have a three-inch basted hem so that they can be easily lengthened or shortened by the customer. We cannot send samples of these materials. For Princess Slips to be worn beneath these dresses, see page 91.

4416—**One-Piece Dress of extra fine quality Batiste**, in white only. The yoke of this beautiful lingerie dress, both front and back, is of handsome Point de Paris insertion varied by embroidered net. The same insertion is lavishly applied down the front and also in back, where the trimming is equally elaborate. Short tucks below the yoke in front and full-length clusters of Princess tucks in back, where the dress closes invisibly. The chic sleeves display clusters of tucks and lace insertion arranged alternately as pictured. The lower part of skirt is finished with horizontal inserts of Point de Paris lace with a deep, full-tucked flounce. Long sleeves only. $12.98

4417—**Two-Piece Dress of excellent quality Lawn**, in white only, with a front attractively embroidered in eyelet effect. Embroidery is also used on the shoulders, on the dainty tucked sleeves, and appears down the front of skirt as pictured. Skirt is completed with a full-tucked flounce headed by a cluster of Princess tucks and embroidery insertion. Waist closes invisibly in front and has a plain tucked back. Tucked Gibson collar edged with lace to match sleeves. Detachable belt. Long sleeves only. $6.98

4418—**One-Piece Princess Dress of Batiste**, in white, light blue or pale pink. This extremely pretty dress is generously trimmed with Val lace insertion as pictured, and displays a Princess panel down the front, of fine tucks and Val lace arranged alternately. The Gibson effect over the shoulders is edged with lace, as are also the

tucked sleeves and collar. Back of waist tucked and trimmed with Val lace. The flounce has two clusters of tucks and is headed by insertion of Val lace. Dress closes invisibly in back. Long sleeves only. $7.98

4419—**One-Piece Princess Dress of finest quality Imported Batiste**, in white only. This superb model exhibits a V-shaped yoke, both front and back, of very handsome imitation Baby Irish insertion and Point de Paris lace. The latter also forms the collar. The Princess panel is of rich embroidery in eyelet design with a wide insert of Point de Paris in the center. The embroidery covers the front of waist and is continued over the shoulders to the waist-line in back. The sleeves are also completed with full-length panels of the same embroidery. The skirt admits insertions of French Val lace all around and is finished with an elaborate lace-trimmed flounce. Dress closes invisibly in back. Long sleeves only. $19.98

4420—**One-Piece Princess Dress of good quality Batiste**, in white only. The panel down the front is of Swiss eyelet embroidery in a pleasing design. The front of waist has a deep yoke of Val and Cluny insertion, and displays alternate squares of Swiss embroidery and tucked batiste outlined by Val. This design is continued down the back to the waist-line. Sleeves are embellished with tucks and inserts of Val lace. Skirt trimmed all around with inserts of Val and finished with a deep tucked flounce. Dress closes invisibly in back. *Can be furnished with long or three-quarter sleeves.* $6.98

These **READY-MADE** Dresses can be furnished only as illustrated and described. Sizes 32 to 44 Bust Measure. The Skirts are made about 40 inches long in front and hang evenly all around. They have a three-inch basted hem so that they can be easily lengthened or shortened by the customer. We cannot send samples of these materials. For Princess Slips to be worn beneath these dresses, see page 91.

4421—One-Piece Princess Dress of finest quality Imported Batiste, in white only. Heavy embroidered dots appear down both front and back of the waist combined with fine Val lace insertion and tucks. V-shaped chemisette effect and Gibson collar of Point de Paris lace. The sleeves display tucked panels outlined by Val lace and embroidered dots. Princess panel down the front of tucks, lace and embroidery. The flounce is elaborately tucked and has insertions of embroidered batiste bordered by Val lace. Dress closes invisibly in back. Long sleeves only. . . $18.98

4422—One-Piece Dress of good quality Linene, in white, cadet blue or natural linen color. Deep V-shaped vest of Swiss embroidery and faggotting, the collar being of embroidery to correspond. Piping in a contrasting color is used very effectively on the Gibson folds over the shoulders, on the girdle and sleeves and down the front of skirt. Waist trimmed with embroidery both front and back. Self-covered buttons to match piping. Dress closes invisibly in back. Long sleeves only. $5.98

4423—Two-Piece Dress of Figured Net, in cream-white only, over Japanese silk. The round yoke both front and back and the vest effect are of fine Val lace insertion combined with inserts of Florentine lace and embroidered dots. Waist displays full-length tucks, and the Gibson outline over the shoulders is edged with a fold of satin Messaline. Tucked sleeves finished with Val lace

and embroidered dots. Waist closes invisibly in back. Skirt has a tucked flounce headed by an inserted panel of tucks which is bordered by Val lace. Attached drop skirt of Japanese silk with lace-edged ruffle and dust ruffle. Plaited girdle of Messaline terminating in back in loops and ends. Long sleeves only. . $19.98

4424—One-Piece Princess Dress of Lawn, in white only. A Princess panel down the front of Swiss eyelet embroidery surrounded by Val lace insertion. Embroidery and Val lace ornament the front, and the round yoke of lawn and Val extends around the back, where clusters of fine tucks are carried down to the waist-line. The sleeves are embellished with panels of embroidery and Val lace paralleled by clusters of tucks. The deep tucked flounce is headed by two parallel rows of insertion. Dress buttons visibly in back. *Can be furnished with long or three-quarter sleeves.* $4.98

4425—One-Piece Dress of Imported Batiste, in white only. Both waist and skirt are embroidered in eyelet effect combined with graduated embroidered dots. The round yoke back and front is of Val lace, as is also the Gibson collar. Dress closes invisibly in back, where the embroidery is exactly like the front. Girdle of embroidery outlined by Val lace. Scallops of embroidery finish the bottom of the skirt, underlaid with a dainty frill formed of three rows of Val lace; the sleeves being also scalloped at the wrist and frilled with Val. Long sleeves only. $15.98

These READY-MADE Dresses can be furnished only as illustrated and described. Sizes 32 to 44 Bust Measure. The skirts are made about 40 inches long in front and hang evenly all around. They have a three-inch basted hem so that they can be easily lengthened or shortened by the customer. We cannot send samples of these materials. For Princess Slips to be worn beneath these dresses, see page 91.

4451   4452   4453   4454   4455

The READY-MADE Tub Suits shown on this page can be furnished only as illustrated and described.   SIZES—32 TO 44 BUST MEASURE.   The skirts are made about 40 inches long in front and hang evenly all around.   They have a three-inch basted hem so that they can be easily lengthened or shortened by the customer.   WE CANNOT FURNISH SAMPLES OF THE MATERIALS.

4451—Jumper Dress and Coat of excellent quality Linon, in white or natural linen color.   The jumper is cut with a low V-shaped neck and is open in back extending in a V to the waistline.   Garment is sleeveless, and piping in a contrasting shade is used at the neck and around armholes.   Jumper and skirt are joined by a stitched belt.   Two piped folds of the material appear around the bottom of the gored, flaring skirt.   Garment is unlined and buttons down the entire front with handsome pearl buttons. The coat is semi-fitted and about 34 inches long in back, where the seams are slashed and trimmed with pearl buttons.   It is in pronounced cutaway effect in front, closing at the bust-line with a single Mother-of-Pearl button.   Tiny pearl buttons and piping trim the collar effect and the cuffs.   Two patch pockets.   Coat is unlined. **$11.98**

4452—Tub Suit of excellent quality Rep, in white or natural linen color.   The jacket is in modified Directoire effect, semi-fitted and about 40 inches long in the back.   Seams in back are slashed and elaborately trimmed with fancy buttons to match those used on the piped sleeves and for the closing in front.   The notched collar is also piped with a contrasting material.   Pockets are simulated on each side by flaps which are piped and trimmed with buttons.   Gored skirt, flaring gracefully at the lower edge and finished smoothly at the top, has a wide fold of the material finished with piping.   Two plaits extend down the front. **$9.98**

4453—Tub Suit of good quality Linen, in white or natural linen color.   This suit is elaborated with Point de Venise insertion extending down the full length of both front and back and applied on all edges.   Coat is semi-fitted, about 36 inches long in the back, where it is trimmed with crochet-covered buttons.   Turn-back cuffs are lace-trimmed.   The gored, flaring skirt displays an insertion of Point de Venise lace to match the jacket.   .   **$11.98**

4454—Tub Suit of good quality Linon, in white or natural linen color.   Single-breasted jacket, semi-fitted, and made about 34 inches long in back, where it is trimmed with pearl buttons. Notched collar and turn-back cuffs.   Four flap pockets.   Coat is unlined.   The skirt has nine gores in flaring outline, with two stitched box-plaits down the front, and a tailored strap of the material around the bottom extending upward in points at the sides.   Pearl buttons provide an attractive completion.   **$4.98**

4455—Tub Suit of very fine Imported English Rep, in white or natural linen color.   A semi-fitting Directoire coat.   Model is collarless and embellished around the neck with a contrasting color, outlined by tabs and a strap of the material; the latter being trimmed with tiny buttons.   This finish is also used on the sleeves. Coat closes across the bust in genuine Directoire style, and is open at the sides in sheath effect.   Back is ornamented with tabs and a button-trimmed strap.   Coat is unlined.   The gored, flaring skirt is finished down the front and around the lower edge with tailored straps, tabs and buttons. **$16.98**

The READY-MADE Tub Suits shown on this page can be furnished only as illustrated and described. SIZES—32 TO 44 BUST MEASURE. The skirts are made about 40 inches long in front and hang evenly all around. They have a three-inch basted hem so that they can be easily lengthened or shortened by the customer. WE CANNOT FURNISH SAMPLES OF THE MATERIALS.

4456—Jumper Dress and Coat of very fine Imported Rep, in white or natural linen color. The coat is semi-fitted, finished with lapped seams and trimmed with self-covered buttons. It is about 34 inches long in back. The turn-back cuffs and simulated collar are outlined with piping in a contrasting color, and finished with Cluny lace. Yoke lining of the material. The jumper dress is sleeveless, and the armholes and low neck are in scalloped effect, ornamented with piping and Cluny insertion. The plain gored skirt is joined to the waist by a belt, and the front displays piping and insertions of Cluny as illustrated, combined with self-covered buttons. The latter are also used on the waist and for the visible closing in back. Dress is unlined. The guimpe pictured is not included. $14.98

4457—Tub Suit of good quality Linen. Colors: white with black stripe, or natural linen color with white stripe; also in plain white or natural linen color. Jacket is semi-fitted and about 29 inches long in back. Notched collar; turn-back cuffs; two patch pockets. Seams are slit and trimmed with pearl buttons. Yoke lining of material. The plain flare skirt is eleven-gored and is finished with a wide fold and pearl buttons. $6.98

4458—Tub Suit of good quality Linon, in white, linen color or cadet blue. Jacket is semi-fitted and displays the fashionable slashed seams in back and also at sides, where pockets are simulated by chic Directoire flaps. Length about 32 inches in back.

Collar, cuffs and pockets are trimmed with straps of contrasting material. Skirt is a fifteen-gored flaring model, finished with three piped folds trimmed with pearl buttons to match those used on jacket. Unlined. $5.98

4459—Tub Suit of excellent quality Pure Linen Crash, in white or natural linen color. Light, cool and extremely serviceable. Jacket is semi-fitted and about 34 inches long in back. Notched collar and turn-back cuffs are trimmed with pearl buttons, and the separate detachable collar and cuffs are of fancy piqué in a contrasting color. Two patch pockets. Plain nine-gored flare skirt is trimmed with a fold and pearl buttons, and finished with three plaits in front. Unlined. $7.98

4460—The Robespierre Model—a stunning creation, distinctly Parisian in style and exquisite in workmanship. The jacket—a pleasing example of the Directoire styles—is semi-fitted and about 39 inches long in back. It is made of heavily braided net, outlined by bands of linen, and is slit at the sides almost to the waist-line. The chic, Incroyable revers and cuffs are made of linen, braided to match. Unlined. The eleven-gored flare skirt is of imported linen, displaying an insertion of braided net down the front, which is continued around the bottom, tapering to points in the back. A charming suit, dainty, yet substantial and serviceable. Can be furnished in white only. $14.98

4461

4462

4463

4464

4465

The READY-MADE Tub Suits shown on this page can be furnished only as illustrated and described. SIZES—32 TO 44 BUST MEASURE. The skirts are made about 40 inches long in front and hang evenly all around. They have a three-inch basted hem so that they can be easily lengthened or shortened by the customer. WE CANNOT FURNISH SAMPLES OF THE MATERIALS.

4461—Tub Suit of fine quality English Rep, in white, natural linen color, or light blue. The coat is extremely smart in cut, being semi-fitted, slashed at the side seams, with a deep box-plait in the back. Length about 38 inches in back. The model is lavishly adorned around the collarless neck and on all edges with Bonnaz embroidery in a fanciful design. The front is in cutaway outline in accordance with some of the very newest ideas. The flare skirt has eleven gores, embellished with Bonnaz embroidery down the front and around the lower edge. Unlined. **$12.98**

4462—Tub Suit of good quality Linon, in white or natural linen color. The jacket is double-breasted and is about 30 inches long in back. It is a semi-fitted model, finished with a mannish notched collar and neat turn-back cuffs. The skirt consists of nine flaring gores and has a wide fold of the material around the bottom. Suit is unlined. **$4.98**

4463—Tub Suit of good quality Imported Rep, in white or light blue. The jacket of this decidedly attractive suit is a semi-fitted model with a front in pronounced cutaway outline. It is about 30 inches long in back and is elaborately trimmed on each side of both front and back, and on the sleeves with imitation Baby Irish insertion. This same lace is applied over the material on all

edges. The nine-gored flaring skirt is ornamented with two parallel rows of Baby Irish insertion to match. Unlined. . . **$9.98**

4464—Tub Suit of good quality Linen, in natural linen color, reseda green, or lavender; with white piqué collar and cuffs. Also in all-white linen. The single-breasted coat is semi-fitted and about 35 inches long in back. Two pockets. The skirt is a fashionable flare model made with eleven gores and has three folds of the material. Unlined. **$6.98**

4465—Tub Suit of finest quality Genuine Imported English Rep, in white or natural linen color. The jacket is a semi-fitted model, made about 37 inches long in back. The front closes with ornamental buttons. Point de Venise lace is applied around the collarless neck, where washable Oriental embroidery to match that used on the turn-back cuffs affords a distinctive touch. Two fancy patch pockets. The skirt is a gored-flaring model with side-plaits introduced on each side and an inverted plait in back. The front displays a stitched strap in plait effect, trimmed with buttons to match those on jacket and simulated button-holes. The fold around the bottom is edged with a tailored strap as pictured. Unlined. **$14.98**

4501   4502

4505   4506   4504   4503   4507

SIZES OF HOUSE DRESSES AND DRESSING SACQUES—32 TO 44 BUST.

4501—Dressing Sacque of fine Dotted Swiss. Colors: white ground with charming floral designs in pink, lavender or blue; also white ground with small black dot. Roll collar with scalloped ruffle headed by embroidery beading threaded with ribbon. Embroidery and ribbon are also used on the chic three-quarter sleeves and at the waist. Tucked to yoke depth in front, with two clusters of tucks extending down the full length of the back. . . . . **98 cents**

4502—Dressing Sacque of fine quality Persian Lawn. Colors: white ground with black figure, white ground with light blue figure, navy blue with white rings or black with white rings. The sleeves are finished with a Van Dyck ruffle prettily trimmed with Val lace and insertion; the dainty pointed collar being also ornamented with the same insertion and lace combined with satin ribbon. Two clusters of fine tucks in back. **$1.49**

4503—One-Piece House Dress of excellent quality Chambray, in blue with white stripe or gray with white stripe; also in plain blue or plain gray. The front displays double box-plaits piped in a contrasting shade, which extend to the waist-line. Piping also finishes the turn-over collar and the box-plait down the front through which the waist buttons visibly. The fulness in the back is arranged in plaits confined at the waist-line by a belt. Sleeves completed with button cuffs. Plain gored skirt, about 43 inches in length, with deep hem. **$1.89**

4504—Two-Piece House Dress of Gingham, in blue with white stripe or gray with white stripe; also in plain blue or plain gray. The waist buttons visibly in front, and is plaited down the full length of both front and back. Soft buttoned cuffs and detachable collar of the material. The plain gored skirt is about 43 inches in length, and has a deep hem. **$2.49**

4505—Two-Piece House Dress of extra fine quality Chambray, in white, navy blue or light blue. The waist buttons in front under a box-plait, on either side of which fine tucks are introduced extending to the waist-line. Tucks to yoke depth on the shoulders in front. The back is also elaborately tucked. Neat buttoned cuffs in a contrasting shade. Detachable stiff linen collar. Tie pictured is not included. The skirt is thirteen-gored, about 43 inches long, and finished with a deep hem. . . **$2.98**

4506—Two-Piece House Dress of superior quality Mohair, in black, navy blue or brown. The waist is plaited to yoke depth in the front, where it buttons invisibly under a box-plait. The back displays two full-length clusters of tucks. Long sleeves finished with buttoned cuffs of the material. A linen collar is included, but we do not furnish the tie shown in illustration. Skirt consists of five gores in flare effect, and is about 43 inches in length. Body of waist is lined. Stitched belt of the material. . **$5.98**

4507—House or Tea Gown of superior quality Cashmere, in garnet, navy blue, brown or gray. A chic and dressy gown made with desirable fulness. The tucked yoke, back and front, is outlined with a Bertha prettily trimmed with shirred satin ribbon and lace. The collar and the cuffs which finish the sleeves are similarly completed with ribbon. Double inverted plait in back, tacked at the waist-line. Lined to the waist. . . **$5.98**

SIZES OF KIMONOS AND DRESSING SACQUES—
32 TO 44 BUST.

4508—Long Kimono of good quality Challis, in navy blue, light blue or red ground with a pretty Persian pattern; ornamented around neck, down fronts and on the three-quarter sleeves with an Oriental border. Belt of similar design. Extra full sweep. $1.29

4509—Dressing Sacque in Marie Antoinette design, of fine quality Dotted Swiss. Colors: white ground with delicate check in blue, pink or lavender with a design of black rings as pictured; also in plain white. Lavishly tucked both front and back and charmingly trimmed down front, on collar, sleeves and around bottom with fine Val lace. Embroidery beading threaded with satin ribbon at neck and waist. Three-quarter sleeves. Extremely chic. $1.98

4510—Dolly Varden Dressing Sacque of fine quality Dotted Swiss, in white only. This charming sacque is tucked to yoke depth both front and back, and is elaborately trimmed with French Val lace, which outlines the Dutch neck and is used around waist, on the peplum, and completes the quaint and graceful sleeves. Garment fastens at the neck with satin ribbon tied in a bow. $2.49

4511—Long Kimono of Japanese Crepe, in Alice blue, navy blue, pink, tan or red ground with a small Persian figure. Garment is edged with satin around the neck and down fronts; satin also trims the sleeves and pocket. The shoulders, fronts, cuffs and pocket display an attractive Persian border, and the belt is of the same pleasing design. Three-quarter sleeves. . . $1.98

4512—Long Kimono of good quality Japanese Crepe, in navy blue, light blue, red or lavender. Shirred yoke both front and back provides extra fulness. Garment is also shirred at the waist-line in back, and the relieved fulness is confined by striped silk ribbon tied in a bow. The same ribbon extends around neck and down fronts and finishes the three-quarter sleeves. Extra wide sweep around bottom. $1.98

4513—Long Kimono of fine quality Japanese Crepe. Colors: light blue, navy blue, lavender or black ground with beautiful floral patterns in harmonizing colors; also in plain colors of navy blue, light blue, red or lavender. Tucked over shoulders in front; prettily trimmed with bands of satin, as pictured, around neck, down front and on the chic three-quarter sleeves. Straps of satin are applied in front and also trim the back. Fulness gathered at waist and confined by an attached girdle of satin. . $2.98

4514—Long Kimono of fine quality China Silk, in light blue, navy blue or red with neat floral designs in harmonizing colors. Shirred yoke, making the garment extra full; also shirred at the waist-line in back and fastening in front with a girdle of satin ribbon; handsomely finished with bands of satin around neck and down fronts. Geisha sleeves are also finished with satin. $4.98

SIZES OF WAISTS—32 TO 44 BUST.

4601—Tailored Shirt Waist of good quality Cross-bar Lawn, in white only. Two wide tucks are taken in the material to yoke depth on each side of the visible buttoned closing in front. Plaits are introduced down the front, forming a panel effect, which are paralleled by full-length clusters of fine tucks. This same pleasing device is used in back, where plaits and tucks are similarly used. The shirt sleeves have stiff laundered cuffs of linen and a detachable turn-over collar is also supplied. We do not furnish the tie in the illustration. Can be furnished with long sleeves only. . . **98 cents**

4602—Waist of good quality Lawn, in white only. A stylish Eton collar of lawn, edged with Val lace, distinguishes this attractive waist. A plastron of embroidery, outlined by tucks, extends down the front beneath which the opening is concealed. The entire front is tucked, as pictured, and is also elaborated with veining. Plain tucked back. Sleeves are finished with chic cuffs, which are neatly tucked. Can be furnished with long sleeves only.
98 cents

4603—Waist of good quality soft Lawn, in white only. This dainty waist displays a panel of Florentine embroidery applied on the front, concealing the buttoned closing. Wide shoulder-pieces of the same embroidery contribute materially to the effectiveness of the design, and tucks extending across the front provide desirable fulness. The sleeves are tucked, as also are the cuffs and Gibson collar, both of which are finished with an edging of Val lace. Three groups of tucks in back. Can be furnished with long sleeves only. . . . . **98 cents**

4604—Waist of good quality Lawn, in white only. A very dressy waist with a yoke effect which consists of panels of Swiss embroidery, tucked lawn and Val lace insertion. Val lace is also used to trim the front as pictured, and edges the Gibson collar and the cuffs, which are neatly tucked. Waist buttons invisibly in back, where Princess tucks to yoke depth are introduced similar to those shown on the front. Can be furnished with three-quarter sleeves only. . . . . **98 cents**

4605—Waist of good quality Lawn, in white only, with a front of all-over Swiss embroidery in eyelet design. The waist is tucked to yoke depth in front, where it buttons invisibly beneath a box-plait. The sleeves are also tucked and ornamented with embroidery as pictured. The Gibson collar and cuffs are edged with Val lace. Plain tucked back. Can be furnished with long sleeves only. . . . . **98 cents**

4606—Waist of Embroidered Lawn, in all-over effect. White only. The embroidery is a very neat eyelet design, and attention is called to the fact that the entire waist, both front and back, as well as the sleeves, is embroidered. Groups of tucks are introduced in front and also in back, where the closing is effected invisibly. The deep cuffs which finish the sleeves are tucked and edged with Val. and the Gibson collar is also lace-edged. Can be furnished with long sleeves only. . . . . **98 cents**

SIZES OF WAISTS—32 TO 44 BUST.

4607—Waist of fine quality Linene, in white only. A very serviceable material which wears well and launders beautifully. The waist is tucked down the entire front, where the waist closes visibly with pearl buttons. Six tucks extend down the back. Shirt sleeves are finished with laundered link cuffs. The detachable stiff linen collar is included, but we do not furnish the tie shown in the illustration. Can be furnished with long sleeves only. **$1.25**

4608—Waist of good quality Batiste, in white only. The use of Cluny insertion on the front of this dainty waist contributes greatly to its charming appearance. Panels of Swiss embroidery are also used as pictured, and short clusters of Princess tucks are introduced on the shoulders. The waist buttons invisibly in back under a box-plait. The back displays four clusters of Princess tucks. The tucked sleeves are finished with cuffs that are finely tucked and edged with Cluny lace to accord with the Gibson collar. Can be furnished with three-quarter sleeves only. **$1.25**

4609—Waist of fine quality Dotted Swiss, in white only. A particularly natty waist made with a plastron front, beneath which the closing is concealed. Full-length clusters of tucks extend down the front paralleled by inserts of Swiss embroidery, and short tucks to yoke depth are also introduced over the shoulders. The sleeves terminate in tucked cuffs frilled with Val lace. The detachable Gibson collar is tucked and edged with lace to correspond. Tucked back. Can be furnished with long sleeves only. **$1.25**

4610—Waist of good quality soft Batiste, in white only. The deep V-shaped front yoke is of Val lace and imitation Irish insertion combined with panels of tucked Batiste. The medallion in the center is of imitation Baby Irish lace, and the yoke is outlined, as pictured, with frills of Val. Inserts of this lace appear down the front, and Irish insertion, the same as that used in the yoke, adds to the charm of the design. The sleeves are tucked, trimmed and edged with Val lace. Tucked in back, where the waist closes invisibly. Can be furnished with long sleeves only. **$1.25**

4611—Tailored Shirt Waist of fine quality Linene, in white only. Waist is neatly tucked as illustrated and displays an entire front of embroidery. It will be noticed that the waist buttons visibly in front on one side—a quaint conceit, which is both new and attractive. The detachable linen collar is included, but we do not furnish the tie shown in the illustration. Link cuffs. Plaited back. Can be furnished with long sleeves only. **$1.25**

4612—Waist of good quality soft Batiste, in white only or in **India Lawn,** in black only. This extremely neat waist buttons invisibly in front under a tucked box-plait. Groups of Princess tucks to yoke depth are introduced on the shoulders and two full-length clusters of the same tucks trim the back. The buttoned cuffs are also tucked and the detachable collar is finished with a tab. Can be furnished with long sleeves only. **$1.25**

SIZES OF WAISTS—32 TO 44 BUST.

4613—Waist of dainty figured Cross-bar Lawn, in white only. A wide plait extends down each side of the visible button closing in front, paralleled by shorter plaits, which are stitched down to yoke depth. Two deep tucks in back. Soft button cuffs of the material and detachable linen collar. Tie shown in the illustration is not included. Can be furnished with long sleeves only. **$1.49**

4614—Tailored Shirt Waist of Pure Linen, in white only. A natty mannish shirt waist, buttoning visibly in front through a box-plait. Four plaits are taken over the shoulders in front, stitched down to yoke depth. Two side-plaits in back simulate a box-plait. Stiff linen link cuffs and detachable turn-over collar. We do not furnish the tie shown in the illustration. Can be furnished with long sleeves only. Remarkable value. . . **$1.49**

4615—Waist of fine Lawn, in white only. The front of this extremely pretty waist is beautifully embroidered in Swiss eyelet effect. The embroidery in the center, which is also applied on the shoulders and sleeves and forms the collar and cuffs, is in a rich Point de Venise design. Short Princess tucks in front; plain tucked back. Val lace outlines the embroidery on sleeves and shoulders, and edges the cuffs and collar. Waist buttons invisibly in back. Can be furnished with three-quarter sleeves only. . . **$1.49**

4616—Tucked Shirt Waist of India Lawn, in black or white. This is undoubtedly one of our smartest designs this season. The entire waist is tucked both front and back, and the front displays groups of tiny pearl buttons. The sleeves are also tucked in Mousquetaire effect. Sleeves and collar are frilled with Val lace. Buttons in back under a plait. Can be furnished with long sleeves only. **$1.49**

4617—Waist of fine quality Lawn, in white only. The front is of handsome Venetian embroidery in all-over effect, varied by plaits which form a plastron, and fine tucks to yoke depth over the shoulders. There are three clusters of tucks extending down the back. Collar and cuffs are tucked and edged with Val lace. Waist closes invisibly in front. Can be furnished with long sleeves only. **$1.49**

4618—Waist of good quality Batiste, in white only. Fine Val lace insertion outlined by hemstitching has been used with artistic results on the front of this elaborate waist. The back, where the closing is concealed, is tucked to yoke depth. The sleeves display Princess tucks below the elbow and are edged with Val lace to match the tucked Gibson collar. Can be furnished with long sleeves only. **$1.49**

SIZES OF WAISTS—32 TO 44 BUST.

4619—Waist of Batiste, in white only. The front of this charming waist is elaborated with insertions of Val lace as pictured, and has two wide bands of Venise embroidery extending down the front meeting in a V at the waist-line. Waist is tucked to yoke depth in front and has four full-length clusters of tucks in back. Waist buttons invisibly in back. Tucked sleeves are finished with cuffs edged with Val lace to match the tucked Gibson collar. Can be furnished with three-quarter sleeves only. **$1.49**

4620—Waist of Batiste, in white only, elaborately trimmed in front with inserts of German Val lace, which are outlined by dainty frills of the same lace. The square yoke is of Val combined with Swiss embroidery insertion. Waist buttons invisibly in back, where fine tucks and Val inserts are introduced to yoke depth. Sleeves are trimmed with lace as pictured, and button at the wrist. Can be furnished with long sleeves only. **$1.49**

4621—Waist of good quality Lawn, in white only. The front is tucked to yoke depth and daintily embroidered as pictured. Waist buttons under a plait in back, where clusters of tucks relieve the plainness. The attractive, tucked sleeves are edged with a frill of Val lace, as is also the Gibson collar. Can be furnished with long sleeves only. **$1.49**

4622—Waist of Batiste, in white only. Inserts of fine Val lace, outlined by delicate hemstitching picturesquely applied on the

front of this stylish waist, contribute greatly to its undeniable charm. Imitation Irish insertion and Val extend down the front in plastron effect, and miniature tucks afford a graceful completion. Waist buttons invisibly in back, where short tucks to yoke depth are introduced. The sleeves are tucked and the cuffs are finished with Val lace to correspond with the Gibson collar. Can be furnished with three-quarter sleeves only. **$1.75**

4623—Waist of Swiss embroidery, in all-over effect. White only. A particularly attractive waist embroidered as pictured both front and back, and on the chic, tucked sleeves which are edged with Val lace. The Gibson collar is of embroidery with a lace edge. Waist is tucked to yoke depth in front and also in back, where it buttons invisibly under a plait. Can be furnished with long sleeves only. **$1.75**

4624—Waist of excellent quality Batiste, in white only. This handsome waist is lavishly ornamented both front and back and also on the sleeves with full-length insertions of Cluny lace. The front displays Princess tucks extending to yoke depth and the same tucks are continued down the back to the waist-line. Waist buttons in back under a plait. The sleeves terminate in tucked cuffs with inserts of Cluny lace and are edged with Val to accord with the tucked Gibson collar. Long sleeves only. **$1.75**

SIZES OF WAISTS—32 TO 44 BUST.

4625—Shirt Waist of Pure Linen, in white only; mannishly finished with detachable stiff linen collar and laundered link cuffs. We do not furnish the tie shown in the illustration. Waist is nattily tucked over the entire front and also has a cluster of tucks down the center of the back. Buttons visibly in front through a plait. Sleeves are tucked below the elbow. Can be furnished with long sleeves only. $1.98

4626—Waist of good quality Persian Lawn, in white only. Fine tucks extend down the front of this dainty waist, which is further ornamented with four sprays of delicate Swiss embroidery in floral and dot effect. The same embroidery appears on the sleeves, which are tucked as illustrated, making them fit the arm closely below the elbow. Back admits tucks of graduated width, and the tucked Gibson collar and the sleeves are edged with Val lace. Waist buttons visibly in front through a plait. Can be furnished with long sleeves only. $1.98

4627—Waist of All-over Embroidered Lawn, in an extremely dainty pattern. White only. This chic little waist is finely tucked to yoke depth both front and back, and buttons invisibly in back under a plait. The collar is of Val lace insertion separated by a band of embroidered lawn. It is daintily frilled with lace to correspond with the sleeves. The latter are tucked below the elbow, making them fit closely in accordance with the prevailing mode. Can be furnished with long sleeves only. $1.98

4628—Waist of fine quality India Lawn, in white only. The front of this charming and serviceable waist is ornamented with three full-length rows of Swiss embroidery, in eyelet effect, interspersed with Princess tucks which extend to yoke depth. Tucks appear down the center of the front concealing the button closing. Four clusters of Princess tucks in back; the same pleasing finish being employed on the sleeves, which are also finished with Val lace to correspond with the tucked collar. Can be furnished with long sleeves only. $1.98

4629—Waist of good quality Persian Lawn, in white only. This extremely pretty waist displays a front of all-over Italian Filet embroidery in a particularly fascinating design. This embroidery wears splendidly. Waist is tucked to yoke depth in front and full-length Princess tucks are used down the back, where the button closing is concealed under a plait. The sleeves are tucked and finished with neatly tucked cuffs adorned with embroidery insertion and edged with Val lace to match the collar. Can be furnished with three-quarter sleeves only. $1.98

4630—Waist of Japanese Crêpe, in white only. The fact that this attractive new material wears so well and launders beautifully accounts for its popularity. Model is trimmed in front with plaits and inserts of imitation crochet lace in Filet effect and closes visibly in front with crochet buttons. Two inserts of lace in back. Sleeves are elaborated with insertion as pictured. Can be furnished with long sleeves only. $1.98

SIZES OF WAISTS—32 TO 44 BUST.

4631—Waist of fine Lawn, in white only. An extremely fetching model with an attractive front, consisting of Swiss embroidery in eyelet effect surrounded by Val lace. Val lace insertion adorns the back, where the plainness is relieved by four full-length clusters of fine tucks. Waist closes invisibly in front beneath a simulated box-plait trimmed with Val insertion. The sleeves are neatly tucked and display inserts of Val, being also frilled with the same lace at the wrist to match the tucked collar. Can be furnished with long sleeves only. $1.98

4632—Waist of fine quality Lawn, in white only. Dainty French Val insertion and shadow embroidery in alternating rows form the front of this becoming and serviceable waist. The sleeves are effectively finished with the same embroidery outlined by Val insertion and hemstitched tucks. These same tucks also appear on the shoulders in front and are continued down the back in four clusters, contributing a charming completion. Waist buttons visibly in back. The sleeves and the tucked Gibson collar are edged with a frill of Val lace. Can be furnished with long sleeves only. $1.98

4633—Shirt Waist of finest quality Corded Madras, in white with fine blue stripe; also in white with black stripe. A splendid material, light weight and admirably adapted for the needs of Summer as it wears well and launders beautifully. Waist is tucked to yoke depth in front, where it closes visibly with pearl buttons through a box-plait. Plain tucked back. Stiff link cuffs of the material. Detachable linen collar. Tie pictured is not included. Can be furnished with long sleeves only. $1.98

4634—Waist of good quality Batiste, in white only. Lavishly trimmed with handsome Point de Paris lace insertion applied on the front, extending in straight lines down the full length of the back. Two rows of the same insertion ornament the sleeves. The latter are finished at the wrist in pointed effect with insertion and edging of Val. Waist is tucked front and back. Gibson collar is of Val lace and Point de Paris insertion. Val lace and Princess tucks form a vest effect in front. Closes invisibly in back. *Can be furnished with long or three-quarter sleeves.* $1.98

4635—Waist of excellent quality French Batiste, in white only. The charm of this simple waist is due to the three sprays of hand embroidery on the front, which are separated by groups of Princess tucks. Full-length clusters of tucks extend down the back, where the waist buttons invisibly. Veining on the shoulders and around the tucked collar lends a dainty finish to the model. Sleeves are tucked as pictured and edged with a frill of Val to accord with the collar. Can be furnished with long sleeves only. $1.98

4636—Waist of good quality Batiste, in black or white. Shadow embroidery furnishes the decorative treatment on the front of this pretty waist. The plastron is outlined by Princess tucks and the same tucks appear to yoke depth, being continued down the full length of the back in four clusters. Sleeves are tucked below the elbow and edged with Val lace to correspond with the tucked collar. Can be furnished with long sleeves only. $1.98

SIZES OF WAISTS—32 TO 44 BUST.

4637—Waist of Imported Batiste, in a fine sheer quality. White only. Tucked in all-over effect both front and back. The sleeves are also tucked and are finished with buttoned cuffs edged with fine Val lace. The tucked Gibson collar is similarly edged with lace and displays a tab trimmed with tiny pearl buttons. The same buttons are a decorative feature of the front. Waist closes invisibly in front under a plait. Can be furnished with long sleeves only. . . . **$1.98**

4638—Waist of fine quality Batiste, in white only. The graceful lines of this model are produced by rows of German Val lace extending down the front, combined with imitation Baby Irish insertion. The yoke consists of panels of Swiss embroidery outlined by Val insertion. The latter lace is also used on the shaped sleeve varied by clusters of dwarf tucks. The lace yoke extends around the back, where Val lace insertion and short clusters of tucks provide a charming completion. Buttons visibly in back. *Can be furnished with long or three-quarter sleeves.* **$2.49**

4639—Waist of fine sheer Batiste, in white only, with a front of dainty Swiss embroidery in all-over effect. A wide band of embroidery insertion extends down the front, beneath which the waist buttons invisibly. Full-length clusters of Princess tucks appear on either side, and four groups of the same tucks are introduced in back combined with two rows of crochet insertion. This insertion trims the tucked sleeves, which are buttoned at the wrist and finished in pointed effect with crochet insertion and lace. Collar of tucked batiste and lace. Plaits are employed on the shoulders in front. Can be furnished with long sleeves only. **$2.49**

4640—Waist of fine French Batiste, in white only. The very handsome yoke and collar of imitation Baby Irish lace is a feature of this tasteful model. Parallel rows of insertion extending down the front interspersed with clusters of tucks, provide the long lines so much desired. Waist is tucked in back and trimmed with Val lace insertion. It buttons visibly in back. The sleeves are particularly chic, being composed entirely of tucked batiste, relieved by inserts of Val lace, and finished in pointed effect with Val to accord with the Gibson collar. Can be furnished with long sleeves only. **$2.49**

4641—Hand-Embroidered Shirt Waist of pure Linen, in white only. This dainty waist is plaited down the front with wider plaits taken over the shoulders. Back displays tucks of graduated width. The model closes visibly in front with pearl buttons through a box-plait, with tucks on either side. Link cuffs and detachable stiff linen collar. Tie shown in the illustration is not included. Can be furnished with long shirt sleeves only. **$2.49**

4642—Waist of sheer French Batiste, in white only. Inserts of imitation Baby Irish lace, outlined by German Val, are used with charming effect on the front of this chic waist. Val lace combined with Cluny insertion form the V-shaped yoke in front and the collar. The front is tucked as pictured, and the back, where the waist buttons visibly, is tucked to yoke depth and trimmed with inserts of Val lace. This lace also appears on the sleeves which are further ornamented with an insert of imitation Baby Irish lace. *Can be furnished with long or three-quarter sleeves.* **$2.49**

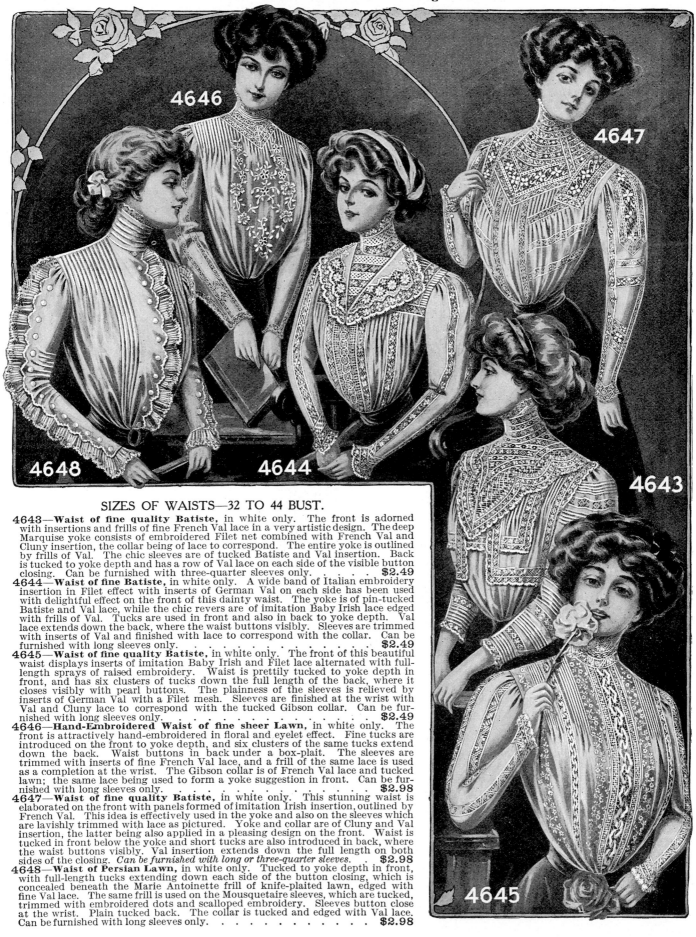

SIZES OF WAISTS—32 TO 44 BUST.

4643—Waist of fine quality Batiste, in white only. The front is adorned with insertions and frills of fine French Val lace in a very artistic design. The deep Marquise yoke consists of embroidered Filet net combined with French Val and Cluny insertion, the collar being of lace to correspond. The entire yoke is outlined by frills of Val. The chic sleeves are of tucked Batiste and Val insertion. Back is tucked to yoke depth and has a row of Val lace on each side of the visible button closing. Can be furnished with three-quarter sleeves only. $2.49

4644—Waist of fine Batiste, in white only. A wide band of Italian embroidery insertion in Filet effect with inserts of German Val on each side has been used with delightful effect on the front of this dainty waist. The yoke is of pin-tucked Batiste and Val lace, while the chic revers are of imitation Baby Irish lace edged with frills of Val. Tucks are used in front and also in back to yoke depth. Val lace extends down the back, where the waist buttons visibly. Sleeves are trimmed with inserts of Val and finished with lace to correspond with the collar. Can be furnished with long sleeves only. $2.49

4645—Waist of fine quality Batiste, in white only. The front of this beautiful waist displays inserts of imitation Baby Irish and Filet lace alternated with full-length sprays of raised embroidery. Waist is prettily tucked to yoke depth in front, and has six clusters of tucks down the full length of the back, where it closes visibly with pearl buttons. The plainness of the sleeves is relieved by inserts of German Val with a Filet mesh. Sleeves are finished at the wrist with Val and Cluny lace to correspond with the tucked Gibson collar. Can be furnished with long sleeves only. $2.49

4646—Hand-Embroidered Waist of fine sheer Lawn, in white only. The front is attractively hand-embroidered in floral and eyelet effect. Fine tucks are introduced on the front to yoke depth, and six clusters of the same tucks extend down the back. Waist buttons in back under a box-plait. The sleeves are trimmed with inserts of fine French Val lace, and a frill of the same lace is used as a completion at the wrist. The Gibson collar is of French Val lace and tucked lawn; the same lace being used to form a yoke suggestion in front. Can be furnished with long sleeves only. $2.98

4647—Waist of fine quality Batiste, in white only. This stunning waist is elaborated on the front with panels formed of imitation Irish insertion, outlined by French Val. This idea is effectively used in the yoke and also on the sleeves which are lavishly trimmed with lace as pictured. Yoke and collar are of Cluny and Val insertion, the latter being also applied in a pleasing design on the front. Waist is tucked in front below the yoke and short tucks are also introduced in back, where the waist buttons visibly. Val insertion extends down the full length on both sides of the closing. *Can be furnished with long or three-quarter sleeves.* . $2.98

4648—Waist of Persian Lawn, in white only. Tucked to yoke depth in front, with full-length tucks extending down each side of the button closing, which is concealed beneath the Marie Antoinette frill of knife-plaited lawn, edged with fine Val lace. The same frill is used on the Mousquetaire sleeves, which are tucked, trimmed with embroidered dots and scalloped embroidery. Sleeves button close at the wrist. Plain tucked back. The collar is tucked and edged with Val lace. Can be furnished with long sleeves only. $2.98

SIZES OF WAISTS—32 TO 44 BUST.

4649—Waist of All-Over Embroidery, in a beautiful open-work design. White only. This neat and dainty waist buttons in front beneath a plait. Short tucks are introduced in front and also extend down the back simulating a box-plait. The sleeves are finished with cuffs and trimmed with Val insertion and edging. The Gibson collar is likewise lace-trimmed. Can be furnished with long sleeves only. **$2.98**

4651—Waist of French Batiste, in white only, lavishly trimmed with Val lace. Two panels of exquisite embroidery are applied on the front, outlined by inserts and frills of Val lace. Pin-tucks form a vest effect down the center of the front, and short tucks combined with full-length inserts of Val, trim the back where the waist buttons invisibly. Sleeves are tucked as pictured, below the elbow and finished with cuffs of Val lace to correspond with the Gibson collar. Can be furnished with long sleeves only. **$2.98**

4652—Waist of excellent quality Batiste, in white only. This beautiful waist is made with a front consisting of three panels of exquisite Filet embroidery interspersed with sprays of shadow embroidery, producing an effect of much charm. The back displays clusters of Princess tucks down the full length combined with rows of French Val insertion. Panels of embroidery sur-

rounded by Val and uniquely tucked as illustrated ornament the sleeves and both collar and sleeves are edged with Val insertion and lace. Waist buttons invisibly in front. Can be furnished with long sleeves only. **$2.98**

4653—Waist of All-Over Embroidered Lawn, in black or white. This is a very effective waist and the artistic beauty of the shadow embroidery makes it particularly desirable. The garment displays tucks of graduated depth and is tucked to yoke depth in back, where it buttons invisibly under a plait. The sleeves are completed with chic, tucked cuffs and the Gibson collar is edged with Val lace. Can be furnished with long sleeves only. **$2.98**

4654—Waist of fine soft India Lawn, in white only. The yoke effect in front as well as the plastron are of imitation Irish Point insertion surrounded by French Val lace. Val lace forms the Gibson collar and is applied in a V at the neck. The back is tucked, trimmed with Val insertion, and buttons visibly with pearl buttons. Sleeves are shaped and close-fitting below the elbow, and the same arrangement of Irish Point and Val insertion as that shown on the front lends them a picturesque charm. Can be furnished with long sleeves only. **$2.98**

4656—Waist of very fine quality Batiste, in white only. Embroidered dots, one of Fashion's newest conceits, have been used on the front of this dressy waist with delightful effect. The yoke is of Val lace and Pompadour tucks, the latter being continued down the front paralleled by rows of Val lace. The waist buttons visibly in back, with two clusters of tucks and a row of Val lace introduced on either side. The prettily tucked sleeves are edged with Val lace to match collar. Can be furnished with long sleeves only. **$3.49**

4650
4655
4659
4657
4658
4660

ncludes all of the Season's artistic
clusive and delightful.

shirt waists for wear with smart
ng wear, for afternoon receptions
lless, and considering the style,
nderfully low.

**4650—Waist of All-Over Em-
broidery,** in an exquisite open-
work pattern. White only. The
distinguishing feature is an attractive chemisette of delicate
Val lace in Filet design. An
insertion of handsome imitation
Baby Irish lace greatly enhances
the fascinating appearance.
Deep cuffs of Val lace to accord
with the Gibson collar. Can
be furnished with long sleeves only. **$2.98**

4655—Waist of fine quality Batiste, in white only. Imitation
Baby Irish insertion in a very rich pattern is the main feature
in the decorative treatment of this exquisite waist. The front
is richly trimmed with this lace and is also ornamented with
embroidery, Cluny insertion and short Princess tucks. Waist
closes visibly in the back, where it is elaborately tucked, and
displays four inserts of Val lace. Sleeves are tucked as
pictured, and adorned with inserts of Val edged with Cluny
and Val lace as is also the collar. Can be furnished with long
sleeves only **$3.49**

4657—Hand-Embroidered Waist of fine quality Batiste, in
white only. A truly charming design, simple and refined, yet very
dainty. Front displays sprays of hand-embroidery and is also
ornamented with fine tucks and insertions of faggotting. The
sleeves and the Gibson collar are also finely tucked and exhibit
similar insertions. Four clusters of Princess tucks in back, where
the waist buttons under a plait. Can be furnished with long
sleeves only. **$3.49**

4658—Waist of fine quality Batiste, in white only. This dressy
waist is practical and decidedly smart. The yoke and collar are

SIZES OF WAISTS—32 TO 44 BUST.

of imitation Baby Irish lace. Crochet insertion in Filet design
appears down the front and on the sleeves. Panels in front are
of Irish lace and Swiss embroidery. The back is tucked and admits two insertions of crochet lace. Buttons visibly in back. Can
be furnished with long sleeves only. **$3.49**

4659—Hand-Embroidered Waist of Handkerchief Linen, in
white only. The front of this dainty and serviceable waist is exquisitely embroidered by hand in a floral design as pictured. The
model buttons visibly in front with fine tucks introduced on either
side. Short tucks on the shoulders in front. Back is neatly trimmed with six full-length clusters of Princess tucks. Stiff linen
cuffs and detachable turn-over collar. Tie shown in illustration
is not included. Can be furnished with long sleeves only. **$3.49**

4660—Waist of fine quality Batiste, in white only. The entire
front of this beautiful lingerie waist is exquisitely embroidered, the
design in the center being in Filet effect. Cluny insertion elabor-
ates the front, where Princess tucks are introduced to yoke depth.
The back is ornamented with imitation Baby Irish and Val insertion and is lavishly tucked. Buttons visibly in back. Sleeves
trimmed with Cluny and embroidery insertions to match that used
on the front. The cuffs are of Cluny and Val lace to accord with
the Gibson collar. Can be furnished with long sleeves only. **$3.98**

SIZES OF WAISTS—32 TO 44 BUST.

4661—Waist of fine Batiste, in white only. Imitation Baby Irish insertion and panels of embroidery form the yoke. The entire waist, front and back, displays insertions of Val lace separated by finely tucked batiste. Closing concealed in back. Sleeves are tucked and trimmed with Val lace. Collar is of Val and net insertion. *Can be furnished with long or three-quarter sleeves.* . **$3.98**

4662—Beau Brummel Waist of fine Batiste, in white only. A panel of Swiss embroidery appears down the front, beneath which the closing is concealed. A knife-plaited frill of Val lace is a feature, and narrow insertions of Cluny lace and rows of Swiss embroidery in block design are used down the full length both front and back. The sleeves are tucked, trimmed with Cluny insertion, and finished with embroidery frilled with lace. Can be furnished with long sleeves only. **$3.98**

4663—Waist of fine quality Batiste, in white only. Square medallions of Swiss embroidery, outlined by Val insertion, are used on the yoke, which also displays insertions of Val and Cluny combined with Princess tucks extending around the back, where the waist buttons visibly between two inserts of Val. Val insertion is lavishly used on the front. The sleeves are trimmed with Val insertion and an embroidery medallion, and are frilled with lace at the wrist to match the Gibson collar. Can be furnished with long sleeves only. **$3.98**

4664—Waist of French Batiste, in white only. Torchon lace and French Val have been used with charming effect in this model. The front displays two panels of raised embroidery, an insert of the same embroidery also appearing in the yoke. Sleeves are trimmed with Torchon and frills of Val. Waist buttons visibly in back, where it is trimmed with lace insertion. Model is tucked over the shoulders front and back, and finely tucked beneath frills extending down the front. Furnished with long sleeves only. **$4.98**

4665—Waist of French Batiste, in white only, finely tucked in all-over effect and elaborated both front and back with full-length insertions of Val lace. The yoke is of imitation Baby Irish lace and the Gibson collar is formed of alternating inserts of net and Val lace. Sleeves are tucked and trimmed with insertions of Val and a frill of the same lace. Buttons invisibly in back. Can be furnished with long sleeves only. **$4.98**

4666—Hand-Embroidered Waist of fine Batiste, in white only. The sprays of embroidery are carefully done by hand. The yoke and Gibson collar are of French Val lace and Thread lace insertion closely resembling real lace. Both back and front display tucks to yoke depth. The waist closes visibly in the back, where there are two full-length inserts of Thread lace. The same lace is applied on the sleeves combined with tucks. A frill of Val lace appears at the wrist to match the collar. Furnished with long sleeves only. **$4.98**

SIZES OF WAISTS—32 TO 44 BUST.

4667—Waist of fine Imported Batiste, in white only, trimmed both front and back with insertions and frills of French Val lace combined with rich Point de Venise insertion. Waist buttons visibly in back, where it is prettily tucked. The shaped sleeves are of finely tucked batiste with insertions and frills of Val. Collar is of Val insertion edged with the same lace. Can be furnished with long sleeves only. **$4.98**

4668—Waist of fine quality Batiste, in white only. Dainty squares of Swiss embroidery, alternated with finely tucked panels of batiste, and outlined by French Val lace insertion, have been utilized with strikingly tasteful effect on the front and also on the sleeves of this dressy waist. The Gibson collar and the yoke effect are also of French Val insertion, and two rows of this attractive lace appear in the back on each side of the visible button closing. Waist is tucked to yoke depth in back, and short groups of Princess tucks contribute to the charm of the front. Sleeves frilled with Val lace. Can be furnished with long sleeves only. **$4.98**

4669—Waist of French Batiste, in solid white; also in white with blue and white embroidery, or white with heliotrope and white embroidery. The front of this fascinating waist is of all-over embroidery in eyelet effect. The floral embroidery has a piquant suggestion of color which is carried out on the frill edging the plaited collar and the cuffs, and also on the chic tie which matches the color of the embroidery. Back is tucked. Waist closes in front under a plait. Sleeves are obliquely tucked and finished with cuffs of embroidery and imitation Irish crochet insertion. Can be furnished with long sleeves only. **$5.98**

4670—Waist of very fine Imported Batiste, in white only. Handsome shadow embroidery covers the entire front, and extends down both sides of the back. It is also introduced in panels on the sleeves, which are further ornamented with five clusters of Princess tucks. Dainty crochet veining trims the model both front and back, and also the sleeves. The chic lace collar displays a Louis XIV frill and a fetching tie of batiste. Closes visibly in front. Can be furnished with long sleeves only. **$5.98**

4671—Waist of very fine Imported Batiste, in white only. This is a truly artistic design, elaborate yet tasteful. Wide bands of imitation Baby Irish lace form a yoke in back, and are brought over the shoulders down to the waist-line in front, meeting in a V. The front is exquisitely embroidered in a dainty floral pattern and is further ornamented with parallel rows of French Val lace insertion, which also trims the back and is applied on the sleeves in combination with clusters of Princess tucks. Gibson collar of Val lace; the same lace being used to frill the sleeves. Tucked to yoke depth in back, where the waist buttons visibly. Can be furnished with long sleeves only. **$6.98**

4672—Marie Antoinette Waist of very fine quality French Batiste, in white only. Front is embellished with Coronation embroidery, done by hand, and crochet buttons. The closing is effected invisibly in front beneath a knife-plaited frill of batiste, edged with French Val lace. Both front and back display Princess tucks and Filet insertion. The Mousquetaire sleeves are tucked, trimmed with insertion, and end in a frill, the Gibson collar being similarly finished. Can be furnished with long sleeves only. **$6.98**

SIZES OF WAISTS—32 TO 44 BUST.

4673—Waist of excellent quality China Silk, in white only. This extremely attractive waist displays plaits over the shoulders and is tucked in box-plait effect down the front and richly trimmed with imitation Baby Irish and Irish crochet insertion. The chemisette and the Gibson collar are of Irish crochet insertion, the collar being also frilled with Val lace to correspond with the tucked cuffs. Pin-tucks are introduced below the chemisette, and the waist is also finely tucked to yoke depth in the back where it buttons invisibly under a plait. Can be furnished with long sleeves only. $2.98

4674—Waist of good quality Japanese Silk, in black or white. This sheer and dainty waist closes in front beneath a plait of silk embroidery in eyelet effect. The entire front is elaborated with full-length clusters of tucks, and also displays clusters of tucks over the shoulders to yoke depth. Plain tucked back. The sleeves are made with tucked buttoned cuffs, which are edged with Val to correspond with the Gibson collar. Can be furnished with long sleeves only. $2.98

4675—Waist of excellent quality China Silk, in black or white. The front of this beautiful waist is heavily silk-embroidered in an artistic design, making the model very dressy in appearance. The garment exhibits clusters of Princess tucks to yoke depth in front, and short tucks are also used to trim the back. The tucked collar and cuffs are edged with Val lace. Waist buttons invisibly in the back. Can be furnished with three-quarter sleeves only. $2.98

4676—Waist of excellent quality Japanese Silk, in white only. The yoke, both front and back, and the Gibson collar consist of Val lace insertion. The front of the yoke is trimmed with handsome medallions of Point de Venise lace in a very rich pattern. Pin-tucks appear below, both front and back, alternated by inserts of Val lace. The sleeves are ornamented with two full-length clusters of tucks and are also trimmed with Val lace and insertion. Waist closes invisibly in back. Can be furnished with three-quarter sleeves only. $3.98

4677—Waist of fine quality China Silk, in white only. Imitation Baby Irish insertion in an attractive Filet pattern, combined with inserts of finely tucked China silk, have been used with charming effect on the front of this handsome waist. The insertion and tucks are continued over the shoulders and down the back, meeting in a V at the waist-line. Waist buttons in back under a plait. The vest effect in front and the Gibson collar are formed of Princess tucks with inserts and frills of German Val lace. Sleeves display Bayadere tucks and are elaborated with three inserts of Baby Irish lace; the same insertion combined with Val lace forming a cuff effect at the wrist. Can be furnished with long sleeves only. $4.98

4678—Waist of fine sheer Japanese Silk, in black or white. This is one of the new all-over tucked waists so fashionable this season. The back is tucked exactly like the front. The model closes invisibly in front beneath a knife-plaited double frill of silk—a chic idea, which is also carried out·on the sleeves and Gibson collar. Silk-braid buttons ornament the front. A silk tie is included. Can be furnished with long sleeves only. $4.98

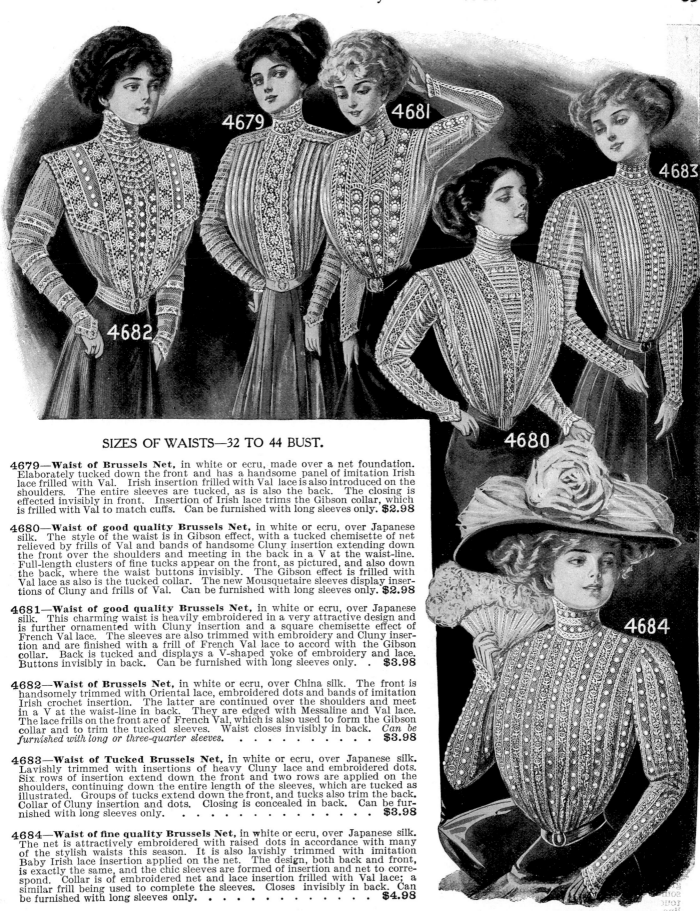

SIZES OF WAISTS—32 TO 44 BUST.

4679—Waist of Brussels Net, in white or ecru, made over a net foundation. Elaborately tucked down the front and has a handsome panel of imitation Irish lace frilled with Val. Irish insertion frilled with Val lace is also introduced on the shoulders. The entire sleeves are tucked, as is also the back. The closing is effected invisibly in front. Insertion of Irish lace trims the Gibson collar, which is frilled with Val to match cuffs. Can be furnished with long sleeves only. **$2.98**

4680—Waist of good quality Brussels Net, in white or ecru, over Japanese silk. The style of the waist is in Gibson effect, with a tucked chemisette of net relieved by frills of Val and bands of handsome Cluny insertion extending down the front over the shoulders and meeting in the back in a V at the waist-line. Full-length clusters of fine tucks appear on the front, as pictured, and also down the back, where the waist buttons invisibly. The Gibson effect is frilled with Val lace as also is the tucked collar. The new Mousquetaire sleeves display insertions of Cluny and frills of Val. Can be furnished with long sleeves only. **$2.98**

4681—Waist of good quality Brussels Net, in white or ecru, over Japanese silk. This charming waist is heavily embroidered in a very attractive design and is further ornamented with Cluny insertion and a square chemisette effect of French Val lace. The sleeves are also trimmed with embroidery and Cluny insertion and are finished with a frill of French Val lace to accord with the Gibson collar. Back is tucked and displays a V-shaped yoke of embroidery and lace. Buttons invisibly in back. Can be furnished with long sleeves only. . **$3.98**

4682—Waist of Brussels Net, in white or ecru, over China silk. The front is handsomely trimmed with Oriental lace, embroidered dots and bands of imitation Irish crochet insertion. The latter are continued over the shoulders and meet in a V at the waist-line in back. They are edged with Messaline and Val lace. The lace frills on the front are of French Val, which is also used to form the Gibson collar and to trim the tucked sleeves. Waist closes invisibly in back. *Can be furnished with long or three-quarter sleeves.* **$3.98**

4683—Waist of Tucked Brussels Net, in white or ecru, over Japanese silk. Lavishly trimmed with insertions of heavy Cluny lace and embroidered dots. Six rows of insertion extend down the front and two rows are applied on the shoulders, continuing down the entire length of the sleeves, which are tucked as illustrated. Groups of tucks extend down the front, and tucks also trim the back. Collar of Cluny insertion and dots. Closing is concealed in back. Can be furnished with long sleeves only. **$3.98**

4684—Waist of fine quality Brussels Net, in white or ecru, over Japanese silk. The net is attractively embroidered with raised dots in accordance with many of the stylish waists this season. It is also lavishly trimmed with imitation Baby Irish lace insertion applied on the net. The design, both back and front, is exactly the same, and the chic sleeves are formed of insertion and net to correspond. Collar is of embroidered net and lace insertion frilled with Val lace; a similar frill being used to complete the sleeves. Closes invisibly in back. Can be furnished with long sleeves only. **$4.98**

SIZES OF WAISTS—32 TO 44 BUST.

4685—Waist of fine **Bridal Net**, in white or ecru, over Japanese Silk. The collar and yoke both front and back are of handsome imitation Baby Irish lace, uniquely trimmed with Irish crochet buttons. Waist is tucked down the full length of both front and back, and the front is embellished with parallel rows of Val and Cluny insertion outlined by frills of Val lace. The sleeves are tucked and prettily trimmed with Val insertion and lace, as pictured. Waist buttons invisibly in back. *Can be furnished with long or three-quarter sleeves.* **$4.98**

4686—Waist of fine **Bridal Net**, in white or ecru, over Japanese Silk. Imitation Baby Irish insertion is employed on this enchanting waist with striking effect. Frills of French Val lace and Cluny insertion also appear on the front as pictured. A feature of the waist is the new Mousquetaire sleeve with a shirred under-piece, full-length panel of insertion and embroidered dots to match those used on the front. The yoke extends around the back where the waist closes invisibly. Can be furnished with long sleeves only. **$4.98**

4687—Waist of **Brussels Net**, in black, ecru, navy blue or smoke gray, over Mousseline de Soie. This waist is a fine net, handsomely trimmed with folds of Messaline in self-tone. Novel touches are given through the addition of a collar of net and Messaline with a ruche of Mousseline de Soie. The fancy scarf is of Messaline. The waist is tucked as pictured, both front and back,

and the tucked sleeves terminate in frills of Mousseline de Soie. Waist closes invisibly in front. Can be furnished with long sleeves only. **$4.98**

4688—Waist of **Ecru Brussels Net**, over net, with trimming of Copenhagen blue, navy blue or wistaria. Entire waist is tucked and on the edge of each tuck colored silk fringe is applied—a fancy which has found great favor on dressy waists this season. The front is trimmed with buttons, and both the collar and sleeves are edged with Val lace. Closes invisibly in back with hooks and eyes. Can be furnished with long sleeves only. **$4.98**

4689—Waist of very fine quality **Bridal Net**, in white or ecru, over Japanese Silk. This charming waist displays the new embroidered dot in all-over effect which has met with the marked approval of fashionable dressers. The waist is tucked down the full length of both front and back, and buttons invisibly in front, beneath a plastron of embroidery. Embroidered dots are employed on the front, collar and sleeves, as well as in the back. The tucked sleeves are trimmed at the wrist with Val lace to accord with the Gibson collar. Can be furnished with long sleeves only. **$4.98**

4690—Waist of fine quality **Brussels Net**, in white or ecru, on net. This elaborate waist, both front and back, consists of bands of Point de Venise insertion combined with insertions of net heavily embroidered in shadow effect. Both back and front are exactly alike. The collar and chemisette effect are of tucked net, trimmed with real Irish crochet insertion. The sleeves are tucked and are completed with Irish insertion and a ruching of net at the wrist to correspond with the Gibson collar. Waist closes invisibly in back. Can be furnished with long sleeves only. **$5.98**

SIZES OF WAISTS—32 TO 44 BUST.

4691—Waist of Brussels Net, in black, white, ecru, navy blue, smoke gray or catawba, over Japanese silk. This dressy waist is plaited over the shoulders and down the back and is ornamented with silk soutache braid in self-color applied in a fanciful design. The jabot is of accordion-plaited net and Messaline. The Gibson collar and the chic close-fitting cuffs are trimmed with soutache braid. The tucked sleeves display four Messaline-covered buttons. Waist closes invisibly in front with hooks and eyes. Can be furnished with long sleeves only. **$5.98**

4692—Waist of superior quality Brussels Net, in black or ecru, over Japanese silk. This waist displays plaits over the shoulders, combined with straps of taffeta trimmed with taffeta-covered buttons. It has two full-length plaits extending down the front on either side of the tucked vest. A medallion of Baby Irish lace and an attractive tie of taffeta silk contribute to the smart appearance. Sleeves are tucked and finished with straps of taffeta and taffeta-covered buttons. The Gibson collar is tucked and edged with taffeta. Waist closes in back invisibly. Can be furnished with long sleeves only. **$5.98**

4693—Waist of excellent quality Brussels Net, in black or ecru, over Japanese silk. The front is plaited as illustrated and is ornamented with straps of Messaline, fancifully applied. A quaint conceit is provided by the use of silk-embroidered rings, laced with Messaline knotted at the ends and finished with silk tassels. The chemisette effect and the Gibson collar are adorned with silk-embroidered dots which are also used on the sleeves in combination with the straps of Messaline and tucks. Sleeves terminate at the wrist with Messaline to correspond with collar. Waist is tucked to yoke depth in the back, where it fastens with hooks and eyes. Can be furnished with long sleeves only. . . . **$6.98**

4694—Waist of all-over Embroidered Bridal Net, in white or ecru, over Japanese silk. Waist is finely tucked down the full length of both the front and back, and closes in front beneath a dainty jabot of Messaline and knife-plaited Val lace, combined with gilt buttons. Messaline tie trimmed with Val lace. The sleeves are tucked and finished at the wrist with Messaline and a knife-plaited frill of French Val, the same completion being employed on the Gibson collar. Can be furnished with long sleeves only. **$6.98**

4695—Princess Waist of very fine quality Bridal Net, in white or ecru, on a net foundation. The yoke and collar of this handsome waist are of imitation Baby Irish lace trimmed with crochet buttons. Model both back and front is lavishly frilled with fine German Val, and panels of tucked net outlined by crochet insertion lend a chic and piquant air. The sleeves are elaborately finished to correspond. Waist closes invisibly in back under a tucked plait. Can be furnished with long sleeves only. **$7.98**

4696—Waist of Filet Net, in ecru, navy blue, brown, smoke gray or catawba, over Japanese silk to match the color of the net. The waist both front and back is handsomely embellished as pictured, with Bonnaz embroidery. Cluny lace insertion in self-color extends down the front and is continued over the shoulders and down the back where the waist buttons invisibly. The chemisette both front and back is of Val lace outlined by rich Persian trimming. Sleeves are tucked as pictured, fancifully trimmed with tiny gilt buttons and frilled with German Val lace to correspond with the Gibson collar. Can be furnished with long sleeves only. **$8.98**

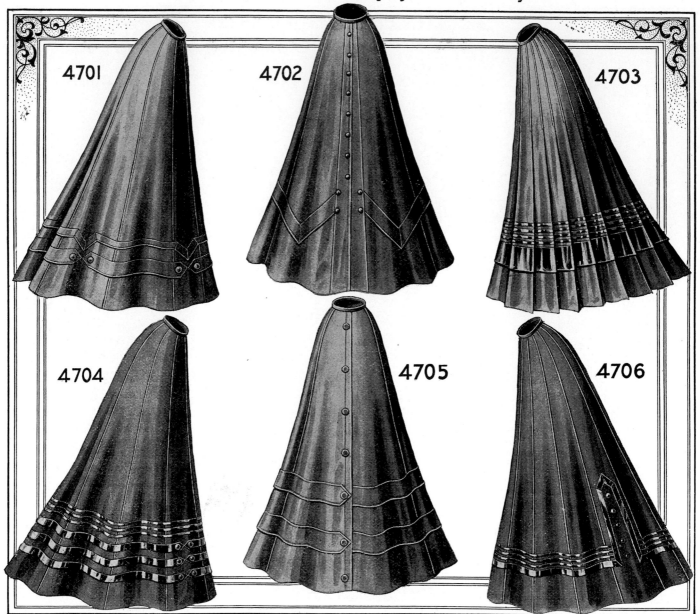

SIZES OF SKIRTS—22 to 30 inches waist measure; 36 to 44 inches front length. Give only waist measure and front length desired. Take measurement from top of skirt band to desired length in front. We cannot supply READY-MADE Skirts in sizes either larger or smaller than those specified. Ladies who desire sizes either larger or smaller are referred to our Made-to-Measure Skirts, pages 9 to 29.

4701—Skirt of good quality light weight Panama Cloth, in black, navy blue or brown. A natty model, strictly man-tailored, which is cut in the popular gored flaring effect. Nine gores are employed in its construction. The trimming consists of two folds of the material with self-covered buttons applied as illustrated. Garment has an inverted plait in back. **$3.98**

4702—Skirt of good quality Panama Cloth, in black, navy blue or brown. This is a beautifully pleasing model, quiet and unassuming in style, yet faultlessly tailored and admirably adapted for general wear. The skirt has seven gores in flaring effect with a plait down the center of the front attractively trimmed with self-covered buttons. A fold of the material in Tunic effect applied as pictured around the bottom. **$3.98**

4703—Skirt of good quality light weight Panama Cloth, in black, navy blue or brown. This is a beautifully tailored, plaited model, in which simplicity and good taste are combined. A fold of taffeta with four parallel straps of the same silk constitutes the effective decorative treatment. The model comprises seven gores, stitched to a little below the hips, with the fulness arranged in fifteen deep side-plaits all around and with a box-plait in front. Unusual value. **$3.98**

4704—Skirt of good quality All-worsted Chiffon Panama Cloth, in black, navy blue or brown. The design of this smart skirt is especially pleasing. It is a nine-gored model hanging in the straight graceful lines demanded by present-day fashions. Ingenuity and good taste are exhibited in the trimming of the skirt, which is particularly effective. It consists of three taffeta folds ending in points in front, paralleled by three narrower straps of taffeta, adorned with taffeta-covered buttons. A deep inverted plait is introduced in back. **$4.98**

4705—Skirt of good quality All-Worsted Panama Cloth, in black, navy blue or brown. This decidedly up-to-date flaring model is an ideal selection for shopping, traveling or general outdoor wear. It is smoothly adjusted over the hips, flaring toward the lower edge in accordance with the latest designs. Two wide folds of the material are applied as pictured, ending in front in a point. A tuck extends down the entire front trimmed with self-covered buttons, but the garment does not button through. An inverted plait in back contributes to the extremely graceful hang of the garment. **$4.98**

4706—Skirt of good quality Mohair, in black or navy blue. A skirt of good style made up in a material noted for its splendid wearing qualities is shown here. It is made with thirteen gores in flaring effect. Straps of satin constitute the trimming device applied around the lower edge as pictured, in parallel rows with a wider strap extending upward on each side of the skirt. . Small satin-covered buttons provide an effective finish. An inverted plait is introduced in back. **$4.98**

The materials used in our READY-MADE Cloth Skirts will be found exactly as described. If you prefer to see a sample we will send it, but delay can be avoided by ordering direct from this Style Book.

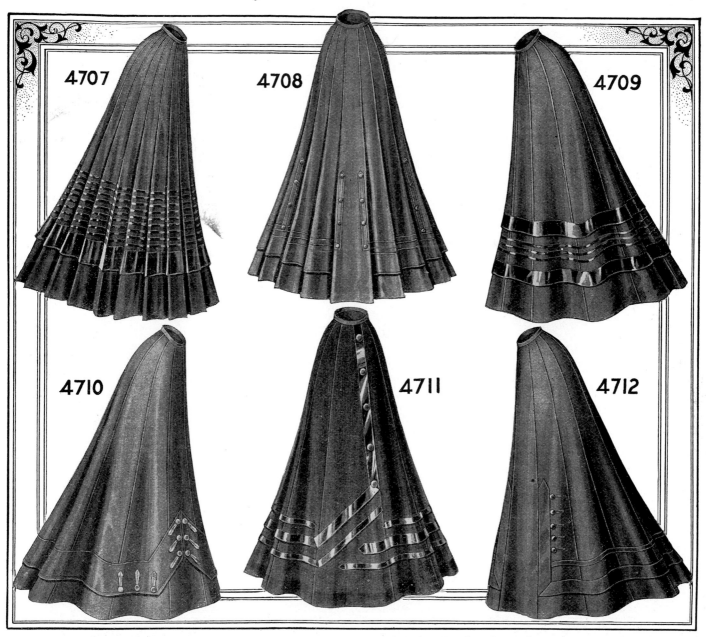

SIZES OF SKIRTS—22 to 30 inches waist measure; 36 to 44 inches front length. Give only waist measure and front length desired. Take measurement from top of skirt-band to desired length in front. We cannot supply READY-MADE Skirts in sizes either larger or smaller than those specified. Ladies who desire sizes either larger or smaller are referred to our Made-to-Measure Skirts, pages 9 to 29.

4707—Skirt of good quality **All-Worsted Panama Cloth,** in black, navy blue or brown. This extremely handsome tailored model is especially adapted for smart outdoor wear. The garment is made with fourteen side-plaits with two box-plaits in front, and consists of seven gores. The trimming device comprises a wide bias fold of taffeta paralleled by nine narrow taffeta straps. Extremely smart. **$4.98**

4708—Skirt of good quality **Chiffon Panama Cloth,** in black, navy blue or brown. A beautiful tailored skirt, which on account of its light weight adapts itself readily to the requirements of summer. The model is constructed with nine gores disposed in fifteen deep side-plaits all around. It is tastefully trimmed on the box-plait in front and also at each side with perpendicular straps of the material and self-covered buttons. A fold and a narrow strap of the material extend around the lower edge, ending in points in back, where there is a deep inverted plait. **$4.98**

4709—Skirt of good quality **All-Wool Chiffon Panama Cloth,** in black, navy blue or brown. This particularly charming example of the new gored flaring models is handsomely trimmed with two wide folds of satin, separated by three narrow, paralleled satin straps, providing a very rich and effective finish. The garment is made with eleven gores, and is beautifully tailored in every detail. **$5.98**

4710—Skirt of good quality **All-Worsted Chiffon Panama Cloth,** in black, navy blue or brown. Nine gores are employed in the construction of this serviceable tailored skirt, which fits smoothly over the hips, and is cut in flaring effect in accordance with the newest ideas. The wide fold of the material, fancifully applied as pictured, ends in points in the back, where a deep inverted plait is admitted. Self-covered buttons combined with satin tabs provide an appropriate decorative finish. . . **$5.98**

4711—Skirt of **All-Worsted Voile,** in black only. Like many of the season's smartest models, this artistically designed skirt is elaborately trimmed with satin. Three folds of satin extend around the lower edge as pictured, ending in points in front, where a satin strap, trimmed with satin-covered buttons, contributes a pleasing finish. The skirt is made with eleven gores in flaring effect.
Without Drop Skirt. **$5.98**
With black Taffeta Silk Drop Skirt attached. . . . **$9.48**

4712—Skirt of excellent quality **Mohair,** in black or navy blue. This attractive skirt is constructed with thirteen gores which fit with perfect smoothness at the top and acquire a gradual flare toward the bottom. A fold and strap of the material appear around the lower edge of the model, the fold being continued in a perpendicular line on each side of the front gore, where soutache loops and satin-covered buttons provide an appropriate decorative completion. Inverted plait in back. **$5.98**

The materials used in our READY-MADE Cloth Skirts will be found exactly as described. If you prefer to see a sample we will send it, but delay can be avoided by ordering direct from this Style Book.

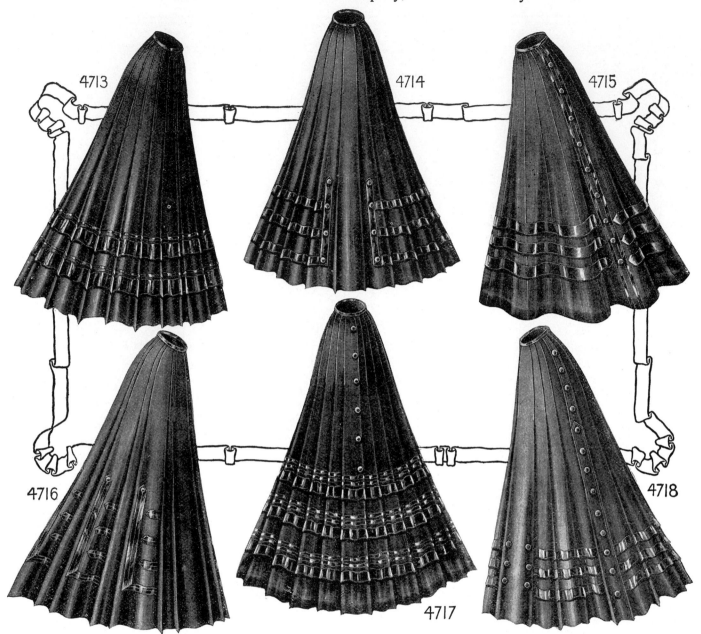

SIZES OF SKIRTS—22 to 30 inches waist measure; 36 to 44 inches front length.   Give only waist measure and front length desired.   Take measurement from top of skirt-band to desired length in front.   We cannot supply READY-MADE Skirts in sizes either larger or smaller than those specified.   Ladies who desire sizes either larger or smaller are referred to our Made-to-Measure Skirts, pages 9 to 29.

4713—Skirt of good quality Chiffon Panama Cloth, in black, navy blue or brown. A stylish skirt made with sixteen deep side-plaits with two box-plaits in front. The trimming is particularly rich and appropriate, consisting of two folds of taffeta, each of which is paralleled by a narrow taffeta strap. **$5.98**

4714—Skirt of excellent quality All-Worsted Panama Cloth, in black, navy blue or brown. This skirt is made with nine gores arranged in seventeen side-plaits with a box-plait in front. Three folds of rich taffeta silk are applied as pictured around the bottom, ending in perpendicular straps in the front, trimmed with taffeta-covered buttons. **$5.98**

4715—Skirt of good quality Voile, in black only. Thirteen gores are employed in the construction of this extremely dressy skirt, which is cut in flaring outline. The three straps which extend around the skirt are of rich black satin ending in points on the left side of the front, where parallel straps of satin extend down the entire length of the garment. Trimmed, as illustrated, with satin covered buttons. **Without Drop Skirt.** **$6.98**
With black Taffeta Silk Drop Skirt attached. . . . **$10.48**

4716—Skirt of good quality Chiffon Panama Cloth, in black, navy blue or brown. A double box-plait in panel effect distinguishes the front of this modish skirt, and groups of side-plaits

all around contribute appreciably to the graceful hang of the garment. The trimming consists of stitched straps of satin picturesquely arranged as illustrated, this device extending entirely around the skirt. A satin-covered button on each point lends a stylish finish. **$6.98**

4717—Skirt of good quality All-Worsted Voile, in black only. This beautiful model is made with eleven gores disposed in nineteen graceful side-plaits. Three folds of satin are applied as pictured, each one paralleled by two narrow satin straps. Six satin-covered buttons appear down the front providing a handsome finish.
Without Drop Skirt. **$6.98**
With black Taffeta Silk Drop Skirt attached. **$10.48**

4718—Skirt of excellent quality All-Worsted Chiffon Panama, in black, navy blue or brown. The popularity of the plaited skirt has not waned, nor does the up-to-date woman fail to appreciate its permanent good points. This beautiful example of the graceful style is made with eleven gores which are arranged in sixteen deep side-plaits. Three folds of taffeta are applied around the bottom as illustrated, the front being trimmed with self-covered buttons. A stitched box-plait, simulating a tailored strap, appears down the left side, ornamented the entire length with self-covered buttons contributing an effect as smart as it is novel. . **$6.98**

The materials used in our READY-MADE Cloth Skirts will be found exactly as described. If you prefer to see a sample we will send it, but delay can be avoided by ordering direct from this Style Book.

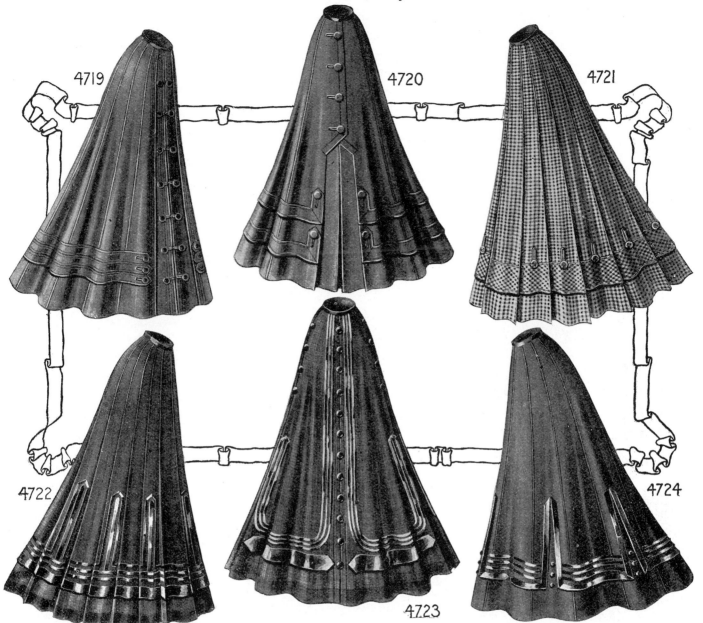

SIZES OF SKIRTS—22 to 30 inches waist measure; 36 to 44 inches front length. Give only waist measure and front length desired. Take measurement from top of skirt-band to desired length in front. We cannot supply READY-MADE Skirts in sizes either larger or smaller than those specified. Ladies who desire sizes either larger or smaller are referred to our Made-to-Measure Skirts, pages 9 to 29.

4719—Skirt of good quality All-Wool Chiffon Panama Cloth, in black, navy blue or brown. A skirt of extremely good style, made with thirteen gores falling gracefully in such a way as to emphasize the slender lines. Three tailored straps of the material are applied around the bottom ending in front in points, trimmed with soutache loops and satin-covered buttons. An inverted plait is introduced in front as pictured, which is also trimmed with similar buttons and loops, and is paralleled by two full-length side plaits. A deep inverted plait in back. **$6.98**

4720—Skirt of excellent quality Chiffon Panama Cloth, in black, navy blue or brown. The skirt is in flare effect, made with eight gores and tailored to fit smoothly over the hips. A chic and Frenchy idea is adopted for the treatment of the front which admits a tuck trimmed with self-covered buttons and soutache loops, and a plaited panel inserted below the knee. The two folds of the material, which end in points in front, are also trimmed with buttons and soutache loops, and terminate in back beneath an inverted plait. **$6.98**

4721—Skirt of excellent quality All-Worsted Panama Cloth, in an attractive black and white Shepherd check; also in black or navy blue. This is a pleasing and graceful nine-gored model. The fulness is stitched down to below the hips, from there falling in deep side-plaits. The wide fold of the material, which is applied at the lower edge, is tastefully embellished all around with self-covered buttons and silk soutache loops. **$6.98**

4722—Skirt of good quality All-Worsted Voile, in black only. This unusually handsome skirt is made with nine gores arranged in eighteen deep side-plaits. The trimming consists of a fold and three narrow parallel straps of satin around the lower edge. The straps of satin extend upward in points on each alternate plait, forming a particularly effective and artistic decoration.
Without Drop Skirt. **$7.98**
With black Taffeta Silk Drop Skirt attached. . . **$11.48**

4723—Skirt of excellent quality All-Worsted Voile, in black only. Tailored straps of satin in parallel lines are applied down the front of this eight-gored skirt, continuing around the bottom in curved outline, and extending upward on each side in a fanciful design as pictured. The inverted plait which appears in front is trimmed with satin buttons, and there is an inverted plait on each side. The fold around the bottom, which ends in points both front and back, is of satin. **Without Drop Skirt.** . . . **$7.98**
With black Taffeta Silk Drop Skirt attached. . . **$11.48**

4724—Skirt of fine quality All-Wool Chiffon Panama Cloth, in black only. This serviceable Panama skirt has thirteen gores in flare effect, and is handsomely trimmed in a unique design with straps of satin which extend in points perpendicularly on each alternate gore. Satin buttons further ornament the model. Three narrow parallel straps of satin are also applied around the bottom of the skirt. **$7.98**

The materials used in our READY-MADE Cloth Skirts will be found exactly as described. If you prefer to see a sample we will send it, but delay can be avoided by ordering direct from this Style Book.

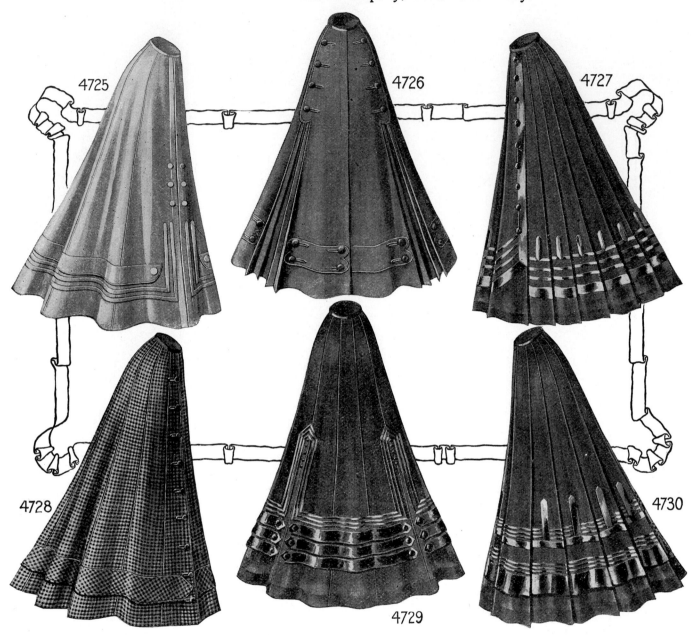

SIZES OF SKIRTS—22 to 30 inches waist measure; 36 to 44 inches front length.   Give only waist measure and front length desired.
Take measurement from top of skirt-band to desired length in front.   We cannot supply READY-MADE Skirts in sizes either larger or
smaller than those specified.   Ladies who desire sizes either larger or smaller are referred to our Made-to-Measure Skirts, pages 9 to 29.

4725—Skirt of good quality All-Wool Serge, in cream-white only.   A stunning white serge skirt constructed on straight, mannish lines appropriate for a garment of this sort, made with eight gores in flaring outline.   An inverted plait extends down the center of the front trimmed with self-covered buttons as illustrated.   A fold of the material paralleled by two narrow straps is applied around the bottom, the straps extending upward on the skirt in front. $7.98

4726—Skirt of excellent quality All-Worsted Chiffon Panama Cloth, in black, navy blue or brown.   This carefully designed model is the acme of good style.   A plait extends down the center of the front, and a double inverted plait is introduced at each side, on which soutache loops and self-covered buttons form an artistic completion.   The deep fold at the lower edge is trimmed with self-covered buttons and soutache loops and terminates at the sides, the back being plain. $7.98

4727—Skirt of excellent quality All-Worsted Voile, in black only.   The fulness is arranged in nineteen side-plaits all around.   The model comprises eleven gores.   Straps of fine quality satin are utilized with artistic effect on the front and all around the lower edge.   Four straps are applied as pictured, extending upward in points on each plait.   Small satin-covered buttons trim the front.
Without Drop Skirt. $7.98
With black Taffeta Silk Drop Skirt attached. . . $11.48

4728—Skirt of excellent quality All-Wool Panama Cloth, in a stylish black and white Shepherd check; also in black or navy blue.   This fetching example of the popular gored flaring skirt is constructed with eleven gores which fit smoothly over the hips, falling in a graceful ripple below.   The front is ornamented with satin loops and satin-covered buttons.   A wide fold which is applied around the bottom is piped with black satin.   An inverted plait and two side-plaits in back. $7.98

4729—Skirt of excellent quality All-Worsted Voile, in black only.   The model pictured here is made with nine gores in flaring outline.   Three straps of taffeta are applied around the bottom, ending at each side in points finished with satin-covered buttons.   The narrow straps of taffeta which further ornament the model appear all around and extend upward in points on each side to a little above the knee.   Small buttons covered with satin supply a touch of distinction.   **Without Drop Skirt.** . . . $7.98
With black Taffeta Silk Drop Skirt attached. . . $11.48

4730—Skirt of excellent quality All-Worsted Voile, in black only.   The charming model shown here is made with nine gores arranged in sixteen deep side-plaits.   The satin trimming is applied around the bottom in the form of a wide and a narrow strap, each paralleled by three narrower satin straps.   Points of satin extend upward on each plait all around.   **Without Drop Skirt.** $8.98
With black Taffeta Silk Drop Skirt attached. . . $12.98

**The materials used in our READY-MADE Cloth Skirts will be found exactly as described.   If you prefer to see a
sample we will send it, but delay can be avoided by ordering direct from this Style Book.**

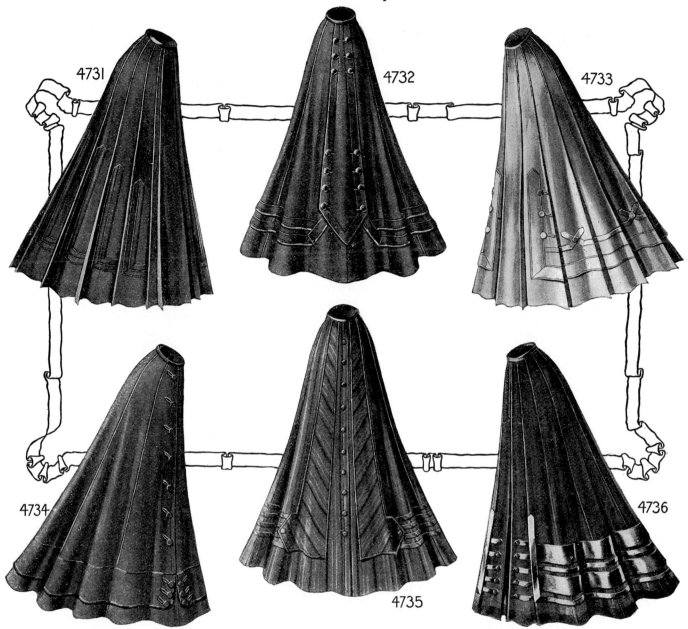

SIZES OF SKIRTS—22 to 30 inches waist measure; 36 to 44 inches front length. Give only waist measure and front length desired. Take measurement from top of skirt-band to desired length in front. We cannot supply READY-MADE Skirts in sizes either larger or smaller than those specified. Ladies who desire sizes either larger or smaller are referred to our Made-to-Measure Skirts, pages 9 to 29.

4731—Skirt of fine quality All-Worsted Chiffon Panama Cloth, in black, navy blue or brown. Simplicity is the key-note of this beautiful man-tailored skirt, which is made with fifteen gores stitched to a short distance below the hips, and from there falling in deep side-plaits all around. Straps of the material ending in points are applied on each plait, as pictured, providing a tailored finish decidedly novel and smart. **$8.98**

4732—Skirt of fine quality All-Worsted Chiffon Panama Cloth, in black only. This skirt is a gored flaring model, beautifully finished. Eleven gores are employed in its construction, smoothly adjusted over the hips with the fulness gracefully flaring at the lower edge. The panel effect in front adds appreciably to the smart appearance, broadening as it does at the lower edge to give a pretty flare. Satin-covered buttons provide an attractive finish. Two stitched folds of the material are applied as pictured, piped with satin ending in back in points and buttons on each side of a deep inverted plait. **$8.98**

4733—Skirt of fine quality All-Wool Serge, in cream-white only. A skirt of this kind is indispensable for Summer wear. Model is made with fifteen gores stitched to a little below the hips and from there falling in side-plaits. A fold of the material is applied around the bottom, above which stitched straps are arranged in a fanciful design, trimmed with self-covered buttons. The folds extend upward on the skirt at each side of the box-plait in front. Buttons and soutache loops provide a stylish completion. . . . **$8.98**

4734—Skirt of fine quality All-Wool Chiffon Panama Cloth, in black or navy blue. A gored flaring model, comprising eight gores. A loose lapped seam extends down the front, which is varied with self-covered buttons and loops of satin. The garment does not button through. A deep fold of the material piped with satin and trimmed with buttons and satin loops is applied around the bottom. **$8.98**

4735—Skirt of fine quality All-Wool Chiffon Panama Cloth, in a fancy gray mixture only. A beautiful, light weight, soft material in a particularly attractive pattern. The model comprises eleven gores in flaring outline with a plait down the center of the front, trimmed with self-covered buttons. Skirt does not button through, however. Two bias stitched folds are also applied down the front, trimmed with a button. Four tailored straps of the material around the bottom; inverted plait in back. **$8.98**

4736—Skirt of excellent quality All-Worsted Voile, in black only. This model is made with eleven gores flaring at the sides, and has an inverted plait both front and back. Two side-plaits are also introduced in front. The garment is richly trimmed around the lower edge with two wide folds and two narrower folds of heavy satin arranged in parallel rows ending as pictured in front with ten small tabs of satin trimmed with satin-covered buttons.
Without Drop Skirt. **$8.98**
With black Taffeta Silk Drop Skirt attached. . . . **$12.98**

The materials used in our READY-MADE Cloth Skirts will be found exactly as described. If you prefer to see a sample we will send it, but delay can be avoided by ordering direct from this Style Book.

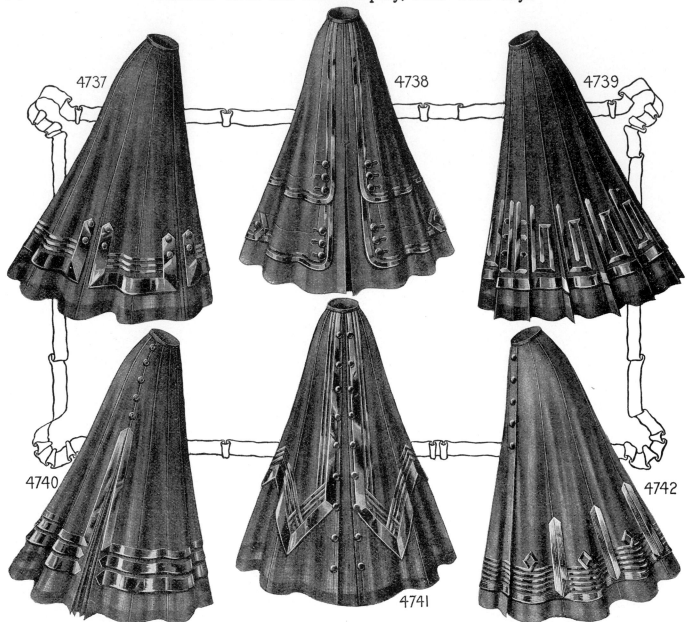

SIZES OF SKIRTS—22 to 30 inches waist measure; 36 to 44 inches front length. Give only waist measure and front length desired. Take measurement from top of skirt-band to desired length in front. We cannot supply READY-MADE Skirts in sizes either larger or smaller than those specified. Our Special Circular illustrating and describing RIDING SKIRTS will be sent free on request.

4737—Skirt of extra fine quality All-Worsted Voile, in black only. Ten gores are employed in this handsome skirt, which is cut in flare effect. Satin is applied in a wide fold extending upward in a point all around the skirt as pictured. Three bands of satin further elaborate the model around the lower edge, and satin buttons are used as a finish. **Without Drop Skirt. . . . $9.98** **With black Taffeta Silk Drop Skirt attached. . . . $13.98**

4738—Skirt of fine quality All-Worsted Chiffon Panama Cloth, in navy blue and black. A tendency toward the Directoire styles is distinctly observable in this particularly striking and handsome model. The garment is a gored flaring model, cut in Tunic effect with two deep flounces as pictured, which are edged with parallel satin straps, and uniquely trimmed with satin-covered buttons and tabs of satin simulating button-holes. Inverted plait down the center of front, and an extra deep inverted plait in back. **$9.98**

4739—Skirt of fine quality All-Worsted Voile, in black only. The straps of satin are applied in Greek border effect all around this handsome dress skirt, and a fold of satin adds to the charming appearance. Thirteen gores are comprised in its construction, stitched to below the hips, with the fulness disposed in side-plaits all around. **Without Drop Skirt. . . . . $9.98** **With black Taffeta Silk Drop Skirt attached. . . $13.98**

4740—Skirt of high grade Imported All-Worsted Voile, in black only. One of the most distinctive models we have shown this season. The skirt is cut with thirteen gores in flaring outline

and is handsomely trimmed with three graduated bands of satin around the bottom as pictured. A double inverted plait in improved sheath effect is introduced at each side of the garment outlined with straps of satin. Satin buttons are applied above this, affording a smart and picturesque finish. **Without Drop Skirt. . . . . $9.98** **With black Taffeta Silk Drop Skirt attached. . . . $13.98**

4741—Skirt of high grade Imported All-Worsted Voile, in black only. An exceptionally dressy and finely tailored garment, smartly cut and beautifully finished. Nine gores are comprised in the skirt, smoothly adjusted over the hips and rippling gracefully below. The front displays two plaits in panel effect ornamented with satin-covered buttons and bordered by bands of satin. These satin bands are fancifully applied around the skirt in Tunic effect as pictured, paralleled by three narrow satin straps. Satin buttons provide a smart finish. **Without Drop Skirt. . . . $9.98** **With black Taffeta Silk Drop Skirt attached. . . $13.98**

4742—Skirt of very fine quality All-Worsted Chiffon Panama Cloth, in black only. There is a certain quiet elegance about this model which the woman of refinement will immediately appreciate. It is made with seven gores and has a deep plait down the front trimmed with satin-covered buttons. Straps of satin finished with tailor stitching furnish the artistic decorative treatment. Straps are applied in parallel rows and also appear on the side gores, as pictured, producing an effect that is attractive and rich. . . **$9.98**

The materials used in our READY-MADE Cloth Skirts will be found exactly as described. If you prefer to see a sample we will send it, but delay can be avoided by ordering direct from this Style Book.

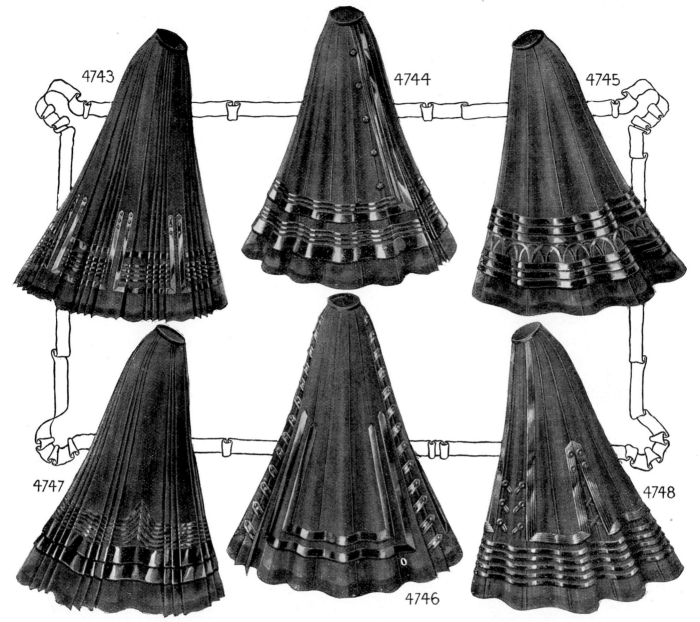

SIZES OF SKIRTS—22 to 30 inches waist measure; 36 to 44 inches front length. Give only waist measure and front length desired. Take measurement from top of skirt-band to desired length in front. We cannot supply READY-MADE Skirts in sizes either larger or smaller than those specified. Our Special Circular illustrating and describing RIDING SKIRTS will be sent free on request.

4743—Skirt of very fine Imported All-Worsted Voile, in black only. The model has thirteen gores stitched to below the hips and falling in groups of side-plaits all around with two box-plaits in back. The bottom is lavishly trimmed with straps of satin arranged in parallel rows, satin being also applied in points on each alternate gore, finished with small buttons, which are covered with satin to match. **Without Drop Skirt.** **$10.98**
With black Taffeta Silk Drop Skirt attached. . . **$14.98**

4744—Skirt of extra fine quality Imported All-Worsted Voile, in black only. The straps of satin which trim this beautiful model are applied down the left side of the front only, and five handsome ornamental buttons of satin add greatly to the rich appearance. Two folds of satin paralleled by narrow satin straps are used to trim the lower part of the skirt, and on the left side a fan-plait is introduced in sheath effect. The skirt is one of the new flaring models, and eleven gores are utilized in its construction.
Without Drop Skirt. **$10.98**
With black Taffeta Silk Drop Skirt attached. . . **$14.98**

4745—Skirt of finest quality Imported All-Worsted Voile, in black only. The skirt is made with eleven gores, snug-fitting over the hips, with long, graceful lines. Folds of black satin extend around the lower part of the model, arranged in two groups of three each, separated by narrow straps of satin uniquely applied.
Without Drop Skirt. **$12.98**
With black Taffeta Silk Drop Skirt attached. . . **$16.98**

4746—Skirt of finest quality Imported All-Worsted Voile, in black only. This elaborate skirt is constructed with fifteen gores in flaring outline, and is trimmed down both sides of the front with graduated tabs of satin and satin-covered buttons. The satin has been utilized with piquant effect around the lower edge as pictured, and is continued upward in points on the skirt to above the knee.
Without Drop Skirt. **$12.98**
With black Taffeta Silk Drop Skirt attached. . . **$16.98**

4747—Skirt of very finest Imported All-Worsted Voile, in black only. This skirt is cut with eleven gores with the fulness stitched to below the hips, and from there falling in groups of side-plaits all around, with two box-plaits in back. The model is trimmed with two wide bands of taffeta, above which six narrow taffeta straps are applied in a particularly attractive effect.
Without Drop Skirt. **$14.98**
With black Taffeta Silk Drop Skirt attached. . . **$18.98**

4748—Skirt of finest quality Imported All-Worsted Voile, in black only. The model is in gored-flaring effect, cut with thirteen gores finished with smart little touches in the way of trimming, and placing it indisputably among our most distinctive styles. Plaits extend down the front in panel effect outlined by tailored straps of satin, which are also applied at the sides perpendicularly on each alternate gore. Fancy buttons and silk braid further embellish the model, which is finished around the bottom with five parallel satin straps. **Without Drop Skirt.** **$14.98**
With black Taffeta Silk Drop Skirt attached. . . **$18.98**

The materials used in our READY-MADE Cloth Skirts will be found exactly as described. If you prefer to see a sample we will send it, but delay can be avoided by ordering direct from this Style Book.

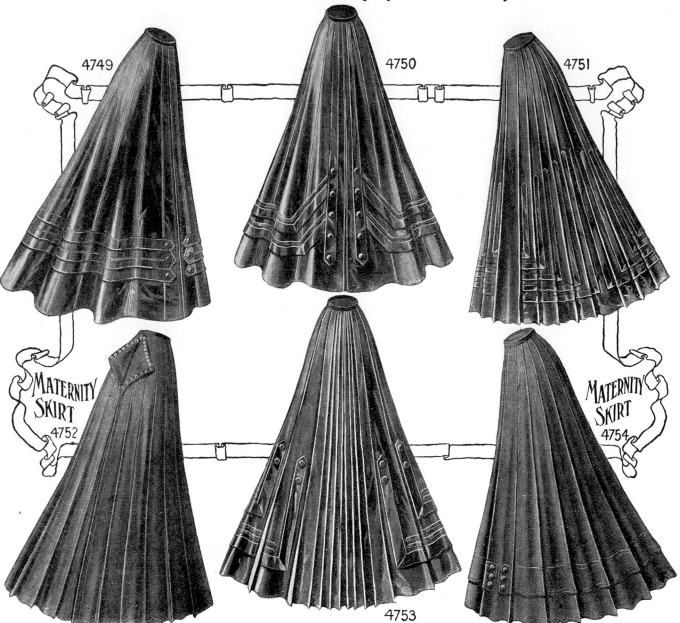

4749   4750   4751

MATERNITY SKIRT 4752

MATERNITY SKIRT 4754

4753

SIZES OF SKIRTS—22 to 30 inches waist measure; 36 to 44 inches front length. Give only waist measure and front length desired. Take measurement from top of skirt band to desired length in front. On Maternity Skirts give front length desired; no waist measure is required. We cannot supply READY-MADE Skirts in sizes either larger or smaller than those specified.

4749—Skirt of good quality Taffeta Silk, in black only. A particularly stylish model, cut in the fashionable eleven-gored effect and displaying an inverted plait down the center of the front. There is also an extra deep inverted plait in back. The trimming consists of four bands of taffeta, applied around the lower edge, ending in front in points trimmed with taffeta-covered buttons. Exceptional value. **$8.98**

4750—Skirt of fine quality Taffeta Silk, in black only. Two bands of taffeta fancifully applied around the lower edge, each one paralleled by a narrow taffeta strap, provide a chic, decorative treatment. A strap also appears on each side of the inverted plait in front. Taffeta-covered buttons are employed to trim the lower part as shown in the picture. Deep inverted plait in back. The skirt is a flare model and is made with twelve gores. **$9.98**

4751—Skirt of fine Taffeta Silk, in a very rich quality. Black only. This particularly pleasing example of the popular plaited styles has the fulness arranged in twenty-four side plaits all around, which are stitched down to below the hips and flare becomingly at the lower edge. Taffeta bands applied in a unique Greek design distinguish the model, the bands extending upward on each plait as illustrated. The design is the same both front and back. **$11.98**

4752—Maternity Skirt of good quality light weight All-Worsted Panama Cloth, in black only. This scientifically designed garment is in side-plaited outline made with a belt like an ordinary skirt, thus dispensing with the customary drawstring or elastic band. The fulness in the back is gracefully arranged in deep inverted plaits. By the aid of hooks and eyelets the waist measure may be increased as required. The ingenious construction of the model causes the fulness to drape evenly both front and back without bulkiness or discomfort. The model is equally appropriate as a maternity skirt or for ordinary wear. Finished with a three-inch basted hem. (See also 4754.). **$5.98**

4753—Skirt of finest quality rich Taffeta Silk, in black only. A deep fan-plait is introduced in front outlined by two narrow box-plaits, the same idea being carried out in back. The fulness at the side is disposed in side-plaits. Bands of heavy satin extending upward in front, finished with satin-covered buttons, trim the model, each band paralleled by two narrow satin straps. **$12.98**

4754—Maternity Skirt of fine quality All-Worsted Chiffon Panama Cloth, in black only. A splendidly made skirt with the fulness falling in side-plaits. Garment is trimmed around the bottom with a wide fold of the material and self-covered buttons. The construction of this model is exactly the same as that of 4752. (Read description 4752.). **$7.98**

The materials used in our READY-MADE Cloth Skirts will be found exactly as described. If you prefer to see a sample we will send it. We cannot furnish samples of the materials used in our Silk Skirts.

MISSES' SKIRTS

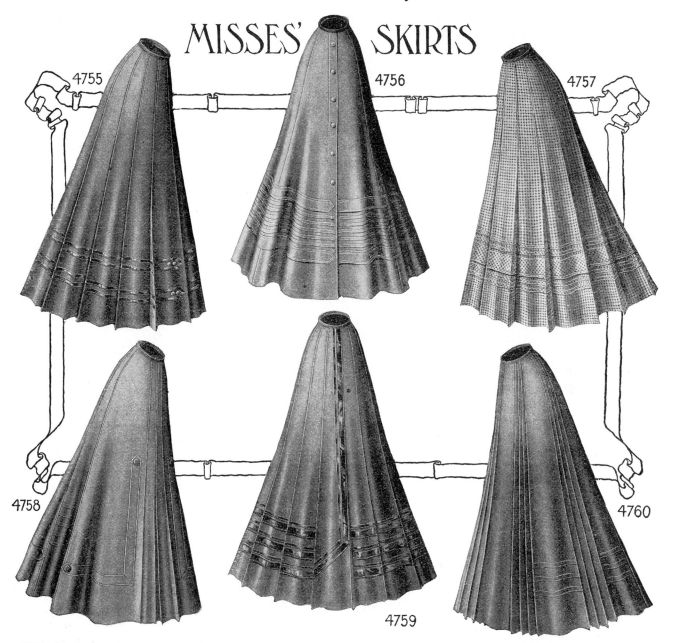

SIZES OF MISSES' SKIRTS—22 to 27 inches waist measure; 32 to 37 inches front length. These Skirts are suitable for misses and small women. The hips are cut in proportion for misses' sizes and vary from 37 to 42 inches according to the size of the waist. Give only waist measure and front length desired. Take measurement from top of skirt-band to desired length in front. We cannot supply READY-MADE Skirts in sizes either larger or smaller than those specified.

4755—Misses' Skirt of good quality All-Worsted Panama Cloth, in black, navy blue or brown. An extremely jaunty skirt made with fifteen gores with the fulness arranged in side-plaits. Four stitched straps of satin appear around the bottom in parallel rows ending in a point on the box-plait in front, where satin-covered buttons are used as a finish. **$3.98**

4756—Misses' Skirt of excellent quality All-Worsted Panama Cloth, in black, navy blue or brown. The five narrow tailored straps of the material which trim the bottom of this natty gored-flaring skirt are outlined by two wider bands which end in points in front. A deep plait extends down the front trimmed with self-covered buttons. **$4.98**

4757—Skirt of excellent quality All-Worsted Panama Cloth, in an attractive black and white Shepherd check; also in plain black, navy blue or brown. A trim plaited model made with thirteen gores stitched to hip depth and falling in side-plaits all around. Four bias straps of the material are applied at the lower edge separated by a wide bias fold. **$4.98**

4758—Skirt of extra fine quality All-Worsted Chiffon Panama Cloth, in black, navy blue or brown. This particularly neat man-tailored skirt is made with nine gores finished at the sides with lapped seams. It has a double inverted plait introduced both front and back outlined by straps of the material which are continued at intervals around the bottom. Narrow tailored straps at the sides impart a chic finish and satin-covered buttons are used as a trimming. **$5.98**

4759—Misses' Skirt of very fine quality All-Worsted Panama Cloth, in black, navy blue or brown. Straps of taffeta have been employed with pleasing effect to trim this stylish and fetching skirt. The straps are applied in parallel rows down the front and around the lower edge as illustrated, making the garment extremely dressy. It is a thirteen-gored model with the fulness becomingly disposed in side-plaits. **$5.98**

4760—Misses' Skirt of finest quality All-Worsted Chiffon Panama Cloth, in black, navy blue or brown. This smart model is made of beautiful material and is flawless as to style and finish. It consists of thirteen gores, with the fulness arranged in groups of deep side-plaits on each alternate gore. **$6.98**

The materials used in our READY-MADE Misses' Skirts will be found exactly as described. If you prefer to see a sample we will send it, but delay can be avoided by ordering direct from this Style Book.

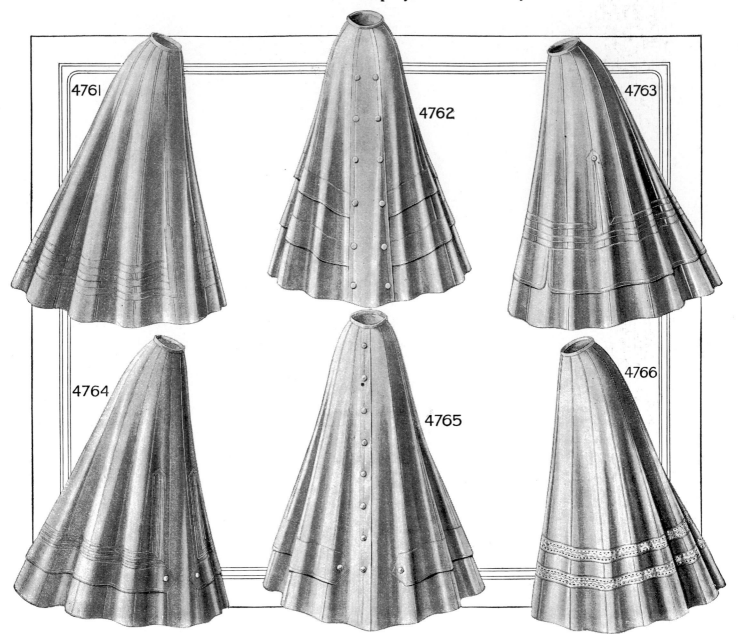

SIZES OF WASH SKIRTS—22 to 30 inches waist measure; 36 to 44 inches front length.   Give only waist measure and front length desired.   Take measurement from top of skirt-band to desired length in front.   We cannot supply these READY-MADE Skirts in sizes either larger or smaller than those specified.   We do not make Wash Skirts to measure.

4761—**Skirt of good quality light weight Linene,** in white or natural linen color. This stylish, serviceable skirt is made in eleven-gored flaring effect, and is neatly trimmed with three tailored straps of the material, arranged in parallel rows around the skirt, ending on the front gore in points as pictured. . . **$1.49**

4762—**Skirt of fine quality light weight Linene,** in white only. An extremely stylish model particularly appropriate for wear during the warm weather. It is cut with seven gores. The front displays a full-length panel attractively trimmed with self-covered buttons, and two wide folds of the material applied in Tunic outline afford a smart completion. **$1.98**

4763—**Skirt of excellent quality light weight Linene,** in white or natural linen color. The natty, tailored skirt shown here answers admirably, all the requirements of summer. It is made with eleven gores in flaring effect and is of generous width. The deep fold of the material, which graces the lower part of the garment, is paralleled · by narrow tailored straps ending in points on the side gores as illustrated. Pearl buttons provide additional ornamentation. **$1.98**

4764—**Skirt of good quality genuine Linen,** in white or natural linen color. This extremely neat and stylish skirt will withstand repeated laundering and will wear splendidly. It is constructed with seventeen tapering gores flaring gracefully at the lower edge. A fold of the material headed by three narrow straps ornament the bottom of the garment, the straps also being displayed perpendicularly on the two front gores. **$2.98**

4765—**Skirt of fine quality Imported Rep,** in white only. This is one of the stylish gored flaring models so popular this season and comprises twelve gores. A deep plait extends down the front trimmed with handsome pearl buttons. The fold of the material which is applied around the bottom, ends in points in front, and is also trimmed with pearl buttons. Exceptional value. . **$2.98**

4766—**Skirt of fine quality Imported English Rep,** in white only. This handsome skirt consists of eleven gores arranged in flaring outline. Two rows of handsome Swiss embroidery insertion in eyelet effect elaborate the lower part of the garment, contributing greatly to its dressy appearance. A very desirable skirt, faultlessly made and finished, which we offer at a remarkably low price. **$3.98**

**The Skirts shown on this page are READY-MADE and can be furnished only as illustrated and described.
We cannot make any alterations in these garments, nor can we send samples of the materials.**

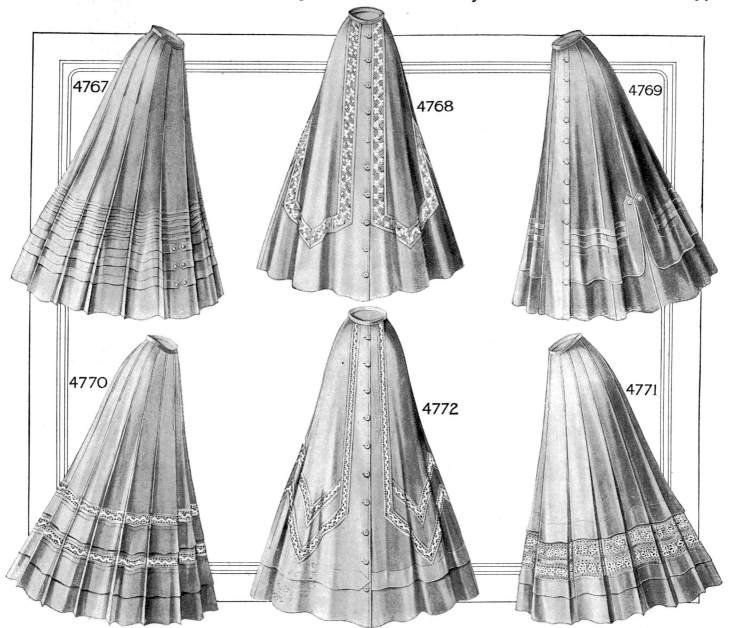

SIZES OF WASH SKIRTS—22 to 30 inches waist measure; 36 to 44 inches front length. Give only waist measure and front length desired. Take measurement from top of skirt-band to desired length in front. We cannot supply these READY-MADE Skirts in sizes either larger or smaller than those specified. We do not make Wash Skirts to measure.

4767—Skirt of excellent quality Pure Linen, in white or natural linen color. This natty model comprises fifteen gores which are stitched to a trifle below the hips, from there being arranged in side-plaits all around. Three bands of the material extend around the lower edge ending in points in front, each point being finished with a pearl button. Five narrow tailored straps appear above the bands, providing a smart finish. Good taste and originality are conspicuous in this model, which is one of the most successful productions of our designers. **$3.98**

4768—Skirt of fine quality Imported Rep, in white only. Few skirts have met with greater favor recently than the charming designs which are made to button in front. This stylish example of the prevailing mode is handsomely trimmed with pearl buttons and wide insertions of heavy Torchon lace, which appears down each side of the button closing and extends upward in points on the sides as pictured. Insertion is also applied in back, where a deep inverted plait is introduced. **$4.98**

4769—Skirt of Pure Irish Linen, in white or natural linen color. This decidedly up-to-date model is cut in flaring outline with ten gores. It buttons visibly down the entire front; handsome pearl buttons being used with admirable effect. The fold of the material, uniquely applied as pictured, is also trimmed with buttons and is paralleled by two narrow stitched straps all around. There is a deep inverted plait in back. **$4.98**

4770—Skirt of extra fine quality Linenette, in white only. An extremely smart and dressy skirt. The material is extra light in weight and wears splendidly. The skirt consists of fifteen gores with the fulness arranged in side-plaits. Two wide folds of the material appear on the lower part, each fold headed by an attractive insertion of Swiss eyelet embroidery. . . . **$4.98**

4771—Skirt of extra fine quality genuine Linen, in white only. Plaited skirts are generally becoming and therefore well liked. This effective example is made with fifteen gores stitched to below the hips, and from there falling in side-plaits. There are two folds of the material around the lower part of the model, which are separated by insertions of English eyelet embroidery. A particularly attractive skirt, the perfect lines and splendid material of which will recommend it to the discriminating. **$5.98**

4772—Skirt of genuine Irish Linen, in a very fine quality. White only. Women are quick to appreciate clothes of character, and the smart model shown here possesses individuality and unusual grace. The skirt is made with four gores with the fulness gracefully adjusted in flare effect. It closes visibly down the front with handsome pearl buttons, and there is a deep inverted plait introduced in back. The trimming consists of rows of Swiss embroidery insertion fancifully applied as illustrated. The fold of the material around the bottom ends in a point in front. **$6.98**

The Skirts shown on this page are READY-MADE and can be furnished only as illustrated and described. We cannot make any alterations in these garments, nor can we send samples of the materials.

SIZES OF PETTICOATS—37 TO 43 INCHES FRONT LENGTH. FOR PARTICULARS REGARDING EXTRA SIZES SEE PAGE 121.

4801—Petticoat of **Gingham**, in blue with white stripe only. Flounce with two gathered ruffles. . . . . . **59 cents**

4802—Petticoat of **Corded Gingham**, in steel gray with white stripe or blue with white stripe. Bias flounce trimmed with three full ruffles. . . . . **98 cents**

4803—Petticoat of **Gingham**, in linen color with white stripe only. Full bias flounce neatly tucked and corded. The gathered ruffle is also trimmed with cording. Dust ruffle beneath. . . . . **98 cents**

4804—Petticoat of **light weight Moreen**, in black only. Flounce has three bouffante ruffles headed by a cluster of pin-tucks. . . . . **98 cents**

4805—Petticoat of **featherweight Rustling Percaline**, with a lustrous finish. Black only. The gathered flounce has two clusters of shirring and is finished with a ruffle of eyelet embroidery. Percaline dust ruffle beneath. . . . **98 cents**

4806—Petticoat of excellent quality **light weight Chambray**, in gray or natural linen color. Pin-tucked flounce with an attractive ruffle of eyelet embroidery. . . . **$1.29**

4814—Petticoat of fine quality **Hydegrade Rustling Heatherbloom**, in black only. The flounce is extra deep and full. It is tucked and shirred, and terminates in a wide ruffle of eyelet embroidery. Dust ruffle. Very rich and tasteful. **$2.98**

4817—Petticoat of fine quality **Hydegrade Rustling Heatherbloom**, in black, navy blue, Havana brown, gray, green or champagne. Extra deep flounce ornamented with pin-tucks, shirring and wide full ruffle of Florentine eyelet embroidery in an artistic and beautiful design. Dust ruffle. A strikingly handsome skirt. **$3.98**

4822—Petticoat of extra fine quality **Taffeta Silk**, in black only. The deep flounce is shirred at the top providing unusual fulness, and is embroidered in eyelet design, not only producing an effect of extreme beauty, but insuring splendid wearing qualities. Flounce of accordion-plaited percaline beneath, finished with a percaline dust ruffle. **$5.98**

5040—Corset Cover of **Cambric**. Front yoke of Torchon lace trimmed with beading and ribbon. Torchon edges neck and arm-holes. Sizes 32 to 44 bust. . . . . . **24 cents**

5041—Corset Cover of **Cambric**, elaborately trimmed in front with inserts of Torchon lace. Neck and arm-holes edged with Torchon. Ribbon beading around neck. Sizes 32 to 44 bust. . . . . **39 cents**

5042—Fitted Corset Cover of good quality **Cambric**. Front yoke of pin-tucks and embroidery insertion. Eyelet embroidery around neck and arm-holes. Sizes 32 to 44 bust. **39 cents**

SIZES OF PETTICOATS—37 TO 43 INCHES FRONT
LENGTH. FOR PARTICULARS REGARDING
EXTRA SIZES SEE PAGE 121.

1906—De Bevoise Brassiere of fine Batiste, in black or white. Edged with Torchon lace and beading threaded with ribbon. Sizes 32 to 48 bust. $1.00

1916—De Bevoise Brassiere of Batiste, in white only. Daintily trimmed with lace. Sizes 32 to 48 bust. **50 cents**

4807—Petticoat of Hydegrade Rustling Heatherbloom, in black, navy blue, Havana brown, gray, green or champagne. The shirred flounce is neatly trimmed with cording and terminates in two gathered ruffles. $1.49

4808—Petticoat of good quality light weight Chambray, in blue or natural linen color. Flounce has two ruffles of eyelet embroidery. Very serviceable. $1.49

4809—Petticoat of Hydegrade Rustling Heatherbloom, in black, navy blue, Havana brown, gray, green or champagne. Full shirred flounce with three gathered tucked ruffles. Dust ruffle. $1.98

4810—Petticoat of Hydegrade Rustling Heatherbloom, in black only. The flounce has two rows of shirring, and is elaborated with a handsome ruffle of eyelet embroidery. Gathered dust ruffle beneath. Excellent value. . . . $1.98

4811—" NATIONAL " Petticoat of featherweight Rustling Percaline, in black, navy blue, Havana brown, gray, green or champagne. Very deep full flounce trimmed with shirrings and pin-tucks. Wide bouffante tucked ruffle, shirred to give unusual fulness. Dust ruffle of nearsilk. . . $1.98

4812—Petticoat of Pure Linen, in natural linen color only. Summer weight. Flounce ending in a deep ruffle of eyelet embroidery. Launders beautifully. Very desirable. $2.49

4818—Petticoat of fine quality Hydegrade Rustling Heatherbloom, in black only. Flounce has two rows of shirring and two taffeta silk ruffles of English eyelet embroidery. $3.98

4821—Petticoat of Taffeta Silk, in a superior quality. In black, navy blue, golden brown, medium gray, hunter's green or champagne. A splendid skirt in tailored effect, completed with a wide bias flounce which is trimmed with five straps of taffeta. Dust ruffle of percaline. $4.98

4824—Petticoat of high grade Rustling Taffeta Silk, in black only. Flounce consists of four gathered ruffles of heavily embroidered silk in eyelet effect. Dust ruffle of Heatherbloom. A very rich and dressy skirt. $6.98

5043—Corset Cover of Cambric. Front yoke consists of four rows of Val lace separated by ribbon beading. Neck and arm-holes are edged with Val. Back trimmed with a row of Val lace. Beading extends around the neck. Sizes 32 to 44 bust. . . . . **49 cents**

SIZES OF PETTICOATS—37 TO 43 INCHES FRONT LENGTH. FOR EXTRA SIZES SEE PAGE 121.

4813—Petticoat of **Hydegrade Rustling Heatherbloom**, in black, navy blue, Havana brown, gray, green or champagne. Two flounces, each of which is headed by shirring, trimmed with tucks and a gathered ruffle. Dust ruffle. **$2.49**

4815—Petticoat of **Hydegrade Rustling Heatherbloom**, in black, navy blue, Havana brown, gray, green or champagne. Flounce finished with two ruffles of fine eyelet embroidery headed by tucks. Dust ruffle. **$2.98**

4816—Petticoat of **Hydegrade Rustling Heatherbloom**, in black, navy blue, Havana brown, gray, green or champagne. Flounce headed by shirrings and pin-tucks, and finished with three gathered ruffles of eyelet embroidery. **$3.98**

4819—Petticoat of **Rustling Taffeta Silk**, in black only. The flounce is shirred and pin-tucked. Gathered ruffle finished with straps of taffeta. Dust ruffle of percaline. . . **$3.98**

4820—Petticoat of good quality **Rustling Taffeta Silk**, in black, navy blue, golden brown, medium gray, hunter's green or champagne. Gathered flounce is pin-tucked and terminates in a ruffle of eyelet embroidery. Under-flounce of accordion-plaited percaline finished with a dust ruffle. **$4.98**

4823—Petticoat of fine **Rustling Taffeta Silk**, in black, navy blue, golden brown, medium gray, hunter's green or champagne. Ornamented with panels of accordion-plaited taffeta outlined by a ruching of pinking. Pin-tucked ruffle, finished with a ruching. Silk dust ruffle. **$5.98**

4825—Petticoat of rich **Rustling Taffeta Silk**, in black, navy blue, golden brown, medium gray, hunter's green or champagne. Elaborate flounce ornamented with accordion-plaited panels and pin-tucks. Wide ruffle trimmed with taffeta straps and also pin-tucked. Dust ruffle of taffeta. . . . **$7.98**

4826—Petticoat of finest **Rustling Taffeta Silk**, in black, navy blue, golden brown, medium gray, hunter's green or champagne. Flounce accordion-plaited and tucked. The accordion-plaited ruffle is finished with an additional gathered bouffante ruffle. Under flounce and dust ruffle of taffeta . . . **$8.98**

4827—Petticoat of finest quality rich **Rustling Taffeta Silk**, in black, light blue, pink, white or lavender. This petticoat has a flounce shirred at the top, trimmed with two rows of handsome Point de Paris lace insertion, and finished with a wide edging of this same beautiful lace. Under-ruffle of taffeta completed with a pin-tucked silk dust ruffle. **$9.98**

5044—**Corset Cover of French Cambric.** Yoke of embroidered lawn. Embroidery around neck and arm-holes. Neck threaded with ribbon. Sizes 32 to 44 bust. . . . **49 cents**

5045—**Corset Cover of Cambric.** Beautiful front yoke of Point de Paris insertion and ribbon beading. Row of Point de Paris insertion in back. Ribbon beading extends around the neck. Sizes 32 to 44 bust. . . . . . . **49 cents**

5085—**Slip of Lawn.** Sizes 32 to 44 bust. . . . **49 cents**

5086—**Slip of China Silk.** Sizes 32 to 44 bust. . . . **$1.98**

These slips button in back. Colors: white, black, pink or light blue. *Can be furnished with long or three-quarter sleeves.*

4851

4852

4853

4854

4855

4856

SIZES OF JACKETS AND COATS—32 TO 44 BUST.

4851—Semi-fitted Coat of superior quality Taffeta Silk, in black only. The collar effect and tie are of Bengaline silk. Vest of fancy garniture. Fancy silk braid trims the model down front and back, and edges the collar and turn-back cuffs. Stitched soutache loops and satin-covered buttons ornament the front and back. Coat is lined with gray satin, and is about 30 inches long in back. . **$9.98**

4852—Coat of fine quality Taffeta Silk, in black only. A modish semi-fitted garment slashed at the sides and back; tabs and satin-covered buttons being applied as a finish. Bengaline silk trims all edges. Persian garniture combined with Bengaline outlines the collarless neck, the same silk being also used on the turn-back cuffs. Front displays silk braid ornaments. Model lined throughout with gray satin and is about 30 inches long in back. . **$11.98**

4853—Semi-fitted Directoire Coat of very fine Taffeta Silk, in black only. The model is slashed at the sides and in back and is bound on all edges with handsome silk braid. The sleeves and the neck are finished with Bengaline silk outlined by fancy braid; trimming of satin-covered buttons and loops of soutache. Front is adorned with motifs of satin. Length in back about 36 inches. Lined throughout with gray satin. **$14.98**

4854—Coat of good quality Taffeta Silk, in black only, with a full loose back and front. The collarless neck is edged with silk braid and folds of taffeta. Silk Hercules and soutache braid are applied down the front and on the turn-back cuffs, where satin-covered buttons are used as a finish. Length in back about 50 inches. Unlined. **$9.98**

4855—Coat of rich lustrous Taffeta Silk, in black only. A beautiful garment handsomely trimmed in scroll effect with silk braid which extends around the collarless neck. Plaits are introduced both front and back giving extra fulness. Robin Hood cuffs. Length in back about 50 inches. Unlined. **$13.98**

4856—Coat of fine quality Chiffon Taffeta Silk, in black only. The distinguishing feature of this coat is the deep shawl collar of Brussels net richly appliquéd with silk braid in a Grecian design, and edged with silk garniture. A chic braid medallion graces the sleeves. Model is plaited both front and back. Yoke lining of taffeta silk. Length in back about 50 inches. **$15.98**

These READY-MADE garments will be found exactly as illustrated and described. We cannot make any alterations nor can we send samples of the materials.

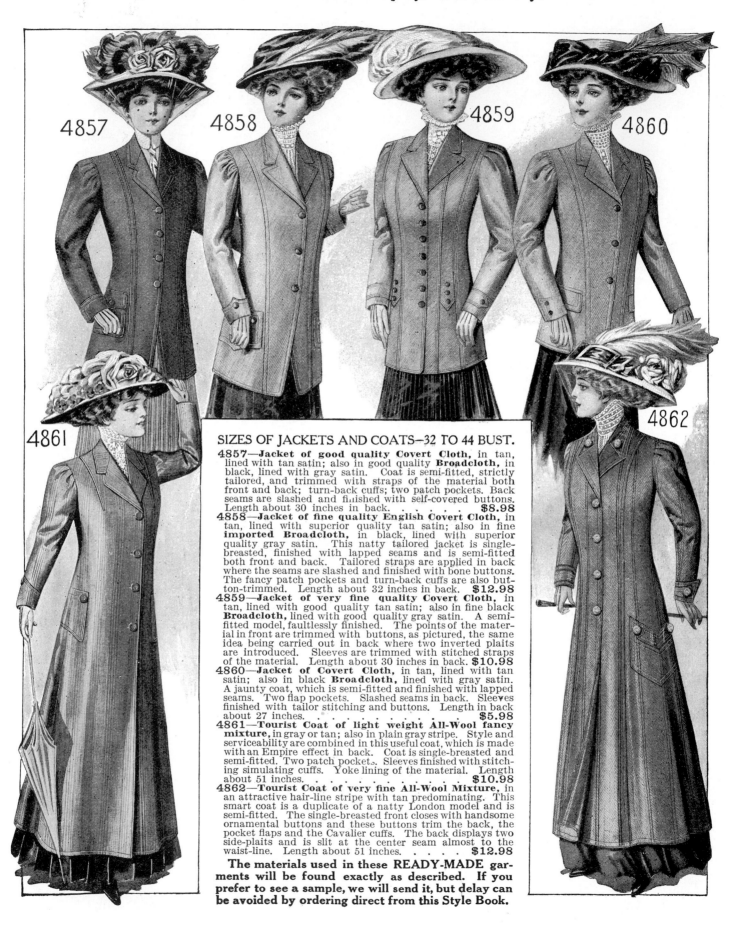

SIZES OF JACKETS AND COATS—32 TO 44 BUST.

4857—**Jacket of good quality Covert Cloth**, in tan, lined with tan satin; also in good quality **Broadcloth**, in black, lined with gray satin. Coat is semi-fitted, strictly tailored, and trimmed with straps of the material both front and back; turn-back cuffs; two patch pockets. Back seams are slashed and finished with self-covered buttons. Length about 30 inches in back. **$8.98**

4858—**Jacket of fine quality English Covert Cloth**, in tan, lined with superior quality tan satin; also in fine **imported Broadcloth**, in black, lined with superior quality gray satin. This natty tailored jacket is single-breasted, finished with lapped seams and is semi-fitted both front and back. Tailored straps are applied in back where the seams are slashed and finished with bone buttons. The fancy patch pockets and turn-back cuffs are also button-trimmed. Length about 32 inches in back. . **$12.98**

4859—**Jacket of very fine quality Covert Cloth**, in tan, lined with good quality tan satin; also in fine black **Broadcloth**, lined with good quality gray satin. A semi-fitted model, faultlessly finished. The points of the material in front are trimmed with buttons, as pictured, the same idea being carried out in back where two inverted plaits are introduced. Sleeves are trimmed with stitched straps of the material. Length about 30 inches in back. **$10.98**

4860—**Jacket of Covert Cloth**, in tan, lined with tan satin; also in black **Broadcloth**, lined with gray satin. A jaunty coat, which is semi-fitted and finished with lapped seams. Two flap pockets. Slashed seams in back. Sleeves finished with tailor stitching and buttons. Length in back about 27 inches. **$5.98**

4861—**Tourist Coat of light weight All-Wool fancy mixture**, in gray or tan; also in plain gray stripe. Style and serviceability are combined in this useful coat, which is made with an Empire effect in back. Coat is single-breasted and semi-fitted. Two patch pockets. Sleeves finished with stitching simulating cuffs. Yoke lining of the material. Length about 51 inches. **$10.98**

4862—**Tourist Coat of very fine All-Wool Mixture**, in an attractive hair-line stripe with tan predominating. This smart coat is a duplicate of a natty London model and is semi-fitted. The single-breasted front closes with handsome ornamental buttons and these buttons trim the back, the pocket flaps and the Cavalier cuffs. The back displays two side-plaits and is slit at the center seam almost to the waist-line. Length about 51 inches. **$12.98**

The materials used in these READY-MADE garments will be found exactly as described. If you prefer to see a sample, we will send it, but delay can be avoided by ordering direct from this Style Book.

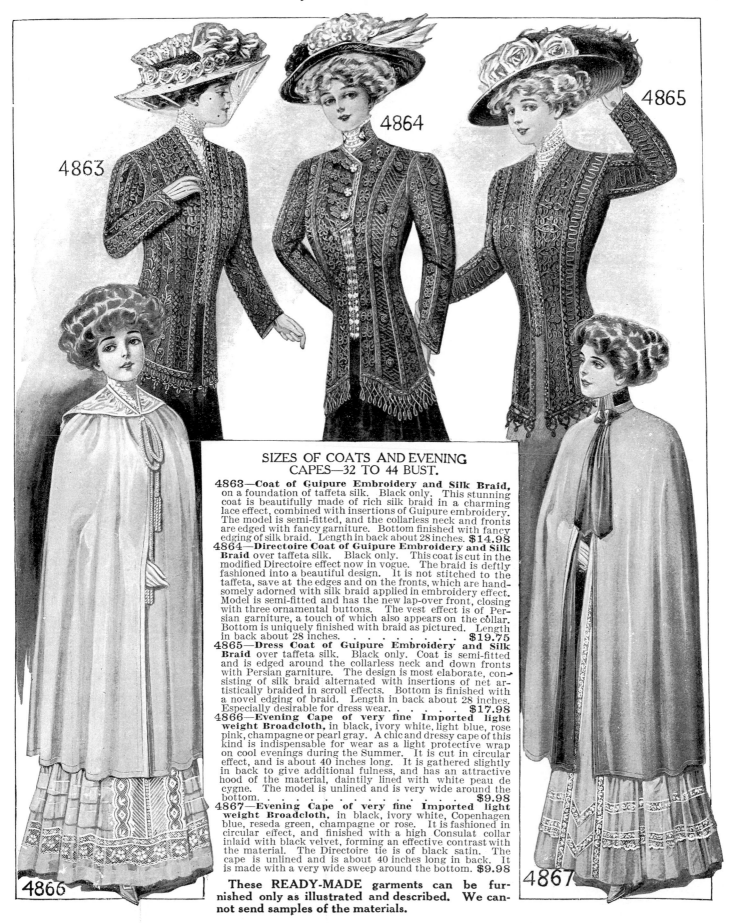

SIZES OF COATS AND EVENING CAPES—32 TO 44 BUST.

4863—Coat of Guipure Embroidery and Silk Braid, on a foundation of taffeta silk. Black only. This stunning coat is beautifully made of rich silk braid in a charming lace effect, combined with insertions of Guipure embroidery. The model is semi-fitted, and the collarless neck and fronts are edged with fancy garniture. Bottom finished with fancy edging of silk braid. Length in back about 28 inches. **$14.98**

4864—Directoire Coat of Guipure Embroidery and Silk Braid over taffeta silk. Black only. This coat is cut in the modified Directoire effect now in vogue. The braid is deftly fashioned into a beautiful design. It is not stitched to the taffeta, save at the edges and on the fronts, which are handsomely adorned with silk braid applied in embroidery effect. Model is semi-fitted and has the new lap-over front, closing with three ornamental buttons. The vest effect is of Persian garniture, a touch of which also appears on the collar. Bottom is uniquely finished with braid as pictured. Length in back about 28 inches. **$19.75**

4865—Dress Coat of Guipure Embroidery and Silk Braid over taffeta silk. Black only. Coat is semi-fitted and is edged around the collarless neck and down fronts with Persian garniture. The design is most elaborate, consisting of silk braid alternated with insertions of net artistically braided in scroll effects. Bottom is finished with a novel edging of braid. Length in back about 28 inches. Especially desirable for dress wear. **$17.98**

4866—Evening Cape of very fine Imported light weight Broadcloth, in black, ivory white, light blue, rose pink, champagne or pearl gray. A chic and dressy cape of this kind is indispensable for wear as a light protective wrap on cool evenings during the Summer. It is cut in circular effect, and is about 40 inches long. It is gathered slightly in back to give additional fulness, and has an attractive hood of the material, daintily lined with white peau de cygne. The model is unlined and is very wide around the bottom. **$9.98**

4867—Evening Cape of very fine Imported light weight Broadcloth, in black, ivory white, Copenhagen blue, reseda green, champagne or rose. It is fashioned in circular effect, and finished with a high Consulat collar inlaid with black velvet, forming an effective contrast with the material. The Directoire tie is of black satin. The cape is unlined and is about 40 inches long in back. It is made with a very wide sweep around the bottom. **$9.98**

These READY-MADE garments can be furnished only as illustrated and described. We cannot send samples of the materials.

SIZES OF TOURIST COATS—32 to 44 bust measure. If these coats are wanted over 44 inches and not more than 48 inches bust measure, there will be an extra charge of 10 per cent.

4901—Duster of Pure Linen, in natural linen color only. Double-breasted front with handsome gilt buttons; turn-back cuffs; two patch pockets. Garment has a full loose back, and is unlined. **$3.98**

4902—Duster of Linene, in tan; or in a fine quality Chambray in gun-metal gray. Double-breasted front with bone buttons; turn-back cuffs; two patch pockets. Full loose back. Unlined. **$2.98**

4903—Storm Coat of Rubberized Soisette, in navy blue, gray, brown, Pongee color or black. Soisette is an attractive, serviceable material, thoroughly shower-proof with a lustrous finish closely resembling silk. This coat is double-breasted, closing with self-covered buttons. It has a loose back. Two patch pockets and turn-back cuffs trimmed with buttons. Yoke lining of the material. Perforated eyelets under the arms for ventilation. **$7.49**

4901
4902

4903

4904

4904—Storm or Tourist Coat of fine quality Rubberized Mohair, in navy blue, brown, gray or black. A handsome coat with double-breasted front and plain loose back. A modish effect is produced by straps over the shoulders, front and back, trimmed with buttons. Mannish stitched cuffs; two patch pockets. Perforated eyelets under the arms for ventilation. . . . **$8.98**

4908—Tourist Coat of finest quality Genuine Cravanetted Roseberry Cloth, in black, navy blue, olive, or smoke gray. Nothing could be finer for a storm or traveling coat than this beautiful new material which resembles silk poplin in finish, is rain-proof, and wears splendidly. Tailored straps of the material encircle the arm-holes in bolero outline. Simulated cuffs and the two patch pockets are trimmed with buttons. Coat is double-breasted, and has a plain loose back. Closes with fancy pearl buttons. Unlined. Perforated eyelets under the arms for ventilation. Remarkable value. **$12.98**

4912—Nell Brinkley Coat of finest quality shadow-striped Satin Messaline, in brown with black stripe, black with black, gray with black or navy blue with black. Very light weight; extremely dressy in appearance; rubberized and shower-proof. Collar and cuffs inlaid with plain Messaline to match stripe. Single-breasted front trimmed with metal buttons. Empire back outlined with straps of the material. Gathered at the sides in Directoire effect beneath Empire girdle, providing graceful fulness below. Cavalier cuffs and collar are trimmed with buttons. Body lined with Duchesse satin. A very stylish coat. Perforated eyelets under arms for ventilation. **$16.98**

4908

4912

The collars of all these READY-MADE Coats may be worn turned down or buttoned close around the neck, as preferred. We will send samples of materials, if desired, but delay can be avoided by ordering direct from this Style Book.

SIZES OF TOURIST COATS—32 to 44 bust measure. See page 121 for particulars regarding extra sizes.

4905—**Coat of genuine light weight Priestley Cravanette Cloth,** in tan or Oxford gray. Coat is double-breasted, and has a full loose back. Turn-back cuffs; two patch pockets. Unlined; shower-proof; equally appropriate in fair or stormy weather. **$9.98**

4906—**Coat of light weight Shower-proof Worsted Material,** in tan or Oxford gray. Double-breasted; full loose back; two pockets; turn-back cuffs. Splendid value. . **$7.98**

4907—**Storm or Traveling Coat of finest quality Imported Mohair,** rubberized and shower-proof, in gray, mode (dark tan), brown, navy blue or black with an attractive stripe the color of the material. Double-breasted. Two patch pockets; collar and Robin Hood cuffs trimmed with soutache loops and buttons. Full loose back. Straps of the material over shoulders in front, ending in points and buttons. Perforated eyelets under the arms for ventilation. **$10.98**

4909—**Automobile or Dress Coat of fine quality Rough Pongee Silk,** rubberized and shower-proof, in natural Pongee color, gun-metal gray, brown, navy blue or black. A very handsome and dressy coat. Double-breasted; full loose back; velvet collar, turned-back cuffs and two pockets. Perforated eyelets under the arms for ventilation. **$14.98**

4910—**Dress Coat of Rubberized Satin-striped Taffeta,** in navy blue with black stripe, garnet with black stripe, black with black, green with black or brown with black. This stylish shower-proof coat is very light in weight and is an admirable selection either for dress wear or for general use. Double-breasted, closing with fancy bone buttons; full loose back; turn-back cuffs. Yoke lining of the material. Perforated eyelets under the arms for ventilation. **$14.98**

4911—**Dress Coat of finest quality Rubberized Satin Messaline,** in black, navy blue, brown or gray (London smoke). Exactly the same style as No. 4910, but plain instead of striped. It is double-breasted, with a plain loose back, and has fancy cuffs trimmed with buttons. Yoke lining of the material. Perforated eyelets under the arms for ventilation. . . **$15.98**

4913—**Evening or Dress Coat of genuine All-Silk Crepe de Chine,** in black, navy blue or gray; rubberized and shower-proof. This exquisite material is a complete novelty. It is very handsome in appearance, gives excellent wear, and is extremely light weight. Double-breasted; fancy buttons. Full loose back. Yoke lining of same material. Perforated eyelets under the arms for ventilation. A coat of extreme elegance which is offered at a very low price. **$17.98**

The collars of all these **READY-MADE** Coats may be worn turned down, or buttoned close around the neck, as preferred. We will send samples of materials, if desired, but delay can be avoided by ordering direct from this Style Book.

SIZES OF CORSET COVERS—32 TO 44 BUST; PETTICOATS—38 TO 44 INCHES FRONT LENGTH.

5001—Petticoat of good Muslin. Flounce trimmed with hemstitched tucks and edged with a ruffle of eyelet embroidery. Dust ruffle beneath. . . . . **59 cents**

5003—Petticoat of good quality Muslin. Flounce of lawn edged with three rows of fine Torchon lace headed with a cluster of Princess tucks. Dust ruffle. . . . . **79 cents**

5005—Petticoat of Cambric. Deep flounce trimmed with clusters of hemstitched tucks and wide ruffle of dotted Hamburg eyelet embroidery. Gathered dust ruffle. . **98 cents**

5006—Petticoat of good quality Cambric. The lawn flounce is unusually elaborate, consisting of four rows of Torchon insertion separated by bands of lawn and trimmed with hemstitched tucks. Gathered dust ruffle. . . **98 cents**

5011—Petticoat of fine Cambric, with a twenty-two inch lawn flounce which displays two wide inserts of handsome Torchon lace, and a lace edging of equal width. Three clusters of Princess tucks add greatly to the attractiveness of the garment. Dust ruffle. **$1.49**

5014—Petticoat of fine soft Nainsook. The flounce is of Persian lawn with a deep ruffle of exquisite Swiss embroidery. The ruffle is headed by two clusters of fine tucks. Gathered dust ruffle of lawn. **$1.79**

5019—Petticoat of fine French Cambric. The deep flounce consists of nine rows of German Val lace headed by a band of finely tucked Persian lawn. A dust ruffle beneath affords protection. **$1.98**

5023—Petticoat of extra fine quality soft French Cambric, with a twenty-four-inch lawn flounce which is beautifully embroidered in Swiss eyelet effect. The flounce is also decorated with clusters of tucks, and veining contributes to the attractive appearance. A dust ruffle is included. **$3.49**

5025—Petticoat of very fine quality Nainsook, finished with an elaborate Du Barry flounce formed of panels of embroidery insertion and Point de Paris lace. This same beautiful lace is applied around the bottom in festoon effect and also on the under-ruffle of lawn. Beneath this an additional ruffle serves to protect the garment from dust. . . . **$3.98**

5053—Corset Cover of fine quality Nainsook. Dainty yoke consists of three rows of Val lace insertion adorned with four medallions of beautiful Swiss embroidery. Neck and arm-holes edged with Val lace. Row of Val insertion in back. Ribbon is drawn through beading at the neck. . . . **98 cents**

5054—Corset Cover of fine quality Nainsook. The yoke is of Val lace insertion alternated with inserts of Swiss eyelet embroidery. Val edges the arm-holes and also the neck, which is threaded with ribbon drawn through beading. Back trimmed with a row of Val insertion. . . . . . . **98 cents**

5055—Fitted Corset Cover of fine Masonville Muslin. Yoke both front and back of eyelet embroidery, which is threaded with baby ribbon. Fine Val lace edges the neck and arm-holes. An unusually attractive design. . . **98 cents**

SIZES OF CORSET COVERS—32 TO 44 BUST; PETTICOATS—38 TO 44 INCHES FRONT LENGTH.

5002—Petticoat of Muslin. Wide tucked flounce with a ruffle of Swiss eyelet embroidery; dust ruffle. . . **79 cents**

5004—Petticoat of good Cambric. Deep flounce terminating in a wide ruffle of eyelet embroidery and headed by four hemstitched tucks. Dust ruffle beneath. . . . **98 cents**

5007—Petticoat of good quality Cambric. Torchon lace insertion in Filet design has been used very effectively on the lawn flounce of this attractive petticoat. There are four rows of lace separated by bands of lawn and headed by a cluster of Princess tucks. Dust ruffle beneath. . . . . **98 cents**

5009—Petticoat of superior Cambric, with a nineteen-inch flounce which is very full at the lower edge, and trimmed with four rows of Torchon insertion, clusters of fine tucks and a Torchon lace edging. Gathered dust ruffle. . . **$1.29**

5012—Petticoat of fine French Cambric, with a deep flounce of India lawn which is trimmed with fine tucks and a deep ruffle of Swiss eyelet embroidery. Dust ruffle. . . . **$1.49**

5013—Petticoat of fine French Cambric. The deep lawn flounce is headed by a row of Val lace insertion run through with satin ribbon, terminating in a bow. The flounce is trimmed with four rows of Val lace insertion and a bouffante ruffle entirely of Val lace. Dust ruffle of lawn. . . **$1.49**

5021—Petticoat of extra fine Cambric. Three rows of Florentine embroidery insertion on the flounce interspersed with hemstitched tucks. The lower edge is completed with a ruffle of the same embroidery. Dust ruffle. . . **$2.98**

5024—Petticoat of fine quality Persian Lawn. The flounce is of Val lace insertion, with panels of tucked lawn. It is edged with lace and headed by an insert of Val beneath which satin ribbon is run, ending in a neat bow. The dust ruffle beneath is edged with lace. **$3.98**

5026—Petticoat of finest quality French Cambric. The flounce is tucked and displays a fifteen-inch ruffle of very handsome Italian open-work embroidery. Lawn dust ruffle beneath with an embroidered edge. **$4.98**

5057—Corset Cover of extra fine Nainsook. The front yoke is formed of Swiss eyelet embroidery outlined by inserts of Medici lace. This exquisite lace also edges the neck and armholes, and two rows of the same insertion trim the back. Ribbon beading around neck and arm-holes. . . . **$1.29**

5059—Corset Cover of very fine Nainsook. The front yoke consists of imitation Baby Irish insertion bordered by Val lace. A row of Val insertion trims the back, and the neck and armholes are finished with ribbon beading and an edging of the same lace. Veining adds to the charming appearance. **$1.49**

5060—Corset Cover of finest quality Nainsook. Yoke, both front and back, of Swiss embroidery panels, surrounded by exquisite Thread lace insertion, very closely resembling real lace. Neck and arm-holes finished with beading and an edging of the same lace. **$1.98**

SIZES OF CORSET COVERS—32 TO 44 BUST;
PETTICOATS—38 TO 44 INCHES FRONT LENGTH.

5008—Petticoat of superior quality Cambric, with a double flounce of eyelet embroidery. The flounces are ornamented with pin-tucks; dust ruffle beneath. **$1.29**

5010—Petticoat of fine Cambric, with wide flounce of dotted Swiss lawn, embroidered in eyelet effect. This embroidery is very pretty and wears splendidly. Dust ruffle. . . **$1.49**

5015—Petticoat of fine Cambric. The lawn flounce, which is twenty-three inches in width, is formed of Point de Paris lace insertions and bands of lawn. The gathered ruffle is of Point de Paris lace and lawn trimmed with tucks. Tucks are used on the flounce. Gathered dust ruffle beneath. . **$1.79**

5016—Petticoat of fine Cambric. The flounce is of lawn elaborated with Princess tucks. Deep gathered ruffle composed of handsome Swiss eyelet embroidery. . . . **$1.98**

5017—Petticoat of fine Cambric. Flounce of Persian lawn decorated with clusters of hemstitched tucks and completed with ruffle of Swiss embroidery. Gathered dust ruffle. **$1.98**

5018—Petticoat of fine Cambric. The deep flounce is made with wide bands of imitation Irish Cluny insertion separated by finely tucked lawn. Lawn dust ruffle. **$1.98**

5020—Petticoat of Cambric, in a particularly fine quality. The flounce is in panel effect with inserts of Val lace separated by tucked bands of lawn. The bouffante ruffle is of Val lace insertion and edging. Lawn dust ruffle. **$2.49**

5022—Petticoat of fine French Cambric. The flounce is of lawn, elaborately tucked and varied by five rows of Val lace insertion. Val insertion threaded with satin ribbon, ending in a chic bow, is used as a heading for the flounce. The ruffle is of lawn in scalloped effect, handsomely edged with Val lace and insertion. Wide lawn dust ruffle. **$2.98**

5027—Petticoat of finest French Cambric. The lawn flounce is made of Duchesse panels of embroidery outlined with Point de Paris lace and alternated with clusters of Princess tucks. The bouffante ruffle is in festoon effect and is formed of Point de Paris. Tucked under-ruffle of lawn edged with the same lace. A bow of satin ribbon. Lawn dust ruffle. **$4.98**

5052—Corset Cover of Cambric. Front yoke consists of four rows of imitation Thread lace insertion separated by ribbon beading. One row of insertion and beading in back. Neck and arm-holes edged with Thread lace. . . . . . **49 cents**

5056—Corset Cover of fine Nainsook. Six medallions of embroidery across front outlined by French Val lace. This same lace extends around neck; neck and arm-holes are frilled with Val lace and threaded with baby ribbon. . . . **$1.29**

5058—Corset Cover of fine soft Nainsook. Front yoke of Swiss embroidery threaded with wide satin ribbon ending in a dainty bow and outlined by Val lace insertion. A row of Val insertion in back. Neck and arm-holes are frilled with the same lace and trimmed with ribbon drawn through beading. **$1.49**

SIZES OF CHEMISES AND SLIPS—32 TO 44 BUST.

5079—Chemise of Nainsook. Yoke is of lawn in Empire effect with vertical inserts of Cluny lace. This lace is also used around arm-holes and neck where beading is threaded with satin ribbon. Beading and ribbon also decorate the bottom of yoke. Garment finished with tucked lawn ruffle edged with Cluny lace. . . . . **98 cents**

5080—Chemise of French Cambric. Yoke in front of Cluny lace and English eyelet embroidery insertion. Ribbon is drawn through the neck, which is bordered with Torchon lace to match the arm-holes. The tucked lawn ruffle is also edged with this lace. **$1.49**

5081—Chemise of fine Nainsook. The low neck is threaded with baby ribbon and edged with two rows of Cluny lace, which also frills the arm-holes. The front displays five panels formed of medallions of embroidery surrounded by Cluny insertion. Tucks and ribbon drawn through beading afford a pleasing finish. Tucked ruffle of lawn edged with Cluny lace. . **$1.79**

5082—Chemise of fine quality Nainsook, in Empire effect. The top in front is of India lawn varied by inserts of Val lace and raised embroidery. Neck and arm-holes edged with Val. Satin ribbon is drawn through the neck and the waist-line. Ruffle of lawn trimmed with tucks and hemstitching and edged with Val lace. **$1.98**

5083—Chemise of very fine quality Nainsook. Yoke in front of Val lace and Cluny insertion with a medallion of embroidery in the center and fine tucks below. Neck and arm-holes threaded with ribbon and edged with Val lace. The lawn ruffle is also trimmed with Val insertion and lace. Fitted back. . **$1.98**

5084—Chemise of finest quality soft Nainsook. Yoke both back and front consists of Cluny insertion in rounded outline separated by Val lace. A butterfly medallion of Swiss embroidery in the center. Val lace frills the yoke and is used around the neck and arm-holes combined with ribbon beading. The front displays a cluster of Tom Thumb tucks. The ruffle is trimmed with Val and tucks. Fitted back. . **$2.49**

5087—Princess Slip of Persian Lawn, in white, pink or light blue. Close-fitting, with front yoke of Cluny insertion separated by lawn inserts. Ribbon beading around the low neck edged with Cluny lace to match arm-holes. Deep lawn ruffle tucked and edged with three rows of Cluny lace. Length from shoulders to hem about 56 inches; buttons in front. . . **$1.98**

5088—Princess Slip of India Lawn, in white, pink or light blue. Garment is fitted; low neck with yoke of Val lace insertion. Neck and arm-holes edged with the same lace. Ribbon beading around neck. Deep flounce of lawn with inserts of Val lace; dust ruffle beneath. Length from shoulder to hem about 56 inches. Closes in back. **$2.98**

5089—Princess Slip of China Silk, in white, pink or light blue. Close-fitting. The low neck and arm-holes are threaded with baby ribbon and edged with Val lace. Three gathered ruffles at the lower edge separated by two clusters of fine tucks. Length from shoulder to hem about 56 inches. Closes in back. **$4.98**

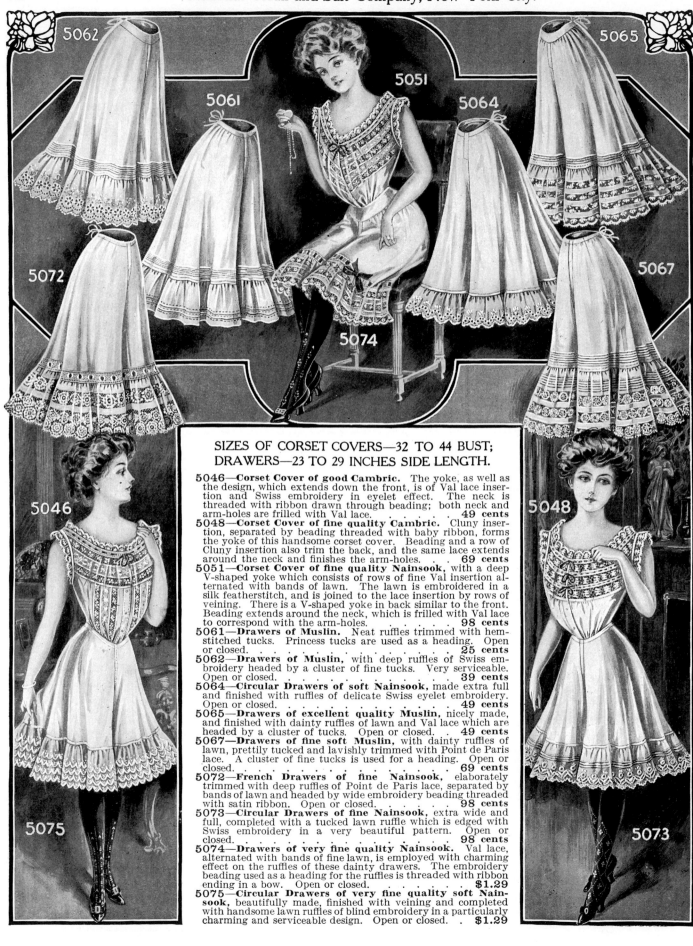

SIZES OF CORSET COVERS—32 TO 44 BUST; DRAWERS—23 TO 29 INCHES SIDE LENGTH.

5046—Corset Cover of good Cambric. The yoke, as well as the design, which extends down the front, is of Val lace insertion and Swiss embroidery in eyelet effect. The neck is threaded with ribbon drawn through beading; both neck and arm-holes are frilled with Val lace. . . . . . **49 cents**

5048—Corset Cover of fine quality Cambric. Cluny insertion, separated by beading threaded with baby ribbon, forms the yoke of this handsome corset cover. Beading and a row of Cluny insertion also trim the back, and the same lace extends around the neck and finishes the arm-holes. . . **69 cents**

5051—Corset Cover of fine quality Nainsook, with a deep V-shaped yoke which consists of rows of fine Val insertion alternated with bands of lawn. The lawn is embroidered in a silk featherstitch, and is joined to the lace insertion by rows of veining. There is a V-shaped yoke in back similar to the front. Beading extends around the neck, which is frilled with Val lace to correspond with the arm-holes. . . . . **98 cents**

5061—Drawers of Muslin. Neat ruffles trimmed with hemstitched tucks. Princess tucks are used as a heading. Open or closed. . . . . **25 cents**

5062—Drawers of Muslin, with deep ruffles of Swiss embroidery headed by a cluster of fine tucks. Very serviceable. Open or closed. . . . . **39 cents**

5064—Circular Drawers of soft Nainsook, made extra full and finished with ruffles of delicate Swiss eyelet embroidery. Open or closed. . . . . **49 cents**

5065—Drawers of excellent quality Muslin, nicely made, and finished with dainty ruffles of lawn and Val lace which are headed by a cluster of tucks. Open or closed. . . **49 cents**

5067—Drawers of fine soft Muslin, with dainty ruffles of lawn, prettily tucked and lavishly trimmed with Point de Paris lace. A cluster of fine tucks is used for a heading. Open or closed. . . . . **69 cents**

5072—French Drawers of fine Nainsook, elaborately trimmed with deep ruffles of Point de Paris lace, separated by bands of lawn and headed by wide embroidery beading threaded with satin ribbon. Open or closed. . . . . **98 cents**

5073—Circular Drawers of fine Nainsook, extra wide and full, completed with a tucked lawn ruffle which is edged with Swiss embroidery in a very beautiful pattern. Open or closed. . . . . **98 cents**

5074—Drawers of very fine quality Nainsook. Val lace, alternated with bands of fine lawn, is employed with charming effect on the ruffles of these dainty drawers. The embroidery beading used as a heading for the ruffles is threaded with ribbon ending in a bow. Open or closed. **$1.29**

5075—Circular Drawers of very fine quality soft Nainsook, beautifully made, finished with veining and completed with handsome lawn ruffles of blind embroidery in a particularly charming and serviceable design. Open or closed. . **$1.29**

SIZES OF CORSET COVERS — 32 TO 44 BUST;
DRAWERS — 23 TO 29 INCHES SIDE LENGTH.

5047—Fitted Corset Cover of fine quality Masonville Muslin. The V-shaped neck of this serviceable garment is finished with Swiss eyelet embroidery. It is splendidly made and fits the figure closely, making it especially desirable for wear with Princess or tight-fitting gowns. . . . . **49 cents**

5049—Corset Cover of fine Nainsook. Panels of lawn exquisitely embroidered and surrounded by Val lace insertion have been utilized with highly pleasing effect on the front of this delightful corset cover. The yoke is entirely of lace, Cluny and Val insertion being used in artistic combination. The neck and arm-holes are edged with Val lace, and beading threaded with ribbon provides desirable fulness. . . . **79 cents**

5050—Corset Cover of fine Cambric. Beautiful yoke of embroidered lawn surrounded by Val insertion. The same lace edges the neck and frills the arm-holes, and two rows of baby ribbon contribute to the daintiness of the garment. **69 cents**

5063—Drawers of good quality Cambric. Tucks are used to form a heading for the full ruffles of lawn, which are edged with Swiss eyelet embroidery. Open or closed. . **49 cents**

5066—Drawers of superior quality Cambric, finished with deep, full lawn ruffles of handsome embroidery in Florentine design. Open or closed. . . . . **69 cents**

5068—Circular Drawers of good quality Nainsook, handsomely finished with full ruffles of lawn trimmed with Cluny insertion. Special value. Open or closed. . . **79 cents**

5069—Drawers of fine Cambric, with lawn ruffles of very fine quality Swiss eyelet embroidery headed by Princess tucks. Open or closed. . . . . **79 cents**

5070—French Drawers of fine soft Nainsook, made with a fitted waist band. Handsomely finished with scalloped ruffles. Val lace is used on these ruffles, and ribbon bows add to the attractive appearance. Open or closed. . . **98 cents**

5071—Drawers of fine quality French Cambric, with deep full ruffles of handsome eyelet embroidery headed by a wide band of eyelet insertion and a cluster of tucks. Very dainty and serviceable. Open or closed. . . . . **98 cents**

5076—Drawers of very fine quality French Nainsook, elaborately finished with ruffles of English eyelet embroidery in Marguerite design. Fine hemstitched tucks trim the ruffles, and are also used as a heading. Open or closed. . **$1.49**

5077—Circular Drawers of Nainsook, in a beautiful, soft quality. The deep, full ruffles are of fine French Val lace with a wide insert of Swiss embroidery. The ruffles are headed by a hemstitching. Open or closed. **$1.69**

5078—Drawers of extra quality French Nainsook, with fitted waist band. The graceful ruffles are in festoon effect, and are formed of lawn with four panels of exquisite Swiss embroidery in each ruffle, combined with German Val insertion and a lace edging. Heading of Val lace. Ribbon bows supply an appropriate completion. **$1.98**

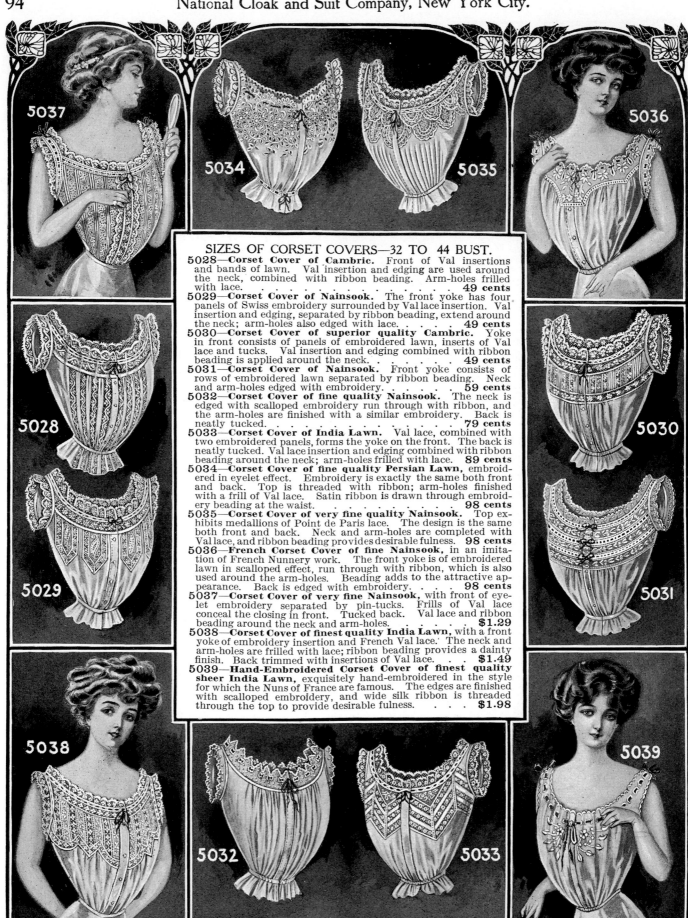

SIZES OF CORSET COVERS—32 TO 44 BUST.

5028—Corset Cover of Cambric. Front of Val insertions and bands of lawn. Val insertion and edging are used around the neck, combined with ribbon beading. Arm-holes frilled with lace. . . . . **49 cents**

5029—Corset Cover of Nainsook. The front yoke has four panels of Swiss embroidery surrounded by Val lace insertion. Val insertion and edging, separated by ribbon beading, extend around the neck; arm-holes also edged with lace. . . . . **49 cents**

5030—Corset Cover of superior quality Cambric. Yoke in front consists of panels of embroidered lawn, inserts of Val lace and tucks. Val insertion and edging combined with ribbon beading is applied around the neck. . . . . . . **49 cents**

5031—Corset Cover of Nainsook. Front yoke consists of rows of embroidered lawn separated by ribbon beading. Neck and arm-holes edged with embroidery. . . . . . . **59 cents**

5032—Corset Cover of fine quality Nainsook. The neck is edged with scalloped embroidery run through with ribbon, and the arm-holes are finished with a similar embroidery. Back is neatly tucked. . . . . **79 cents**

5033—Corset Cover of India Lawn. Val lace, combined with two embroidered panels, forms the yoke on the front. The back is neatly tucked. Val lace insertion and edging combined with ribbon beading around the neck; arm-holes frilled with lace. **89 cents**

5034—Corset Cover of fine quality Persian Lawn, embroidered in eyelet effect. Embroidery is exactly the same both front and back. Top is threaded with ribbon; arm-holes finished with a frill of Val lace. Satin ribbon is drawn through embroidery beading at the waist. . . . . . **98 cents**

5035—Corset Cover of very fine quality Nainsook. Top exhibits medallions of Point de Paris lace. The design is the same both front and back. Neck and arm-holes are completed with Val lace, and ribbon beading provides desirable fulness. **98 cents**

5036—French Corset Cover of fine Nainsook, in an imitation of French Nunnery work. The front yoke is of embroidered lawn in scalloped effect, run through with ribbon, which is also used around the arm-holes. Beading adds to the attractive appearance. Back is edged with embroidery. . . . . **98 cents**

5037—Corset Cover of very fine Nainsook, with front of eyelet embroidery separated by pin-tucks. Frills of Val lace conceal the closing in front. Tucked back. Val lace and ribbon beading around the neck and arm-holes. **$1.29**

5038—Corset Cover of finest quality India Lawn, with a front yoke of embroidery insertion and French Val lace. The neck and arm-holes are frilled with lace; ribbon beading provides a dainty finish. Back trimmed with insertions of Val lace. . . **$1.49**

5039—Hand-Embroidered Corset Cover of finest quality sheer India Lawn, exquisitely hand-embroidered in the style for which the Nuns of France are famous. The edges are finished with scalloped embroidery, and wide silk ribbon is threaded through the top to provide desirable fulness. . . . **$1.98**

SIZES OF GOWNS—32 TO 44 BUST.

5098—Gown of Cambric. Front yoke of handsome eyelet embroidery. V-shaped neck finished with a frill of the same embroidery, which also completes the sleeves. . . **79 cents**

5099—Gown of fine Muslin, with a square front yoke in Marguerite effect, composed of Swiss embroidery insertion separated by embroidery beading threaded with ribbon. Embroidery frills the neck and sleeves. Mother Hubbard back. **89 cents**

5100—Gown of Cambric in Pompadour design. The chic sleeves, as well as the trimming on front yoke, are of Val lace insertion and are elaborated with ribbon beading. Beading extends around neck which is edged with Val lace. . . **98 cents**

5101—Gown of Cambric, trimmed around the low neck and on the short sleeves with Val lace. Front displays three panels of eyelet embroidery outlined by Val insertion—a device, which is also used with charming effect on the sleeves. Baby ribbon is drawn through beading around the neck. . . . **98 cents**

5107—Gown of fine French Cambric. The Gretchen yoke is of embroidery combined with Val lace insertion. Beading and a lace edging are used to finish the neck, and the dainty sleeves are made of Val lace separated by bands of lawn. . **$1.29**

5108—French Gown of Nainsook, with front yoke of lawn, exquisitely embroidered, and outlined with narrow featherstitch braid. The same braid finishes the sleeves which are frilled with embroidery to correspond with the neck. Ribbon bow at the neck. Mother Hubbard back. **$1.29**

5114—Gown of fine Nainsook, in Madame Butterfly effect. Handsome yoke formed of rows of German Val lace and rich Cluny insertion. There is an embroidered medallion in the center with clusters of Princess tucks below. The butterfly sleeves are finished with two rows of Val lace insertion and a lace edging. Ribbon beading is used around the neck. . . . **$1.98**

5115—Gown of Nainsook. Embroidery insertion combined with Val and Cluny is used on the square yoke effect in front. The same lace is used around the neck and wide silk ribbon run through beading affords a dainty finish. The sleeves, which are short, are trimmed with lace and are extremely artistic in design. Fine tucks are used on either side of a handsome medallion of embroidery which is frilled with Val lace. **$2.49**

5116—Gown of very fine quality soft Nainsook. Yoke of German Val lace and eyelet embroidery outlined by veining. The dainty sleeves are of lace and eyelet embroidery. Ribbon is drawn through beading at the neck. Handsome bow of satin ribbon. Val lace insertion extends around the neck which is also frilled with an edging of the same lace. . . . **$2.98**

5117—Gown of finest quality French Nainsook. The yoke is of Val lace with inserts of tucked lawn and a medallion of exquisite embroidery in the center. Yoke is outlined by veining. Val lace threaded with satin ribbon extends around the low neck, finished in front with two chic bows. The dainty sleeves display inserts of Val lace and are prettily lace-edged. . **$2.98**

SIZES OF GOWNS AND COMBINATION GARMENTS — 32 TO 44 BUST.

5091—Combination Drawers and Corset Cover of Lawn. Front and back of corset cover are almost entirely of English eyelet embroidery. Val lace edges the arm-holes which are threaded with ribbon, same being also drawn through top of corset cover. The drawers are circular, finished with ruffles, edged with Val lace. Open only. **$1.49**

5093—Combination Drawers and Corset Cover of fine, soft Nainsook, finished with a deep front yoke of Val lace and insertions of embroidered lawn. Val lace extends around neck, and both neck and arm-holes are finished with ribbon beading and an edging of Val. Circular drawers completed with lawn ruffles daintily trimmed with Val lace and insertion. Embroidery beading at the waist threaded with ribbon. Open only. **$1.98**

5094—Combination Drawers and Corset Cover of fine Persian Lawn. Front of corset cover is of handsome eyelet embroidery. Both back and front are exactly the same. Top is threaded with ribbon, and Val lace and ribbon are used around the arm-holes. Embroidery beading at the waist through which satin ribbon is drawn. Drawers are extra full and finished with eyelet embroidery. Open only. **$2.98**

5096—Gown of Muslin, with a V-shaped yoke of embroidery neatly tucked. The neck and sleeves are completed with a pretty frill of embroidery. Mother Hubbard back. . . **59 cents**

5103—Gown of Cambric, with a square front yoke of eyelet embroidery insertion and hemstitched tucks. Yoke is trimmed with featherstitch braid and the neck and sleeves are frilled with Swiss embroidery. Gown buttons at side of front. Mother Hubbard back. . . . . **98 cents**

5106—Gown of Nainsook, with pointed yoke of baby tucks and open-work embroidery. This pleasing design is finished with a square neck of embroidery beading and ribbon, frilled with eyelet embroidery to match sleeves. **$1.29**

5109—Gown of fine quality Nainsook, with a rounded neck which is threaded with ribbon and edged with Val lace. The yoke effect in front consists of four panels of delicate embroidery outlined by Val lace with Princess tucks below. The bell sleeves are of lawn and Val lace insertion. **$1.49**

5110—Gown of fine quality soft Nainsook. We know that you will be delighted with the splendid quality of the material of which this neat model is made. The Dutch neck is frilled with embroidery and outlined with wide embroidery beading run through with ribbon. The sleeves are finished with a ruffle of embroidered lawn. **$1.49**

5111—Gown of French Cambric, with a front yoke of open-work embroidery insertion in Filet effect and inserts of tucked lawn. Wide embroidery beading, threaded with satin ribbon, borders the yoke, and the same dainty finish is used on the sleeves. Both neck and sleeves are frilled with embroidery. Mother Hubbard back. **$1.98**

SIZES OF GOWNS AND COMBINATION GARMENTS—32 TO 44 BUST.

5090—Combination Drawers and Corset Cover of Cambric. An insert of Swiss embroidered lawn and Val lace with a Filet mesh, forms the yoke in front. Val lace frills the neck and arm-holes, and ribbon beading around the neck and at the waist takes up the fulness. The drawers have ruffles of embroidered lawn trimmed with Val lace. Open only. . . . . **98 cents**

5092—Combination Drawers and Corset Cover of fine soft Nainsook. Front yoke of Val lace in Filet effect and inserts of lawn. Neck and arm-holes edged with lace and ribbon beading. A frill of Val lace down front. Ribbon beading around the waist. The drawers are circular and finished with lawn ruffles, edged with Val lace. Open only. **$1.49**

5095—Combination Drawers and Corset Cover of finest quality Persian Lawn. The corset cover is composed of all-over Swiss eyelet embroidery. Back and front of corset cover are exactly alike. Ribbon is drawn through the neck. Arm-holes frilled with Val lace. Embroidery beading at waist threaded with satin ribbon. Drawers are in yoke effect with deep flounce of Swiss eyelet embroidery. Open only. . . **$3.98**

5097—Gown of good quality Muslin. Marguerite yoke in front of fine Torchon lace and ribbon drawn through beading, which also extends around the back. Neck finished with Torchon lace. Sleeves display a lawn ruffle edged with Torchon. **79 cents**

5102—Gown of Cambric, with a Gretchen yoke in front formed of rows of Cluny insertion and India lawn. The bell sleeves are also of bands of Cluny insertion and lawn and are edged with lace to match the neck. Ribbon beading at the neck. **98 cents**

5104—French Gown of Nainsook. The front yoke is of embroidered lawn, laced with ribbon and outlined with veining. Neck and sleeves are edged with embroidery. . . **98 cents**

5105—Gown of Nainsook. The front yoke is of eyelet embroidery in raised effect varied by veining. Ribbon beading at the neck frilled with Val lace. A lace-trimmed ruffle finishes the sleeves. . . . . **98 cents**

5112—Gown of fine quality Nainsook. The round embroidered front yoke is an excellent imitation of French Nunnery work. The sleeves are outlined with ruffles tucked and edged with embroidery. Particularly attractive. Special value. **$1.98**

5113—Gown of fine soft Nainsook. The rounded low-cut neck is edged with Val insertion and lace, threaded with baby ribbon. Yoke in front in Van Dyke effect outlined by inserts of blind embroidery, Cluny and Val lace. The sleeves are similarly finished with embroidery and lace, and threaded with ribbon. The front is tucked as illustrated. **$1.98**

5125—Vest of Swiss Ribbed Cotton; low neck; sleeveless, finished with crochet lace and beading. Sizes 30 to 40 bust only.
                 13 cents; 2 for 25 cents

5126—Vest of Cotton; Richelieu ribbed; low neck; sleeveless; trimmed with fine quality crochet lace yoke and beading. Splendid value. Sizes 30 to 40 bust only. . . . . 19 cents

5127—Vest of good quality Egyptian Cotton; Richelieu ribbed; daintily finished with crochet lace and beading; low neck; sleeveless. Sizes 30 to 40 bust only. . . . . . . 25 cents

5128—Vest of Mercerized Cotton; Swiss ribbed; low neck; sleeveless; edged with crochet beading threaded with ribbon.
Sizes 30 to 40 bust. . . . . 25 cents
Sizes 42, 44, 46 bust. . . . . 29 cents

5130—Vest of Lisle-finished Sea Island Cotton, of excellent quality; Richelieu ribbed; low neck; sleeveless; prettily trimmed with Cluny lace and silk ribbon beading.
Sizes 30 to 40 bust. . . . . . 35 cents; 3 for $1.00
Sizes 42, 44, 46 bust. . . . . 40 cents

5132—Vest of extra quality Mercerized Lisle Thread; Spring needle rib; low neck; sleeveless. Handsome trimming of Cluny lace forming a yoke, edged with ribbon beading. Sizes 30 to 40 bust only. . . . . 49 cents

5133—Vest of fine quality Mercerized Lisle Thread, in white, pink, or light blue; low neck; sleeveless; finished with ribbon beading. Sizes 30 to 40 bust only. . . . . . 49 cents

5134—Vest of excellent quality Lisle Thread; fine ribbed; shaped waist. Low neck; sleeveless; finished with ribbon beading.

Sizes 30 to 40 bust. . . . . 49 cents
Sizes 42, 44, 46 bust. . . . . 59 cents

5136—Vest of good quality Sea Island Cotton, same style as 5134. Sizes 30 to 40 bust. . . . . 25 cents
Sizes 42, 44, 46 bust. . . . . 29 cents

5159—Union Suit of Cotton; fine ribbed; trimmed with Cluny lace and ribbon beading. Low neck; sleeveless; finished with Torchon lace. Open only. Sizes 30 to 40 bust. . . 49 cents
Sizes 42, 44, 46 bust. . . . . 59 cents

5161—Union Suit of fine Lisle Thread, made knee length; beautifully shaped; snug-fitting at the knee; low neck; sleeveless; trimmed with Baby Irish insertion in yoke and ribbon beading; narrow edge of Torchon lace. Sizes 30 to 40 bust. 98 cents
Sizes 42, 44, 46 bust. $1.15

5163—Union Suit of Sea Island Cotton, similar to illustration 5161. Sizes 30 to 40 bust. . . . . 49 cents
Sizes 42, 44, 46 bust. . . . . 59 cents

5165—Union Suit of fine Lisle Thread; Cluny insertion in front and back; finished with handsome ruffles and edging of Torchon lace and beading; low neck; sleeveless. Open only. Fitted to shape. Sizes 30 to 40 bust. . . . . 98 cents
Sizes 42, 44, 46 bust. $1.25

5167—Union Suit of extra quality Lisle Thread; very fine rib; fitted to shape. Low neck; sleeveless. Edged with ribbon beading. The drawer part is finished with Torchon lace. Open only.
Sizes 30 to 40 bust. . . . . 98 cents
Sizes 42, 44, 46 bust. $1.15

5140
5138
5142
5143
5145
5147
5169
5171
5172
5174
5149
5151
5153
5155
5157

5138—Vest of fine quality Lisle Thread; high neck; short sleeves; shaped waist. Sizes 30 to 40 bust. . . . **49 cents**
Sizes 42, 44, 46 bust. . . . . **59 cents**
5140—Vest of Cotton, same style as 5138.
Sizes 30 to 40 bust . . . . **25 cents**
Sizes 42, 44, 46 bust. . . . . **29 cents**
5142—Vest of Mercerized Lisle Thread, soft quality; Swiss ribbed; low neck; sleeveless. Trimmed with silk crochet lace and ribbon. A beautiful garment. Sizes 30 to 40 bust only. **98 cents**
5143—Vest of Pure Silk; Swiss ribbed; low neck; sleeveless; trimmed with silk crochet beading and wash silk ribbon. One of the finest garments made. Sizes 30 to 40 bust. . **98 cents**
Sizes 42, 44, 46 bust. **$1.35**
5145—Vest of finest quality Mercerized Lisle Thread; very fine rib; shaped to insure a snug fit; finished with silk crochet beading and wash ribbon. Sizes 30 to 40 bust. . . **98 cents**
Sizes 42, 44, 46 bust. **$1.19**
5147—Vest of fine, soft Silk and Lisle Mixture, same style as 5145. Low neck; sleeveless; edged with silk crochet beading. A beautiful garment. Sizes 30 to 40 bust. . . **98 cents**
Sizes 42, 44, 46 bust. **$1.19**
5149—Drawers of fine Combed Cotton Yarn, finished with crochet lace. Open only. Sizes 20 to 30 waist. . **25 cents**
Sizes 32, 34, 36 waist. . . . . **29 cents**
5151—Drawers of fine quality Combed Egyptian Cotton; very fine rib; handsomely trimmed with ruffles of Point de Paris lace. Open only. Sizes 20 to 30 waist. . . . . **49 cents**
Sizes 32, 34, 36 waist. . . . . **59 cents**

5153—Drawers of Egyptian Lisle; knee length; snug fit at the knee. Open only. Sizes 20 to 30 waist. . . . . **49 cents**
Sizes 32, 34, 36 waist. . . . . **59 cents**
5155—Drawers of Egyptian Cotton, same style as 5153. Sizes 20 to 30 waist. . . . . **25 cents**
Sizes 32, 34, 36 waist. . . . . **29 cents**
5157—Drawers of fine Lisle Thread, with ruffles of Torchon lace. Open only. Sizes 20 to 30 waist. . . . . **98 cents**
Sizes 32, 34, 36 waist. **$1.19**
5169—Union Suit of finest quality Lisle Thread. A very handsome garment; low neck; sleeveless; finished with finest quality Torchon lace ruffles and silkateen crochet beading. Fine ribbed. Open only. Sizes 30 to 40 bust. **$1.25**
Sizes 42, 44, 46 bust. **$1.49**
5171—Union Suit of finest quality Lisle Thread; fine rib; low neck is trimmed with Torchon lace yoke and ribbon beading. Sleeveless. Drawer parts are finished with Torchon lace. Open only. Sizes 30 to 40 bust only. **$1.25**
5172—Union Suit of soft Egyptian Lisle, in a splendid, durable quality. Low neck; sleeveless; finished with crochet beading and silk wash ribbon. Drawer parts are attractively trimmed with fine Torchon lace. Open only. Sizes 30 to 40 bust. . **$1.49**
Sizes 42, 44, 46 bust. **$1.75**
5174—Union Suit of finest quality Mercerized Lisle; wears better than silk. Very fine rib. Low neck; yoke trimmed with silkateen crochet lace and beading. Sleeveless. Drawer parts trimmed with beautiful Mechlin lace. Sizes 30 to 40 bust. **$1.98**
Sizes 42, 44, 46 bust. **$2.25**

301—Nemo Military Belt Corset; for medium figures. In white Batiste only. Sizes 18 to 30. . . . . $3.00
304—Nemo Military Belt Corset; for medium figures. Same model as 301, but with the new "Flatning Back." In white Batiste only. Sizes 18 to 30. . . . . $3.00
This corset has a medium high bust and long hip. The military belt attachment constantly reminds the wearer to stand erect, and gives perfect poise. The "Flatning Back" is a new departure. It produces the flat, curveless appearance demanded by the styles of to-day.

312—Nemo Self-Reducing Corset; for tall, stout figures. In white or drab Coutil. Sizes 19 to 36. . . . . . $3.00
314—Nemo Self-Reducing Corset; same model as 312; for short, stout figures. White or drab Coutil. Sizes 19 to 36. $3.00
The Nemo Self-Reducing corset makes the figure look smaller and more shapely, re-moulds the abdomen into graceful lines, and imparts a grateful sensation of perfect support and complete ease.

318—Nemo Self-Reducing Corset; with the new "Flatning Back"; for short, stout figures. In white or drab Coutil. Sizes 19 to 36. . . . . $3.00
320—Nemo Self-Reducing Corset; with the new "Flatning Back"; same model as 318; for tall, stout figures. In white or drab Coutil. Sizes 19 to 36. . . . . $3.00
No matter how stout you may be, this model will improve your figure. It has long slender hips, medium high bust and beautifully curved waist. The new "Flatning Back" device gives the long, flat back effect so much desired by fashionable women.

351—Nemo Back-Resting Corset; for medium and slender figures. In white Coutil only. Sizes 19 to 26. . . . $3.50
Brings relief and comfort to women who suffer from tired, aching backs, and gives the wearer the long sloping back and slender hip effect—the new Directoire form at its best.

2704—National Corset; for average and slender figures. In white Batiste only. Sizes 18 to 30. . . . . $1.50
A graceful model, with medium low bust, and the new French hip, long and gently sloping in accordance with Fashion's demands.
2715—National Corset; for medium and stout figures. In white Batiste only. Sizes 18 to 30. . . . . $2.50
A truly fashionable shape, designed for long service; willowy and slender in contour, with medium high bust and extra long hip. Six hose supporters and a skirt hook.
2716—National Girdle-top Corset; for medium and slender figures; in extra fine imported white Batiste only. Sizes 18 to 26. . . . . $2.00
2717—National Girdle-top Corset; same as 2716. In cheaper Batiste. White only. Sizes 18 to 26. . . . . $1.50
A beautifully modeled corset with a low girdle top, and extra long, slender hip. It is an admirable selection for warm weather and provides an ideal foundation for dainty summer gowns.
Silk Corset Laces, in white, pink or light blue. . . 25 cents

Before ordering corsets, be sure to read note regarding sizes on page 121.

2718

2703
2713

2701
2702

2714

2719

2709
2710

2721

2701—National Corset; for medium figures. In white Batiste only. Sizes 18 to 30. . . . .$1.00

2702—National Corset; same model as 2701; for short figures. In white Batiste only. Sizes 18 to 30. . . . . . . $1.00
Both of these corsets are straight-front models with tapering waist and slender hip.

2703—National Corset; for youthful, slender figures. Low bust; slender, shapely waist; deep hip. In white Batiste only. Sizes 18 to 26. (See also 2713.) $1.00

2709—National Reinforced Belt Corset; for tall, stout figures. In white Coutil only. Sizes 19 to 36. . . . $3.00

2710—National Reinforced Belt Corset; same model as 2709, but with lower bust; for short, stout figures. In white Coutil only. Sizes 19 to 36. . . . . $3.00
This model re-shapes the form into the long, slender, willowy lines required by present-day fashions, without discomfort or danger to health. It retains its shape and wears splendidly. The Reinforced Belt which supports the abdomen and reduces the hips, is a device found only in this corset. A skirt hook is included.

2713—National Corset; for slender and medium figures. In imported white Batiste only. Sizes 18 to 26. . . . $2.00
A graceful, durable corset, which imparts symmetry to the figure. It has the popular girdle top and the new long habit hip. A skirt hook is included.

2714—National Corset; for slender and medium figures. In white Batiste only. Sizes 18 to 30. . . . . . . $2.00
A sensible, serviceable model, conservative in its shaping, which is recommended for long wear. It has a medium high bust, long hip, and is provided with a skirt hook.

2718—National Corset; for slender and medium figures. In handsome Mercerized Brocaded Coutil; white only. Sizes 18 to 26. . . . . $3.00
If you wish a dainty corset in a splendid material, with low girdle top, and long Directoire hip and back, you will find this model in every way satisfactory.

2719—National Corset; for average and slender figures. In white Batiste only. Sizes 19 to 26. . . . . . $3.00
This is the correct corset for women who wish to acquire the new Directoire hip effect in modified form. It has a medium high bust, and though not extreme in its shaping, displays the straight long back and hips characteristic of the late Parisian designs. Six hose supporters.

2721—National Corset; for stout figures. In white Coutil only. Sizes 19 to 36. . . . . $2.00
This corset is built on scientific lines and is anatomically correct in its shaping. It may be worn with absolute comfort. Attention is called to the new "Abdominal Straps" which reduce the hips, support the abdomen, and assist in re-shaping the form to give an appearance of slenderness. Model has medium high bust and deep hip.

Silk Corset Laces, in white, pink or light blue. . . 25 cents

Before ordering corsets, be sure to read note regarding sizes on page 121.

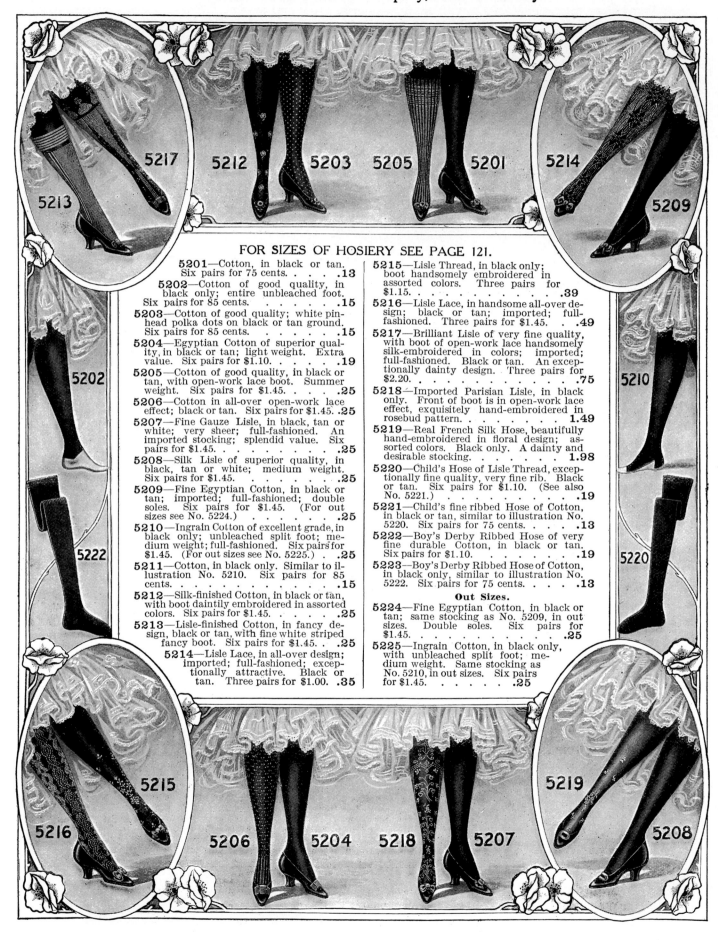

FOR SIZES OF HOSIERY SEE PAGE 121.

5201—Cotton, in black or tan. Six pairs for 75 cents. 13

5202—Cotton of good quality, in black only; entire unbleached foot. Six pairs for 85 cents. 15

5203—Cotton of good quality; white pinhead polka dots on black or tan ground. Six pairs for 85 cents. 15

5204—Egyptian Cotton of superior quality, in black or tan; light weight. Extra value. Six pairs for $1.10. 19

5205—Cotton of good quality, in black or tan, with open-work lace boot. Summer weight. Six pairs for $1.45. 25

5206—Cotton in all-over open-work lace effect; black or tan. Six pairs for $1.45. .25

5207—Fine Gauze Lisle, in black, tan or white; very sheer; full-fashioned. An imported stocking; splendid value. Six pairs for $1.45. 25

5208—Silk Lisle of superior quality, in black, tan or white; medium weight. Six pairs for $1.45. 25

5209—Fine Egyptian Cotton, in black or tan; imported; full-fashioned; double soles. Six pairs for $1.45. (For out sizes see No. 5224.) 25

5210—Ingrain Cotton of excellent grade, in black only; unbleached split foot; medium weight; full-fashioned. Six pairs for $1.45. (For out sizes see No. 5225.) .25

5211—Cotton, in black only. Similar to illustration No. 5210. Six pairs for 85 cents. 15

5212—Silk-finished Cotton, in black or tan, with boot daintily embroidered in assorted colors. Six pairs for $1.45. 25

5213—Lisle-finished Cotton, in fancy design, black or tan, with fine white striped fancy boot. Six pairs for $1.45. . .25

5214—Lisle Lace, in all-over design; imported; full-fashioned; exceptionally attractive. Black or tan. Three pairs for $1.00. .35

5215—Lisle Thread, in black only; boot handsomely embroidered in assorted colors. Three pairs for $1.15. 39

5216—Lisle Lace, in handsome all-over design; black or tan; imported; full-fashioned. Three pairs for $1.45. . .49

5217—Brilliant Lisle of very fine quality, with boot of open-work lace handsomely silk-embroidered in colors; imported; full-fashioned. Black or tan. An exceptionally dainty design. Three pairs for $2.20. 75

5218—Imported Parisian Lisle, in black only. Front of boot is in open-work lace effect, exquisitely hand-embroidered in rosebud pattern. 1.49

5219—Real French Silk Hose, beautifully hand-embroidered in floral design; assorted colors. Black only. A dainty and desirable stocking. 1.98

5220—Child's Hose of Lisle Thread, exceptionally fine quality, very fine rib. Black or tan. Six pairs for $1.10. (See also No. 5221.) 19

5221—Child's fine ribbed Hose of Cotton, in black or tan, similar to illustration No. 5220. Six pairs for 75 cents. 13

5222—Boy's Derby Ribbed Hose of very fine durable Cotton, in black or tan. Six pairs for $1.10. 19

5223—Boy's Derby Ribbed Hose of Cotton, in black only, similar to illustration No. 5222. Six pairs for 75 cents. 13

Out Sizes.

5224—Fine Egyptian Cotton, in black or tan; same stocking as No. 5209, in out sizes. Double soles. Six pairs for $1.45. 25

5225—Ingrain Cotton, in black only, with unbleached split foot; medium weight. Same stocking as No. 5210, in out sizes. Six pairs for $1.45. 25

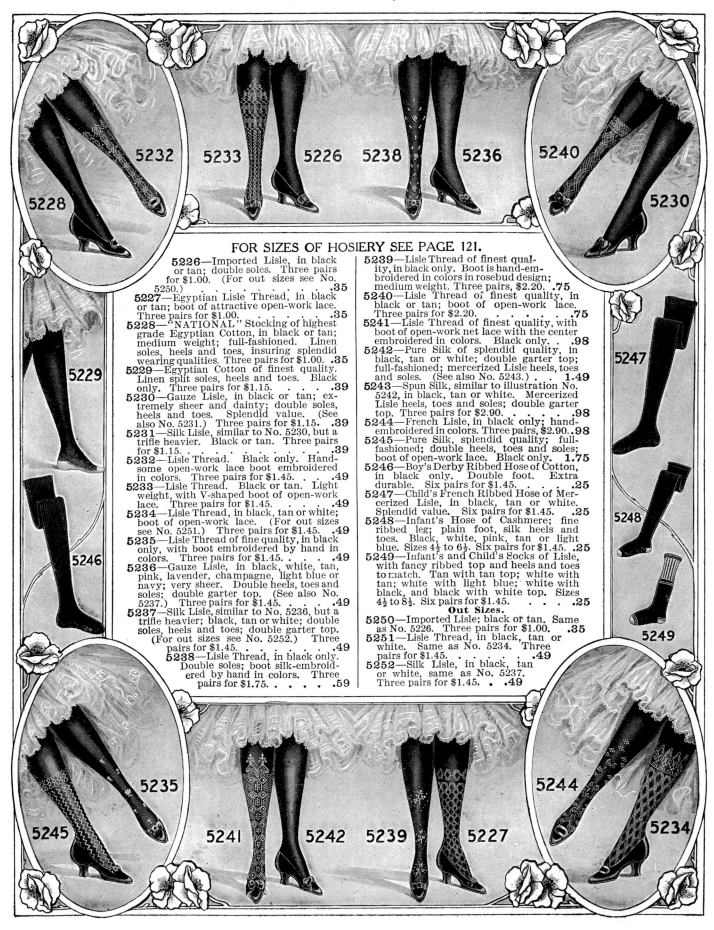

FOR SIZES OF HOSIERY SEE PAGE 121.

5226—Imported Lisle, in black or tan; double soles. Three pairs for $1.00. (For out sizes see No. 5250.) 35

5227—Egyptian Lisle Thread, in black or tan; boot of attractive open-work lace. Three pairs for $1.00. 35

5228—"NATIONAL" Stocking of highest grade Egyptian Cotton, in black or tan; medium weight; full-fashioned. Linen soles, heels and toes, insuring splendid wearing qualities. Three pairs for $1.00. .35

5229—Egyptian Cotton of finest quality. Linen split soles, heels and toes. Black only. Three pairs for $1.15. 39

5230—Gauze Lisle, in black or tan; extremely sheer and dainty; double soles, heels and toes. Splendid value. (See also No. 5231.) Three pairs for $1.15. .39

5231—Silk Lisle, similar to No. 5230, but a trifle heavier. Black or tan. Three pairs for $1.15. 39

5232—Lisle Thread. Black only. Handsome open-work lace boot embroidered in colors. Three pairs for $1.45. . . .49

5233—Lisle Thread. Black or tan. Light weight, with V-shaped boot of open-work lace. Three pairs for $1.45. 49

5234—Lisle Thread, in black, tan or white; boot of open-work lace. (For out sizes see No. 5251.) Three pairs for $1.45. .49

5235—Lisle Thread of fine quality, in black only, with boot embroidered by hand in colors. Three pairs for $1.45. . . .49

5236—Gauze Lisle, in black, white, tan, pink, lavender, champagne, light blue or navy; very sheer. Double heels, toes and soles; double garter top. (See also No. 5237.) Three pairs for $1.45. 49

5237—Silk Lisle, similar to No. 5236, but a trifle heavier; black, tan or white; double soles, heels and toes; double garter top. (For out sizes see No. 5252.) Three pairs for $1.45. 49

5238—Lisle Thread, in black only. Double soles; boot silk-embroidered by hand in colors. Three pairs for $1.75. 59

5239—Lisle Thread of finest quality, in black only. Boot is hand-embroidered in colors in rosebud design; medium weight. Three pairs, $2.20. .75

5240—Lisle Thread of finest quality, in black or tan; boot of open-work lace. Three pairs for $2.20. 75

5241—Lisle Thread of finest quality, with boot of open-work net lace with the center embroidered in colors. Black only. . .98

5242—Pure Silk of splendid quality, in black, tan or white; double garter top; full-fashioned; mercerized Lisle heels, toes and soles. (See also No. 5243.) . . 1.49

5243—Spun Silk, similar to illustration No. 5242, in black, tan or white. Mercerized Lisle heels, toes and soles; double garter top. Three pairs for $2.90. 98

5244—French Lisle, in black only; hand-embroidered in colors. Three pairs, $2.90. .98

5245—Pure Silk, splendid quality; full-fashioned; double heels, toes and soles; boot of open-work lace. Black only. 1.75

5246—Boy's Derby Ribbed Hose of Cotton, in black only. Double foot. Extra durable. Six pairs for $1.45. 25

5247—Child's French Ribbed Hose of Mercerized Lisle, in black, tan or white. Splendid value. Six pairs for $1.45. .25

5248—Infant's Hose of Cashmere; fine ribbed leg; plain foot, silk heels and toes. Black, white, pink, tan or light blue. Sizes 4½ to 6½. Six pairs for $1.45. .25

5249—Infant's and Child's Socks of Lisle, with fancy ribbed top and heels and toes to match. Tan with tan top; white with tan; white with light blue; white with black, and black with white top. Sizes 4½ to 8½. Six pairs for $1.45. 25

Out Sizes.

5250—Imported Lisle; black or tan. Same as No. 5226. Three pairs for $1.00. .35

5251—Lisle Thread, in black, tan or white. Same as No. 5234. Three pairs for $1.45. 49

5252—Silk Lisle, in black, tan or white, same as No. 5237. Three pairs for $1.45. . .49

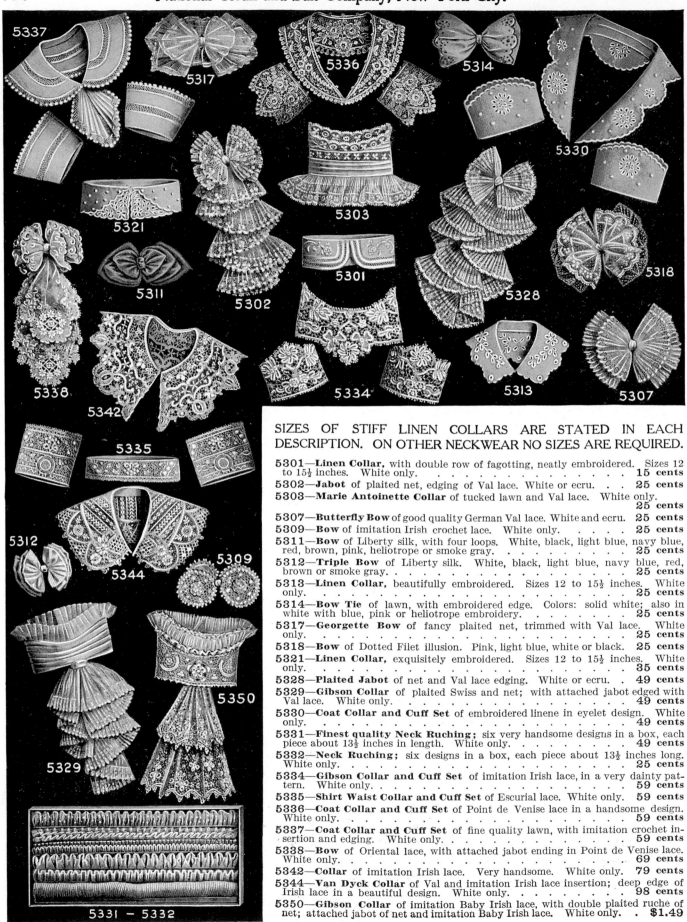

SIZES OF STIFF LINEN COLLARS ARE STATED IN EACH DESCRIPTION. ON OTHER NECKWEAR NO SIZES ARE REQUIRED.

5301—Linen Collar, with double row of fagotting, neatly embroidered. Sizes 12 to 15½ inches. White only. . . . . **15 cents**

5302—Jabot of plaited net, edging of Val lace. White or ecru. . . **25 cents**

5303—Marie Antoinette Collar of tucked lawn and Val lace. White only. . . . . **25 cents**

5307—Butterfly Bow of good quality German Val lace. White and ecru. **25 cents**

5309—Bow of imitation Irish crochet lace. White only. . . . . **25 cents**

5311—Bow of Liberty silk, with four loops. White, black, light blue, navy blue, red, brown, pink, heliotrope or smoke gray. . . . . **25 cents**

5312—Triple Bow of Liberty silk. White, black, light blue, navy blue, red, brown or smoke gray. **25 cents**

5313—Linen Collar, beautifully embroidered. Sizes 12 to 15½ inches. White only. . . . . **25 cents**

5314—Bow Tie of lawn, with embroidered edge. Colors: solid white; also in white with blue, pink or heliotrope embroidery. . . . . **25 cents**

5317—Georgette Bow of fancy plaited net, trimmed with Val lace. White only. . . . . **25 cents**

5318—Bow of Dotted Filet illusion. Pink, light blue, white or black. **25 cents**

5321—Linen Collar, exquisitely embroidered. Sizes 12 to 15½ inches. White only. . . . . **35 cents**

5328—Plaited Jabot of net and Val lace edging. White or ecru. . **49 cents**

5329—Gibson Collar of plaited Swiss and net; with attached jabot edged with Val lace. White only. . . . . **49 cents**

5330—Coat Collar and Cuff Set of embroidered linene in eyelet design. White only. . . . . **49 cents**

5331—Finest quality Neck Ruching; six very handsome designs in a box, each piece about 13½ inches in length. White only. . . . . **49 cents**

5332—Neck Ruching; six designs in a box, each piece about 13½ inches long. White only. . . . . **25 cents**

5334—Gibson Collar and Cuff Set of imitation Irish lace, in a very dainty pattern. White only. **59 cents**

5335—Shirt Waist Collar and Cuff Set of Escurial lace. White only. **59 cents**

5336—Coat Collar and Cuff Set of Point de Venise lace in a handsome design. White only. . . . . **59 cents**

5337—Coat Collar and Cuff Set of fine quality lawn, with imitation crochet insertion and edging. White only. . . . . **59 cents**

5338—Bow of Oriental lace, with attached jabot ending in Point de Venise lace. White only. . . . . **69 cents**

5342—Collar of imitation Irish lace. Very handsome. White only. **79 cents**

5344—Van Dyck Collar of Val and imitation Irish lace insertion; deep edge of Irish lace in a beautiful design. White only. . . . . **98 cents**

5350—Gibson Collar of imitation Baby Irish lace, with double plaited ruche of net; attached jabot of net and imitation Baby Irish lace. White only. . **$1.49**

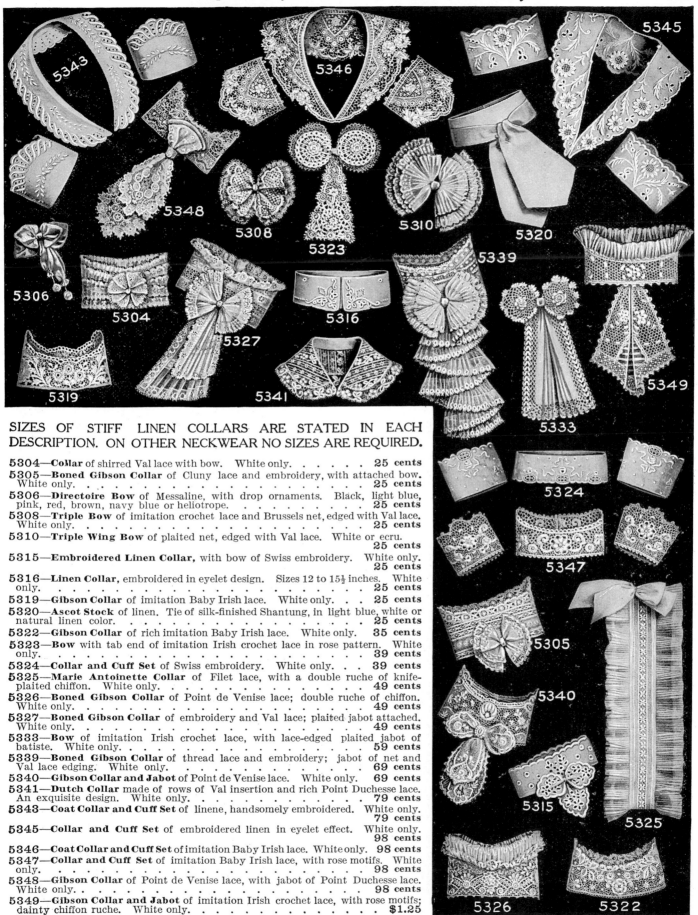

SIZES OF STIFF LINEN COLLARS ARE STATED IN EACH DESCRIPTION. ON OTHER NECKWEAR NO SIZES ARE REQUIRED.

5304—**Collar** of shirred Val lace with bow. White only. . . . . . 25 cents

5305—**Boned Gibson Collar** of Cluny lace and embroidery, with attached bow. White only. . . . . 25 cents

5306—**Directoire Bow** of Messaline, with drop ornaments. Black, light blue, pink, red, brown, navy blue or heliotrope. . . . . 25 cents

5308—**Triple Bow** of imitation crochet lace and Brussels net, edged with Val lace. White only. . . . . 25 cents

5310—**Triple Wing Bow** of plaited net, edged with Val lace. White or ecru.
25 cents

5315—**Embroidered Linen Collar**, with bow of Swiss embroidery. White only.
25 cents

5316—**Linen Collar**, embroidered in eyelet design. Sizes 12 to 15½ inches. White only. . . . . 25 cents

5319—**Gibson Collar** of imitation Baby Irish lace. White only. . . 25 cents

5320—**Ascot Stock** of linen. Tie of silk-finished Shantung, in light blue, white or natural linen color. . . . . 25 cents

5322—**Gibson Collar** of rich imitation Baby Irish lace. White only. 35 cents

5323—**Bow** with tab end of imitation Irish crochet lace in rose pattern. White only. . . . . 39 cents

5324—**Collar and Cuff Set** of Swiss embroidery. White only. . . 39 cents

5325—**Marie Antoinette Collar** of Filet lace, with a double ruche of knife-plaited chiffon. White only. . . . . 49 cents

5326—**Boned Gibson Collar** of Point de Venise lace; double ruche of chiffon. White only. . . . . 49 cents

5327—**Boned Gibson Collar** of embroidery and Val lace; plaited jabot attached. White only. . . . . 49 cents

5333—**Bow** of imitation Irish crochet lace, with lace-edged plaited jabot of batiste. White only. . . . . 59 cents

5339—**Boned Gibson Collar** of thread lace and embroidery; jabot of net and Val lace edging. White only. . . . . 69 cents

5340—**Gibson Collar and Jabot** of Point de Venise lace. White only. 69 cents

5341—**Dutch Collar** made of rows of Val insertion and rich Point Duchesse lace. An exquisite design. White only. . . . . 79 cents

5343—**Coat Collar and Cuff Set** of linene, handsomely embroidered. White only.
79 cents

5345—**Collar and Cuff Set** of embroidered linen in eyelet effect. White only.
98 cents

5346—**Coat Collar and Cuff Set** of imitation Baby Irish lace. White only. 98 cents

5347—**Collar and Cuff Set** of imitation Baby Irish lace, with rose motifs. White only. . . . . 98 cents

5348—**Gibson Collar** of Point de Venise lace, with jabot of Point Duchesse lace. White only. . . . . 98 cents

5349—**Gibson Collar and Jabot** of imitation Irish crochet lace, with rose motifs; dainty chiffon ruche. White only. $1.25

IN ORDERING SWEATERS, STATE SIZE AND COLOR DESIRED.

5401—Child's and Infant's Pony Coat of Worsted; single-breasted; button front; two pockets. Colors: cardinal with gray edge; navy blue with red; gray with red; or in solid white. Sizes 20, 22, 24 and 26 chest. . . . . **98 cents.**

5402—Misses' or Boy's Pony Coat of Worsted; single-breasted; button front; two pockets. Colors: cardinal with gray edge; navy blue with red; gray with red; or solid white. Sizes 28, 30 and 32 chest. **$1.49**

5403—Infant's or Child's Sweater of very soft fine pure Worsted, in white with either pink or blue stripe around the neck, sleeves and bottom; also in solid white or solid cardinal. High neck; long sleeves; button front. Sizes 20, 22, 24 and 26 chest. **$1.25**

5404—Sweater in Pony style of extra fine quality Wool, in vertical stitch; pearl buttons; two pockets. Colors: white, cardinal or Oxford gray. Sizes 32 to 44 bust. **$2.35**

5405—Mannish Pony Coat of very finest quality Wool, made with a double edge around neck and down front; closes with handsome pearl buttons; three pockets. An ideal sweater for outdoor sports or atheletic exercises. Colors: white, cardinal or gray. Sizes 32 to 44 bust. **$3.49**

5406—Pony Sweater of fine soft Worsted Yarn in raised herringbone stitch; roll collar; double-breasted; closes with fine pearl buttons; two pockets. A well-made, serviceable sweater. Splendid value. Colors: white, cardinal, gray or navy blue. Sizes 32 to 44 bust. **$3.98**

5407—Pony Sweater of highest quality Zephyr Worsted, in a very attractive zigzag stitch. One of the finest sweaters made. Garment is single-breasted; closes with handsome pearl buttons and is scalloped around the neck and down the front, as illustrated. Two pockets. Colors: white, cardinal or gray. Sizes 32 to 44 bust. **$4.98**

5408—Misses' Pony Coat of very fine Zephyr Worsted Yarn, in Marseilles stitch. Double-breasted; roll collar; pearl buttons; two pockets. Colors: white, gray or navy blue. Sizes 28, 30 and 32 bust only. **$2.49**

5409—Misses' Sweater of Wool; doubled-breasted; roll collar; pearl buttons; two pockets. Colors: white, cardinal, gray or navy blue. Sizes 28, 30 and 32 bust only. **$1.85**

Girl's Dresses can be supplied in lengths from 26 to 42 inches, measuring in the back from neck-band to bottom of skirt. When ordering, give only this measurement and we will send correct size.

5451—Girl's Princess Dress of good quality striped washable Gingham, in brown and white, light blue and white, or navy blue and white. Waist box-plaited both front and back. Neatly piped to match stripe. Kilted skirt. $1.98

5452—Girl's One-Piece Sailor Dress of washable Linene, in cadet blue, navy blue, solid white or natural linen color. Sailor collar, belt, shield and cuffs trimmed with straps of white linene. Shield, collar and right sleeve embroidered with emblems. Sailor tie. Kilted skirt. $2.49

5453—Girl's Dress of fine quality French Chambray, in navy blue, light blue or rose pink. Trimmed around the Dutch neck, armholes and belt with parallel rows of soutache braid fancifully applied. Plaited front finished with pearl buttons; kilted skirt. The guimpe of tucked lawn and embroidery is included. $2.98

5454—Girl's Princess Dress of pure Linen, in navy blue, light blue, rose pink, white or natural linen color. Swiss eyelet embroidery insertion outlines the Dutch neck and appears down the panel front and on the cuffs. Embroidery also joins the waist and skirt. $3.98

5455—Girl's Dress of India Lawn, in white only. Neatly tucked both front and back, and trimmed with Swiss embroidery insertion and ruffles of the same exquisite embroidery. Skirt trimmed with fine tucks and hemstitching. Buttons in back. $2.49

5456—Girl's Dress of fine quality Dotted Swiss, in white only. Trimmed with Val lace and inserted medallions of embroidery, as illustrated. The skirt is tucked. Low neck. $2.98

5457—Girl's Party Dress of fine sheer Organdie, in white only. Elaborately trimmed with Val lace insertion and edging. The dainty Bertha is also lace-trimmed and ornamented with ribbon rosettes. Sash of satin ribbon. $4.98

5458—Guimpe of fine Lawn, trimmed with hemstitched tucks and Swiss embroidery insertion. Tucked back; long sleeves. Sizes 6 to 14 years.
59 cents

Dresses are made with a deep hem so that they may be easily lengthened or shortened by the customer.

The READY-MADE Misses' Dresses shown on this page can be furnished in four sizes: **Size R** is made with 32 inch bust measure and 33 inch skirt length from waist to bottom of skirt in front. **Size S** is made with 34 inch bust measure and 34 inch skirt length. **Size T** is made with 36 inch bust measure and 36 inch skirt length. **Size U** is made with 38 inch bust measure and 38 inch skirt length. All skirts are made with a three-inch basted hem so that they can be readily lengthened or shortened by the customer. Order according to the letter indicating the sizes which most nearly meet your requirements.

5501—Misses' Two-Piece Outing Suit of good quality Rep, in white with light blue trimming; also in natural linen color or cadet blue. This is an extremely natty little suit which is just the thing for wear during the Summer months as it washes splendidly, wears well and looks cool and becoming. The natty blouse buttons visibly in front through a plait and has a breast pocket on the left side. The detached shield is finished with a Gibson collar, and an additional roll collar and tie are chic accessories. The cuffs fasten with a button. The nine-gored flare skirt has an attached belt of the material, and lapped seams afford a smart completion. Unlined. **$5.98**

5502—Misses' One-Piece Jumper Dress of striped Lawn, with separate waist included. Colors: pink and white, black and white, navy blue and white, light blue and white, or tan and white. The jumper is cut with a low neck both front and back and daintily trimmed with insertions of Swiss embroidery. The Mandarin sleeve effect also displays insertions of embroidery. The waist is of fine lawn prettily tucked and trimmed with Val lace. A dainty medallion of embroidery lends charm to the front. The skirt, which is attached to the jumper by an embroidery belt, is in side-plaited outline with a bias fold around the bottom. Dress closes invisibly in back and is unlined. **$2.98**

5503—Misses' One-Piece Lingerie Dress of very fine Imported Batiste, in white, pink, light blue or champagne. A charming dress, exquisitely made, which is ideal for evening wear or formal occasions. The yoke and collar are of Cluny and Val insertion combined with panels of Baby Irish lace. This same beautiful lace outlined by insertion and frills of Val forms the epaulettes over the shoulders. The body of waist both front and back is tucked and trimmed with Val. The sleeves are three-quarter length, exquisitely lace-trimmed to accord with the waist. The skirt is finely tucked to hip depth and is joined to the waist by an Empire girdle of lace. The deep tucked flounce is headed by Val insertion, which also adorns the front, as pictured. An unusually pleasing and dainty dress of exceptional value. Dress closes in back and is unlined. **$12.98**

5504—One-Piece Dress of good quality light weight Linon, in cadet blue trimmed with white; also in solid white or natural linen color. The yoke and Gibson collar are of Swiss eyelet embroidery, the collar being completed with a frill of Val lace. Waist is plaited to the waist-line both front and back and ornamented with buttons. The sleeves are piped and trimmed with small buttons, piping being also used effectively on the belt which joins the waist and skirt. The latter is in flare outline with plaits simulating a panel in front, and an inverted plait at the sides and back. Buttons similar to those on the waist provide an appropriate completion. Dress closes invisibly in back. Unlined. . . **$4.98**

5505—Misses' Wash Suit of pure Linen, in white, cadet blue or natural linen color. The jacket of this extremely natty suit is single-breasted and is about 32 inches long in back. The closing is effected visibly with pearl buttons, the latter being employed with pleasing effect on the envelope pockets. The notched collar and natty turn-back cuffs are provided with additional collar and cuffs of white English Rep which may be easily detached and laundered when necessary. The chic eleven-gored skirt is a flare model and has a wide bias fold of the material applied around the lower edge. Suit is unlined. **$6.98**

5506   5507   5508   5509   5510

The READY-MADE Misses' Dresses shown on this page can be furnished in four sizes: **Size R** is made with 32 inch bust measure and 33 inch skirt length from waist to bottom of skirt in front. **Size S** is made with 34 inch bust measure and 34 inch skirt length. **Size T** is made with 36 inch bust measure and 36 inch skirt length. **Size U** is made with 38 inch bust measure and 38 inch skirt length. All skirts are made with a three-inch basted hem so that they can be readily lengthened or shortened by the customer. Order according to the letter indicating the sizes which most nearly meet your requirements.

5506—Misses' One-Piece Lingerie Princess Dress of superior quality Batiste, in white, pink, light blue or champagne. This dainty little dress is appropriate for evening wear, and its pleasing style and artistic trimming make it an especially desirable selection. The yoke both back and front is of tucks and Val lace. The yoke in front is deepened by beautiful imitation Point de Venise lace with a handsome medallion in the center. Two rows of Venise insertion extend down the front with V-shaped inserts of Val between. The sleeves are tucked in clusters and trimmed with Val lace, the same lace being also used in back and on the tucked Princess girdle. The skirt is finished with a full, tucked flounce headed by two rows of Val insertion. Both the sleeves and collar are attractively frilled with lace. Dress is unlined and closes invisibly in back. **$6.98**

5507—Misses' Two-Piece Dress of good quality Lawn, in white with a fine black check; in white with fine light blue check; also in plain white. Light dainty dresses of this material are favored for general wear, for comfort and becomingness and also because they may be easily laundered. This neat dress has a waist elaborately trimmed with Val lace insertion which is applied on the front as pictured, combined with inserts of plain tucked lawn. The back is also trimmed with Val. This lace frills the Gibson collar and the tucked sleeves and appears with charming effect in perpendicular lines on the skirt. The full bouffante flounce is ornamented with tucks and headed by an insertion of Val. Separate belt of the material. Dress is unlined. Closes invisibly in back. **$3.98**

5508—Misses' Regulation Two-Piece Sailor Suit of Linen, in white with blue trimming; cadet blue with white trimming; also in natural linen color with white trimming. This is an extremely serviceable and attractive suit which may be worn to advantage for out door recreation. It is recommended for general wear as the material launders splendidly. The blouse is made with a broad sailor collar which is trimmed with straps of the material in a contrasting shade and furnished with a tie of linon. The detachable shield and the right sleeve are embroidered with nautical emblems, the shield being headed with a collar which is finished with straps to match the cuffs. Left sleeve is neatly piped. The skirt is a side-plaited model, which closes down the entire front with pearl buttons. Dress is unlined. **$4.98**

5509—Misses' Two-Piece Dress of fine quality Dotted Swiss, in white only. This is a particularly desirable dress made of a sheer and dainty Summer fabric, cool, attractive to the eye and easily laundered. The yoke both front and back is formed of rows of fine Val lace prettily finished with lace frills. Val insertion adorns the front and also the sleeves. The skirt is a flaring model, with a deep flounce, which is tucked and trimmed with Val lace insertion. Separate crushed girdle of the material is included. Unlined. Dress closes invisibly in back. Exceptional value. **$8.98**

5510—Misses' Jumper Dress and Coat of fine quality Imported Rep, in white, light blue or natural linen color. This natty suit is simple in design but correct in style, and will be found in every way a pleasing selection. The jumper is sleeveless, made in Princess effect with a V-shaped low neck and a panel down the entire front. Swiss eyelet embroidery insertion in a very handsome design borders the neck and is used around the arm-holes in Mikado outline. The jumper is plaited both front and back and is joined to the gored-flaring skirt by a belt of the same Swiss embroidery. The lace guimpe pictured is not included. The coat is semi-fitted, double-breasted and finished with a mannish notched collar and Cavalier cuffs trimmed with pearl buttons. It is about 30 inches long in back. Three pockets. Both coat and dress are unlined. Dress closes invisibly in back. **$8.98**

5513

5512

5514

5515

5516

5517

The READY-MADE Misses' Suits shown on this page can be furnished in four sizes : **Size R** is made with 32 inch bust measure and 33 inch skirt length from waist to bottom of skirt in front. **Size S** is made with 34 inch bust measure and 34 inch skirt length. **Size T** is made with 36 inch bust measure and 36 inch skirt length. **Size U** is made with 38 inch bust measure and 38 inch skirt length. All skirts are made with a three-inch basted hem so that they can be readily lengthened or shortened by the customer. Order according to the letter indicating the sizes which most nearly meet your requirements.

5512—Misses' Regulation Sailor Suit of very fine quality All-Wool Serge, in navy blue or brown. The sailor collar of this trim suit is embroidered in red and adorned with white braid to correspond with the buttoned cuffs. The detachable shield is also embroidered and braid-trimmed. The tie is of silk. The left sleeve and pocket are neatly piped, and the right sleeve is embroidered in red with a nautical emblem. The gored skirt has two side-plaits in front and closes through a buttoned placket on one side of the front. It is laced in back to insure a snug fit. A separate belt of the material is included. $12.98

5513—Misses' Suit of superior quality Mohair, in navy blue or dark green; with a fine hair-line shadow stripe of the same color. The material used in this exceptionally smart tailored suit is very stylish, and the model will command admiration wherever it is worn. The jacket is semi-fitted and is made with a double-breasted front. It is about 26 inches long in back, where the seams are slit and trimmed with buttons. Two flap pockets are convenient features. The notched collar of the material adds to the mannish air. Cuffs are simulated by stitching, and buttons provide an attractive finish. Jacket is lined throughout with good quality satin. Skirt comprises thirteen gores with the fulness disposed in side-plaits all around. (See also 5513X.) $11.98

5513X—Misses' Tailored Suit of superior quality Mohair, in navy blue or brown, exactly the same as 5513, but in plain colors, without stripe. $11.98

5514—Jumper Dress and Coat of fine quality All-Wool light weight Fancy Striped Serge, in navy blue or brown. The jumper of this desirable suit, though extremely stylish, is beautifully simple. It is sleeveless, with a low neck which is finished with a collar effect handsomely edged with satin, soutache loops and tiny buttons. A chic satin tie is included, caught with an ornamental tie clasp. Waist is attached to the flare skirt by a stitched belt of the material. The skirt is ornamented with a fold of the material and displays a plait down the center of the front.

The semi-fitted coat is single-breasted and about 29 inches long in back, where the seams are slit. Three pockets. The notched collar and turn-back cuffs are edged with satin, finished with satin-covered buttons and loops. Lined throughout with good quality satin. $17.98

5515—Misses' One-Piece Dress of good quality Figured Chiffon Silk, in navy blue, brown, or reseda green; with a pretty white figure. The yoke both front and back, the collar and the sleeves below the elbow are of rich Cluny insertion combined with dotted net. Collar and sleeves are edged with a narrow fold of the material and Val lace. Waist is tucked both front and back and embellished with knife-plaited frills of the material around the yoke and down front. Plain gored skirt is attached to waist by a stitched belt. Sleeves are tucked. Dress is unlined and closes invisibly in back. A decidedly chic and dressy garment. $12.98

5516—Tailored Suit of good quality All-Worsted Panama Mixture, in gray or tan. The jacket is single-breasted and semi-fitted. It is about 27 inches long in back, where the seams are slashed and trimmed with self-covered buttons. Notched collar of the material and unique button-trimmed cuffs. Two flap pockets. Lined throughout with good quality satin. The skirt is in nine-gored flaring outline with plaits in front simulating a panel, ornamented at the lower edge with self-covered buttons. $9.98

5517—Jumper Dress and Coat of excellent quality All-Wool Serge, in navy blue, brown, or reseda green. The jumper of this smart suit is sleeveless and the low-cut neck both front and back is edged with fancy braid. Jumper and skirt are joined by a belt of the material. The skirt is made with thirteen gores, arranged in side-plaits all around. The jacket is double-breasted and about 26 inches long in back. The plainness of the notched collar is relieved by fancy braid and tiny gilt buttons. Ornamental buttons trim the back where the seams are slit, and are also used for the closing in front. Turn-back cuffs display braid and buttons to match the collar. Two flap pockets. Lined throughout with satin. $13.98

5518 5519 5520 5521 5522 5523

The READY-MADE Misses' Suits shown on this page can be furnished in four sizes: **Size R** is made with 32 inch bust measure and 33 inch skirt length from waist to bottom of skirt in front. **Size S** is made with 34 inch bust measure and 34 inch skirt length. **Size T** is made with 36 inch bust measure and 36 inch skirt length. **Size U** is made with 38 inch bust measure and 38 inch skirt length. All skirts are made with a three-inch basted hem so that they can be readily lengthened or shortened by the customer. Order according to the letter indicating the sizes which most nearly meet your requirements.

5518—Misses' Suit of very fine quality Shangtung Silk, in navy blue, brown, reseda green, natural Pongee color or catawba. This handsome material is both cool and attractive. The jacket is single-breasted and about 26 inches long in back. The seams at the sides and in back are slashed. The notched collar is inlaid with taffeta in a contrasting color, and the chic turn-back cuffs and pocket flaps are piped with taffeta to match. Lined throughout with fine quality satin. The skirt has nine gores in flaring effect, with inverted plait front and back and a fold of the material around the bottom, which is piped with taffeta to match jacket. **$14.98**

5519—Jumper Suit and Coat of fine quality All-Wool Serge, in navy blue, brown or reseda green. The jumper is cut with a low square neck in front and is open down the back in V-effect to the waist-line; the model is sleeveless. Guimpe is not included. Jumper is plaited over the shoulders and handsomely trimmed both front and back with tailored straps of satin. Fancy buttons lend a trim completion to the front, and larger buttons of similar design are used on the skirt as pictured. Skirt has eleven flaring gores with a panel effect in front and a wide fold around the lower edge. The single-breasted jacket is semi-fitted, about 29 inches long in back. The collar is inlaid with satin and trimmed with silk braid ornaments and fancy buttons. Satin buttons finish the box-plaited sleeves and also appear on the pockets combined with soutache loops. Seams in back are slit, and also adorned with buttons and loops. Lined throughout with satin. . . **$14.98**

5520—Misses' Tailored Suit of fine quality All-Worsted Chiffon Panama Cloth, in navy blue or brown. The jacket of this jaunty suit is about 29 inches long in the back. It is a single-breasted model in cutaway outline, semi-fitted, and made with slashed seams in back, which are trimmed with buttons. The notched collar is finished with a detachable embroidered collar of white linen, and the sleeves display embroidered linen cuffs to match. Two patch pockets which are button-trimmed. The skirt has nine gores with two plaits down the front ornamented with buttons, and a group of side-plaits introduced on each side. Inverted plait in back. **$12.98**

5521—Misses' One-Piece Princess Dress of very fine quality Figured Chiffon Silk, in navy blue, Copenhagen blue or rose; with a charming white figure. The yoke both front and back and the guimpe sleeves of this very dressy little gown are of imitation Irish crochet lace in a very pleasing design. The yoke is bordered by a strap of the material, piped with taffeta to match and trimmed with small taffeta-covered buttons. An insert of tucked taffeta provides a pretty effect in the front. Sleeves are edged with taffeta. A piped Empire girdle of the material joins waist and skirt; the latter is arranged in side-plaits and finished with two tucks around the bottom. Dress is unlined and closes invisibly in back. **$14.98**

5522—Misses' Tailored Suit of good quality Fancy Mixed Suiting, in gray or tan; **also in good quality Serge,** in plain navy blue or brown. The single-breasted jacket is semi-fitted and is made about 26 inches long in back. The notched collar, the turn-back cuffs and the pocket flaps display tabs of broadcloth in a contrasting color outlined by fancy braid. Seams in back are slit and trimmed with fancy buttons to match those used on the cuffs and collar and for the closing in front. Lined throughout with good quality satin. The skirt is of the flare variety with a plait down the left side of the front which is finished with buttons. A wide fold of the material ornaments the bottom. . . **$11.98**

5523—Misses' Tailored Suit of very fine quality All-Wool Serge, in navy blue, brown or reseda green. No illustration can do justice to the splendid style and finished workmanship of this beautiful suit. The jacket is semi-fitted and is about 28 inches long in back, where the seams are slit and trimmed with small silk buttons. The same buttons appear on the sleeves and pocket flaps; the latter being piped with satin to match the material. The collar is especially ornate, being composed of rich Persian brocade combined with satin and outlined by silk braid. A Directoire tie of satin ending in chic gilt tassels is included. Jacket fastens as pictured with one handsome ornamental button. Lined throughout with fine quality satin. The nine-gored, flaring skirt has a wide fold of the material ending in front and trimmed with silk buttons, ... **$14.98**

In ordering the Blouse Suits shown on this page, give the boy's age and state whether he is large or small for his age.   If these questions are answered correctly, no measurements will be necessary.

5601—Boy's Russian Blouse Suit of good quality striped Cotton Cheviot, in cadet blue with white stripe, navy blue and white stripe; also in plain white with blue collar, and in solid white.   Washable; fast colors.   Sizes 2½ to 7 years. $1.25

5602—Boy's Sailor Suit of good quality French Chambray, in natural linen color or cadet blue; also in blue and white stripe.   Washable; fast colors.   Sizes 3 to 10 years. $1.25

5603—Boy's Cadet Blouse Suit of fine durable Galatea Cloth, in white, cadet blue or natural linen color.   Washable; fast colors.   Sizes 2½ to 7 years. $1.69

5604—Boy's Sailor Blouse Suit in excellent quality Khaki Cloth, natural color; also in **Cotton Crash,** in natural linen color.   This suit includes two pair of bloomers and a cap of the same material.   Suit is washable and will wear splendidly.   Fast colors.   Extraordinary value.   Sizes 3 to 10 years. . . $1.75

5605—Boy's Russian Blouse Suit of excellent quality durable French Chambray, in white, cadet blue or natural linen color.   Fast colors.   Sizes 2½ to 7 years. $1.98

5606—Boy's Sailor Suit of very fine English Chambray, in blue, natural linen color or solid white; very durable; launders beautifully; fast colors.   Sizes 3 to 10 years. .   . . $1.98

5607—Boy's Russian Blouse Suit of fine quality Linene, in white with cadet blue collar, solid cadet blue, solid navy blue or in natural linen color.   This material wears splendidly and withstands repeated washing.   Sizes 2½ to 7 years. $2.49

5608—Boy's Sailor Suit of pure Linen, in natural color only, with either blue or white sailor collar.   A very natty little wash suit combining style and serviceability.   Sizes 3 to 10 years. $2.49

5618—Boy's Double-Breasted Suit of fine quality All-Wool blue Serge; also in **an attractive brown Woolen Mixture;** or in a **stone-gray Woolen Mixture**.   This stylish suit has two pair of trousers consisting of one pair of knickerbockers and one pair of plain knee pants.   Coat and trousers lined throughout.   Exceptionally well made.   Suitable for boys from 8 to 16 years.   Do not order by age, but refer to sizes given on page 121, under the heading of Boy's Double-Breasted Suits. $4.98

5613
5611
5609
5612
5615
5614
5617
5610
5619
5620
5616

In ordering the Blouse Suits shown on this page, give the boy's age and state whether he is large or small for his age. If this information is given correctly, no measurements will be necessary.

5609—Boy's Russian Blouse Suit of extra fine quality washable Linene, in natural linen color, solid cadet blue or solid brown; fast colors. A very attractive style. Sizes 2½ to 7 years. $2.49

5610—Boy's Sailor Suit of genuine English Percale, in blue with white stripe; also in solid navy blue, solid linen color or in white with cadet blue collar. Fast colors; washable. Sizes 3 to 10 years. $2.98

5611—Boy's Russian Blouse Suit of very fine quality English Rep, in white with cadet blue collar; also in solid white or solid cadet blue. This material is recommended for long wear and launders splendidly. Fast colors. Sizes 2½ to 7 years. $2.98

5612—Boy's Russian Blouse Suit of fine quality English Rep, in white with cadet blue collar; also in solid white, solid linen color, or solid cadet blue. Sailor collar with scalloped embroidered edge; washable; fast colors. Sizes 2½ to 7 years. $2.98

5613—Boy's Russian Blouse Suit of very fine quality English Percale, in solid white only. Light weight and cool; washable, durable and dressy. Collar and belt trimmed with embroidery insertion. Sizes 2½ to 7 years. $2.98

5614—Boy's Sailor Suit of fine quality English Rep, in white with cadet blue collar; also in solid cadet blue or solid linen color. A particularly neat and attractive suit. Washable; fast colors. Sizes 3 to 10 years. . . $3.49

5615—Boy's Russian Blouse Suit of very fine English Rep, in cadet blue, tan or pink. Washable; fast colors. Sizes 2½ to 7 years. $3.49

5616—Boy's Double-Breasted Suit of genuine Khaki Cloth, in natural color; in **pure Linen**, in natural color; also in **fine white Duck**. A fine suit for Summer wear which is both neat in appearance and serviceable. Washable; fast colors. Suitable for boys from 8 to 16 years. Do not order by age, but refer to sizes given on page 121, under the heading of Boy's Double-Breasted Suits. . . . $2.98

5617—Boy's Knickerbocker Pants of genuine Khaki Cloth, in natural color; in **pure Linen**, in natural linen color; also in **white Duck**. Sizes 8 to 16 years. In ordering give waist measure desired. . . . . 98 cents

5619—Boy's Sailor Blouse Suit in very fine All-Wool blue Serge; also in an Imported Fancy brown Woolen Mixture, or stone-gray Woolen Mixture. A very natty little suit; beautifully finished. Sizes 3 to 10 years. $4.98

5620—Boy's Sailor Blouse Suit of All-Wool blue Serge; also in a Fancy brown Woolen Mixture, or stone-gray Woolen Mixture. Sizes 3 to 10 years. $3.98

5701—Infant's Dress of Cambric. Front yoke of embroidery insertion and tucks. Embroidery ruffle headed by tucks. Sizes 6 months to 3 years. **69 cents**

5702—Infant's Dress of Lawn. Yoke of pin-tucks and embroidery insertion. Bottom finished with insertion. Sizes 6 months to 3 years. . . **98 cents**

5703—Child's French Dress of Lawn. Trimmed with Val insertion and embroidery. Sleeves edged with Val lace. Sizes 2 to 6 years. . . **98 cents**

5704—Child's Dress of Lawn, for boy or girl. Box-plaited back and front. Trimmed with eyelet embroidery insertion. Sizes 2 to 6 years. . . **$1.29**

5705—Child's Dress of Persian Lawn. Front trimmed with pin-tucks and Val insertion. Skirt has ruffle of lawn with Val lace and insertion. Tucked back. Sizes 2 to 6 years. **$1.29**

5706—Infant's Dress of Nainsook. Front yoke of Val lace and embroidery with ruffle of Val lace. Tucked lawn ruffle edged with lace and trimmed with Val insertion. Sizes 6 months to 3 years. . **$1.49**

5707—Child's French Dress of very fine Lawn. Yoke, both back and front, of embroidery and Val insertion; trimmed with tucks, embroidery and Val lace. Skirt has three rows of insertion and edging of Val. Sizes 2 to 6 years. **$1.75**

5708—Infant's Dress of fine Nainsook. Yoke front and back of pin-tucks, insertion and Val lace. Lavishly trimmed with fine tucks and Point de Paris lace. Sizes 6 months to 3 years. **$1.98**

5709—Infant's Dress of fine Lawn, beautifully embroidered in Swiss eyelet effect. Yoke and sleeves of Val lace and embroidery. Sizes 6 months to 3 years. **$1.98**

5710—Child's Dress of fine quality Lawn, embroidered in Swiss eyelet effect. Yoke of Val lace and ribbon beading. The sleeves and waist are ornamented with beading; tucked front; two ribbon rosettes. Sizes 2 to 6 years. **$2.98**

5711—Child's Dress of finest quality sheer India Lawn, lavishly tucked back and front, and trimmed as pictured with fine Swiss embroidery. Embroidery insertion extends around waist. Satin ribbon rosettes. Plain tucked back. Sizes 2 to 6 years. . . **$3.98**

5715—Child's Russian Dress of fine Poplin, in light blue, pink, white or tan; for boy or girl. Plaited both front and back. Front, sleeves and collar trimmed with handsome white embroidery insertion. Sizes 2 to 6 years. **$2.49**

5712—**Child's Dress of Linene,** in natural linen color, light blue or navy blue. Piped in a contrasting shade. Dutch neck. Sizes 2 to 6 years. . . . 98 cents

5713—**Child's Dress of Hydegrade Galatea Cloth,** in a neat check. Colors: tan, pink or navy blue. Piped to match check. Sizes 2 to 6 years. . $1.25

5714—**Child's Dress of Scotch Plaid Chambray,** with either red or blue prevailing. Kilted skirt; belt and collar of white piqué. Sizes 2 to 6 years. . $1.98

5716—**Child's Rompers of Irish Linen,** in pink, linen color or cadet blue. Neatly piped and trimmed with embroidery. Sizes 1 to 6 years. . 98 cents

5717—**Child's Rompers of Linene,** in tan, cadet blue or pink. Sizes 1 to 6 years. . . . 59 cents

5718—**Child's Rompers of Irish Linen,** in natural linen color, cadet blue or pink. Prettily piped in a contrasting color. Sizes 1 to 6 years. . 98 cents

5719—**Child's Rompers of Linene,** in tan, cadet blue or pink. Sizes 1 to 6 years. . . . 49 cents

5720—**Child's Coat of light weight Serge,** in scarlet or navy blue. Collar and cuffs, white piqué. Collar trimmed with medallions of lace. Pearl buttons. Lined throughout. Sizes 2 to 6 years. $1.98

5721—**Child's Coat of All-Wool,** black and white check; detachable collar and cuffs of embroidered piqué. Lined throughout. Sizes 2 to 6 years. $2.49

5722—**Child's Coat of Pongee,** in champagne color only. Collar and cuffs trimmed with soutache braid and Venise lace. Lined throughout. Sizes 2 to 6 years. $2.49

5723—**Child's Coat of light weight Broadcloth,** in red, navy blue or castor. Collar and cuffs of broadcloth in a contrasting color edged with fancy silk braid. Plaits down each side of front and back. Lined throughout. Sizes 2 to 6 years. . $2.98

5724—**Child's Coat of fine Cheviot,** in red, navy blue or castor. Pearl buttons. Extra, detachable collar and cuffs of piqué ornamented with lace. Lined throughout. Sizes 2 to 6 years. $3.98

5725—**Infant's Long Cloak of fine Cashmere,** in cream color only. Deep double cape embroidered in white silk. Collar effect trimmed with ribbon, silk soutache and fancy braid. Embroidered at bottom with white silk. Lined throughout. $3.49

5726—**Infant's Short Coat of fine Cashmere,** in cream color only. Same as 5725, but made short. Lined throughout. Sizes 1 to 3 years. . . $3.49

5741—**Bonnet of Embroidered Lawn,** with panel of Swiss eyelet embroidery; ruching and frills of Val lace; ribbon rosette. Sizes 12 to 16 inches. **49 cents**

5742—**Bonnet of Lawn,** tucked and edged with Val; two bands of embroidery. Sizes 12 to 16 inches. **49 cents**

5743—**Embroidered Bonnet of Silk,** finished with net. Lined with silk. Sizes 12 to 16 inches. . . **49 cents**

5744—**French Bonnet of Dotted Swiss,** trimmed with embroidery and Val. Sizes 12 to 16 inches. . **59 cents**

5745—**Bonnet of Lawn,** with panel of embroidery and Val lace; ruching of Val. Sizes 12 to 16 inches. **75 cents**

5746—**Bonnet of Tuscan Straw;** natural color; ribbon loops in pink or blue. Sizes 13 to 16 inches. **79 cents**

5747—**Poke Bonnet of Embroidered Lawn;** ruffle of Swiss embroidery. Sizes 14 to 16 inches. . **89 cents**

5748—**French Bonnet of All-Over Eyelet Embroidery.** Val lace edging. Sizes 12 to 16 inches. . . . **98 cents**

5749—**French Bonnet of Lawn,** with rows of Filet embroidery frilled with Val. Sizes 12 to 16 inches. **98 cents**

5750—**Bonnet of Japanese Silk,** embroidered in white; Val lace ruching; four silk ribbon rosettes; lined with silk. Sizes 12 to 16 inches. . . . . **98 cents**

5751—**Tam O' Shanter of Japanese Silk;** ruching of Val lace. Sizes 19 and 20 inches. White only. . **98 cents**

5752—**Boy's Hat of white Japanese Silk.** Wire edge; ribbon rosettes. Sizes 19 and 20 inches. . **98 cents**

5753—**Bonnet of Tucked Lawn;** ruffle of embroidery; satin ribbon loops. Sizes 14 to 16 inches. . . **98 cents**

5754—**Normandy Bonnet of Embroidery;** trimming of Val lace and ribbon. Sizes 13 to 16 inches. **98 cents**

5755—**French Bonnet of Tuscan Straw,** in natural color; daintily trimmed with ruche and rosettes in pink or blue. Sizes 14 to 16 inches. . . . . **98 cents**

5756—**Poke Bonnet of Dotted Swiss;** full ruffle of eyelet embroidery with ribbon loops, net ruching and rosebuds. Sizes 14 to 16 inches. **$1.25**

5757—**Bonnet of Tuscan Straw,** in natural color; lined with silk; ribbon bows and rosettes; chiffon ruche; trimmed in pink or blue. Sizes 13 to 16 inches. . . . **$1.25**

5758—**Poke Bonnet of Tuscan Straw,** in natural color, lined with silk; ribbon and rose buds; chiffon ruche; trimmed in pink or blue. Sizes 14 to 16 inches. . . **$1.49**

5759—**Bonnet of Embroidered Lawn,** ribbon rosettes in pink or blue. Sizes 14 to 16 inches. . . . **$1.75**

5760—**Kate Greenaway Bonnet of braided Tuscan Straw and Lawn,** in pink or blue; satin ribbon and two ribbon rosettes. Sizes 14 to 16 inches. . . . **$1.75**

5761—**Poke Bonnet of Lawn Embroidery,** ruche edged with Val lace. Bows of satin ribbon in pink or blue. Sizes 14 to 16 inches. **$1.98**

5762—**Poke Bonnet of Tuscan Straw,** in natural color; lined with pink or blue silk; chiffon ruche; trimmed with ribbon and rosebuds. Sizes 14 to 16 inches. . . **$1.98**

5763—**Child's Hat of Chip Straw,** with silk ribbon streamers. Sizes 19 and 20 inches. **$1.98**

Use this Order Blank only for Ready-Made Goods

SHOWN ON PAGES 30 TO 116 INCLUSIVE

(Order Blanks for our **Made-to-Measure** Garments shown on pages 9 to 29 will be found in the FRONT of this Style Book)

NATIONAL CLOAK AND SUIT CO.

207 TO 217 WEST TWENTY-FOURTH STREET
NEW YORK CITY

I send you this order with the understanding that if the goods sent me are not entirely satisfactory, I may return them in good condition within three days of their receipt, at your expense, and you will refund my money, or you will exchange them for other merchandise, whichever I prefer.

Mrs or Miss.. No. .... Street or Avenue

(If married, use husband's initials.)

Town.. County.. State..

(State here your post-office address.)

In what town is your Express Office?.. What is the name of Express Company?..

Enclosed find $...................

(Read paragraphs 6 and 7, page 6, regarding Our Terms and How To Remit.)

Do not write anything in this space.

Important—Read Carefully

BEFORE MAILING THIS ORDER GO OVER IT VERY CAREFULLY TO MAKE SURE THAT YOU HAVE GIVEN THE CORRECT STYLE NUMBERS, COLORS AND SIZES. SEE PAGE 121, ABOUT SIZES, Etc.

Our Terms.

¶ We do a strictly cash business and carry no charge accounts.

¶ We prepay express charges or postage to any part of the United States, provided an amount sufficient to cover the full list price of the goods desired accompanies the order.

¶ If you wish goods sent C. O. D. we require a deposit of at least one-third of the amount of your order, in which case they will be sent by express C. O. D. for the balance. On such shipments the customer must pay the express charges and the express company's charge for sending the money to us. We do not ship C. O. D. without the required deposit. Goods sent C. O. D. must go by express.

¶ All orders for points outside the United States must be fully paid for in advance.

Insure Your Mail Packages.

¶ For a slight extra charge we will insure the safe delivery of our packages sent you by mail. If the goods are lost, write us that they were not delivered, have your Postmaster certify to your statement, and we will duplicate your order without extra charge. Write the word "INSURE" plainly on your order.

Rates of Mail Insurance.

Orders for less than $5.00	5 cents
" from $ 5.00 to 10.00	10 "
" " 10.01 " 15.00	15 "
For each additional $5.00 worth of Merchandise add	5 "

No Alterations On Ready-Made Goods.

¶ We cannot make any alterations on the goods shown on pages 30 to 116 of our Style Book. They are Ready-Made and can be furnished only as illustrated and described, and in only such sizes as are stated in the descriptions.

Please send your Style Book to my friends named below:

NAME	ADDRESS
....	....
....	....
....	....

Additional Order Blanks furnished on request

FILL IN PARTICULARS, CUT OUT THIS SHEET AND SEND IT TO US.

NATIONAL CLOAK AND SUIT CO.

207 TO 217 WEST TWENTY-FOURTH STREET, NEW YORK CITY

BEFORE MAILING THIS ORDER GO OVER IT VERY CAREFULLY TO MAKE SURE THAT YOU HAVE GIVEN THE CORRECT STYLE NUMBERS, COLORS AND SIZES.   SEE PAGE 121, REGARDING SIZES, Etc.

NOTE:—Give color, size, bust, waist or length as called for in the description of each article you order.

Have you read how to order correct sizes of Ready-Made Goods on page 121?................

May we substitute if our stock of your selection is sold out?................ Should it be necessary to do so, we will, with your permission select for you a similar article of the same or greater value without extra charge, with the understanding that if not entirely satisfactory you may return it at once at our expense.

QUANTITY	STYLE	SIZE (See Note) above	COLOR (See Note) above	LENGTH	ARTICLE	PRICE	
		State Size	State Color			$	cts.
		State Size	State Color				
		State Size	State Color				
		State Size	State Color				
		State Size	State Color				
		State Size	State Color				
		State Size	State Color				
		State Size	State Color				
		State Size	State Color				
		State Size	State Color				
		State Size	State Color				
		State Size	State Color				
		State Size	State Color				
		State Size	State Color				
		State Size	State Color				
		State Size	State Color				
		State Size	State Color				
		State Size	State Color				
		State Size	State Color				
		State Size	State Color				
		State Size	State Color				

FILL IN BOTH SIDES OF THIS ORDER BLANK WITH INK.   DON'T USE A PENCIL.

FILL IN PARTICULARS, CUT OUT THIS SHEET AND SEND IT TO US.

SHOWN ON PAGES 30 TO 116 INCLUSIVE

(Order Blanks for our **Made-to-Measure** Garments shown on pages 9 to 29 will be found in the FRONT of this Style Book)

NATIONAL CLOAK AND SUIT CO.
207 TO 217 WEST TWENTY-FOURTH STREET
NEW YORK CITY

I send you this order with the understanding that if the goods sent me are not entirely satisfactory, I may return them in good condition within three days of their receipt, at your expense, and you will refund my money, or you will exchange them for other merchandise, whichever I prefer.

Mrs.
or Miss.. No.. Street or Avenue

(If married, use husband's initials.)

Town.. County .... State ....

(State here your post-office address.)

In what town is your **Express Office ?**.. What is the name of Express Company ? ....

Enclosed find $....................

Important—Read Carefully

(Read paragraphs 6 and 7, page 6, regarding Our Terms and How To Remit.)

Do not write anything in this space.

BEFORE MAILING THIS ORDER GO OVER IT VERY CAREFULLY TO MAKE SURE THAT YOU HAVE GIVEN THE CORRECT STYLE NUMBERS, COLORS AND SIZES. SEE PAGE 121, ABOUT SIZES, Etc.

Our Terms.

¶ We do a strictly cash business and carry no charge accounts.

¶ We prepay express charges or postage to any part of the United States, provided an amount sufficient to cover the full list price of the goods desired accompanies the order.

¶ If you wish goods sent C. O. D. we require a deposit of at least one-third of the amount of your order, in which case they will be sent by express C. O. D. for the balance. On such shipments the customer must pay the express charges and the express company's charge for sending the money to us. We do not ship C. O. D. without the required deposit. Goods sent C. O. D. must go by express.

¶ All orders for points outside the United States must be fully paid for in advance.

Insure Your Mail Packages.

¶ For a slight extra charge we will insure the safe delivery of our packages sent you by mail. If the goods are lost, write us that they were not delivered, have your Postmaster certify to your statement, and we will duplicate your order without extra charge. Write the word "INSURE" plainly on your order.

Rates of Mail Insurance.

Orders for less than $5.00 . . . . . 5 cents
" from $ 5.00 to 10.00 . . . . . 10 "
" " 10.01 " 15.00 . . . . . 15 "
For each additional $5.00 worth of Merchandise add 5 "

No Alterations On Ready-Made Goods.

¶ We cannot make any alterations on the goods shown on pages 30 to 116 of our Style Book. They are Ready-Made and can be furnished only as illustrated and described, and in only such sizes as are stated in the descriptions.

Please send your Style Book to my friends named below:
NAME   ADDRESS

----------------------------------   ---

----------------------------------   ---

----------------------------------   ---

FILL IN PARTICULARS, CUT OUT THIS SHEET AND SEND IT TO US.

NATIONAL CLOAK AND SUIT CO.

207 TO 217 WEST TWENTY-FOURTH STREET, NEW YORK CITY

BEFORE MAILING THIS ORDER GO OVER IT VERY CAREFULLY TO MAKE SURE THAT YOU HAVE GIVEN THE CORRECT STYLE NUMBERS, COLORS AND SIZES.   SEE PAGE 121, REGARDING SIZES, Etc.

NOTE:—Give color, size, bust, waist or length as called for in the description of each article you order.

Have you read how to order correct sizes of Ready-Made Goods on page 121?................

May we substitute if our stock of your selection is sold out?................ Should it be necessary to do so, we will, with your permission, select for you a similar article of the same or greater value without extra charge, with the understanding that if not entirely satisfactory you may return it at once at our expense.

QUANTITY	STYLE	SIZE (See Note above)	COLOR (See Note above)	LENGTH	ARTICLE	PRICE	
		State Size	State Color			$	cts.
		State Size	State Color				
		State Size	State Color				
		State Size	State Color				
		State Size	State Color				
		State Size	State Color				
		State Size	State Color				
		State Size	State Color				
		State Size	State Color				
		State Size	State Color				
		State Size	State Color				
		State Size	State Color				
		State Size	State Color				
		State Size	State Color				
		State Size	State Color				
		State Size	State Color				
		State Size	State Color				
		State Size	State Color				
		State Size	State Color				
		State Size	State Color				
		State Size	State Color				

FILL IN BOTH SIDES OF THIS ORDER BLANK WITH INK.   DON'T USE A PENCIL.

FILL IN PARTICULARS, CUT OUT THIS SHEET AND SEND IT TO US.

SIZES OF READY-MADE GOODS.

When ordering READY-MADE goods, please observe these rules governing measurements and sizes required.

Don't guess at your size. Send measurements as called for below. Be sure to use an accurate tape-measure.

Belts: Sizes 22 to 30 inches waist measure.

Boys' Blouse Suits are made to fit boys from 2½ to 10 years of age. In ordering give the boy's age. State whether he is large or small for his age. (If these questions are answered correctly, no measurements will be necessary.)

Boys' Double-Breasted Suits: (Pages 112–113.) These suits are made to fit boys from 8 to 16 years of age, and can be furnished in six sizes as follows:

	Chest	Waist	Inside Sleeve
Size J	26 inch	26 inch	12¾ inch
K	27½ "	27½ "	14 "
L	29 "	28½ "	15¼ "
M	30 "	29 "	16 "
N	31 "	29½ "	16½ "
O	32 "	30 "	17 "

Order according to the letter indicating the size which most nearly meets your requirements.

Brassieres: (Page 81.) Sizes 34 to 48 inches bust. Order by bust measure only.

Chemises: Sizes 32 to 44 inches bust. Order by bust measure only.

Coats, Children's: (Page 115.) Sizes 2 to 6 years. Order by age only.

Combination Suits, Muslin: (Pages 96–97.) Sizes 32 to 44 inches bust. Order by bust measure only.

Corsets: Order by size—not by waist measure. The size of your corset should be about four inches smaller than your waist measure taken over your dress. If your waist measure is 24 inches, order corset size No. 20. If your waist measure is 26 inches, order corset size No. 22, and so on.

Corset Covers: Sizes 32 to 44 inches bust. Order by bust measure only.

Drawers, Knit: Sizes 20 to 30 inches waist; extra sizes 32 to 36 inches waist. Order by waist measure only.

Drawers, Muslin: Sizes 23 to 29 inches side length. Take measurement down side from waist to length desired. Order by side length only.

Dresses, Children's: (Pages 114–115.) Sizes 2 to 6 years. Order by age only.

Dresses, Girls': (Page 107.) Girls' dresses can be supplied in lengths from 26 to 42 inches, measuring in the back from neckband to bottom of skirt. When ordering, give only this measurement and we will send correct size.

Dresses, Infants': (Pages 114–115.) Sizes 6 months to 3 years. Order by age only.

Dresses, Ladies' Ready-Made: (Pages 38 to 46.) Sizes 32 to 44 inches bust. Give bust and waist measures only. The skirts of these dresses are about 40 inches long in front and made to hang evenly all around. They have a three-inch basted hem, so that they can be easily lengthened or shortened by the customer.

Dresses, Misses': (Pages 108–109.) Misses' wash dresses are made in four sizes. Use same scale of measurements as that given for misses' suits in the next column.

Hats, Little Boys': Page 116. Can be furnished in sizes 19 and 20 inches only. Measure around inside of hat-band.

Hosiery: Order by size according to the following schedule. Be sure that you ask for a size sufficiently large.

Children's Hosiery:

Size Shoe:	5–5½	6–6½	7–7½	8–8½
Size Hose:	5	5½	6	6½
Size Shoe:	9–10	10½–12½	13–1½	2–3
Size Hose:	7	7½	8	8½
Size Shoe:	4–5	5½–6	6½–7½	
Size Hose:	9	9½	10	

Ladies' Hosiery:

No. 2 ladies' shoe requires about 8½ hose.
No. 3 " " " " 9 "
No. 4 " " " " 9 "
No. 5 " " " " 9½ "
No. 6 " " " " 9½ "
No. 7 " " " " 10 "

House Dresses: Sizes 32 to 44 inches bust. Order by bust measure only.

Infants' Bonnets and Caps: Start at side of chin marked "A" in illustration, and measure in front of ears and over fore part of head to other side of the chin marked "B." The number of inches is the size needed. Do not measure underneath the chin.

Jackets and Coats, Ladies': Sizes 32 to 44 inches bust. Order by bust measure only.

Kimonos and Dressing Sacques: Sizes 32 to 44 inches bust. Order by bust measure only.

Neckwear, Linen Collars: Sizes 12 to 15½ inches; give size desired. On other neckwear no measurements required.

Night Gowns: Sizes 32 to 44 inches bust. Order by bust measure.

Petticoats, Black and Colored: (Pages 80 to 82.) Lengths 37 to 43 inches; hip measure up to 50 inches. Order by front length only. Take measurement down front from waist to length desired. Petticoats priced at less than $2.98 cannot be supplied in extra large sizes. On garments quoted at $2.98 and over, we will make petticoats more than 43 inches long or more than 50 inches hip measure for an additional charge of one-third above prices quoted.

Petticoats, Muslin: (Pages 88 to 90.) Sizes 38 to 44 inches front length. Take measurement in front from waist to desired length. Order by front length only.

Rain Coats: Sizes 32 to 44 inches bust; extra sizes 46 and 48 inches bust will cost 10 per cent. additional; extra lengths 10 per cent. additional; extra bust and extra length, 20 per cent. additional. Order by bust measure only.

Shirt Waists: Sizes 32 to 44 inches bust. Order by bust measure only.

Skirts, Ready-Made: (Pages 68 to 79.)

Ladies' Skirts: waist measures 22 to 30 inches; front lengths 36 to 44 inches. See "Note."

Misses' Skirts: waist measures 22 to 27 inches; front lengths 32 to 37 inches.

NOTE: Give only waist measure and front length desired. Take measurement from top of skirt-band to desired length in front. We cannot supply Ready-Made skirts in sizes either larger or smaller than those specified. Ladies who desire skirts either larger or smaller are referred to our Made-to-Measure skirts, pages 9 to 29.

Maternity Skirts: (Page 76.) Front lengths from 38 to 44 inches. Order by length only; no waist measure necessary. These skirts have a three-inch basted hem so that they may be easily lengthened by the customer.

Slips: (Pages 82 and 91.) Sizes 32 to 44 inches bust. Order by bust measure only.

Suits, Misses': (Pages 110–111.) Misses' suits are made in four sizes, as follows:

Size R: 32 inch bust measure and 33 inch skirt length from waist to bottom of skirt in front.
Size S: 34 inch bust measure and 34 inch skirt length.
Size T: 36 " " " 36 " " "
Size U: 38 " " " 38 " " "

Order according to the letter indicating the size which most nearly meets your measurements. The skirts of these suits are made with a wide basted hem so that they can be readily lengthened or shortened by the customer.

Sweaters: (Page 106.)
Infants': Sizes 20 to 24 inches chest. Order by chest measure only.
Children's: " 22 to 26 " " " " " "
Misses': " 28 to 32 " " " " " "
Ladies': " 32 to 44 " bust. " " bust " "

Tub Suits, Ladies': (Pages 47 to 49.) Sizes 32 to 44 inches bust. Order by bust measure only.

Undervests, Knit: Sizes 30 to 40 inches bust; extra sizes 42, 44 and 46 inches bust. Order by bust measure only.

Union Suits: Sizes 30 to 40 inches bust; extra sizes 42, 44 and 46 inches bust. Order by bust measure only.

Waists: Sizes 32 to 44 inches bust. Order by bust measure only.

LARGEST LADIES'
OUTFITTING ESTABLISHMENT
IN THE WORLD

NATIONAL CLOAK & SUIT CO.

207 TO 217 WEST 24TH ST.   NEW YORK CITY.